Chicano Tattoo Design Book

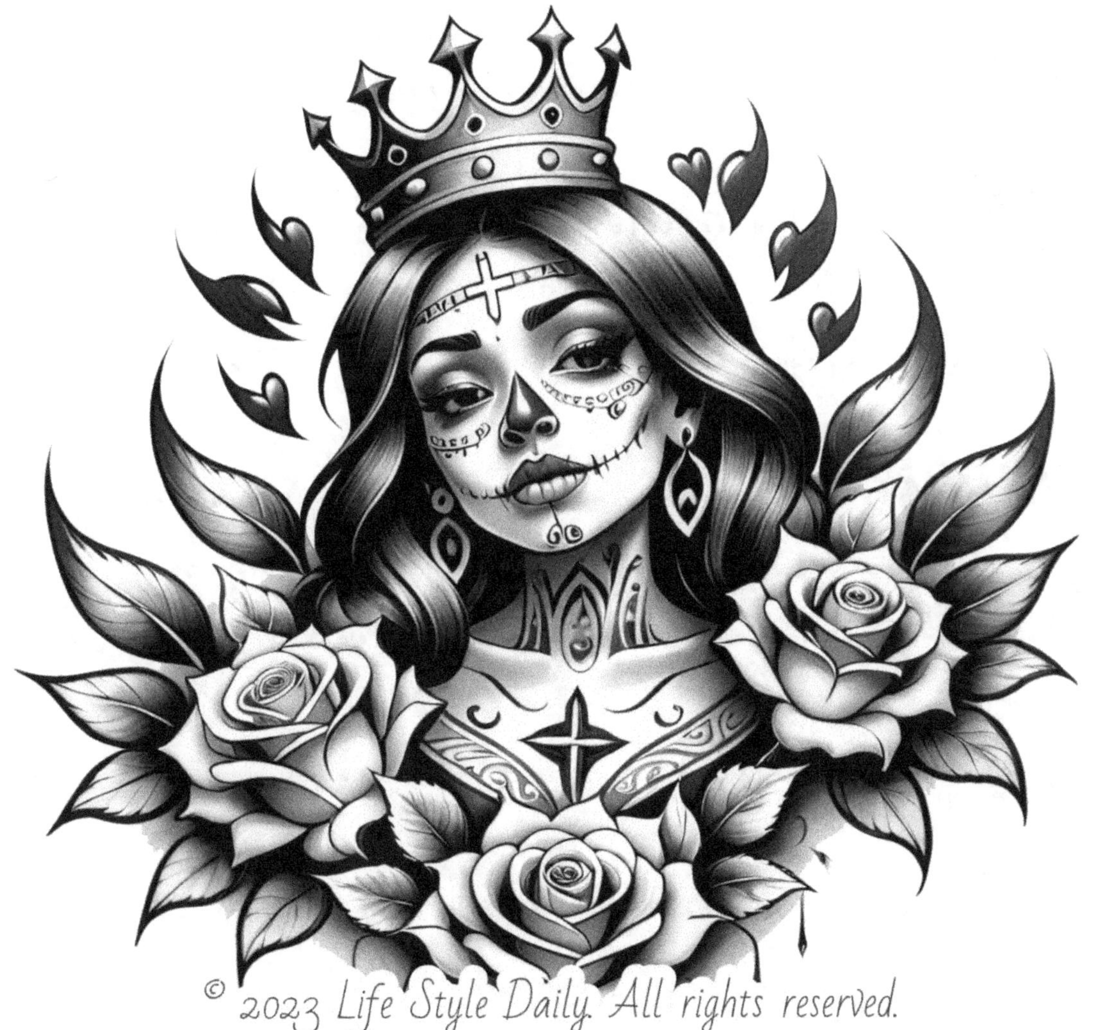

Table Of Contents

Introduction to "Chicano Tattoo Design Book"

Welcome to the vibrant and profound world of Chicano tattoo art, a realm where each ink stroke carries a deep cultural significance and personal story. This book, "Chicano Tattoo Design Book," is designed to be a comprehensive guide and source of inspiration for artists and enthusiasts alike, delving into the rich tapestry of symbols, motifs, and themes that define this unique style.

Chicano tattoos originated within the Chicano communities in the United States, emerging as a powerful form of self-expression among Mexican Americans. They are more than mere decorations: they are a form of cultural assertion and personal identity. Rooted in the historical and contemporary struggles, celebrations, and everyday lives of the Chicano people, these tattoos often feature intricate patterns, poignant imagery, and a stark black and grey palette enriched occasionally with vibrant colors.

In this book, we explore a multitude of themes ranging from spiritual symbols blending Catholic and indigenous influences, to street art capturing the gritty reality of urban life, to personal motifs of love, loss, and resilience. Each chapter is dedicated to a specific theme, such as Rebellion, Honor, Music, Nature, and Heritage, providing not only a gallery of designs but also the stories and meanings behind them.

Whether you're a tattoo artist seeking inspiration for your next piece, a cultural scholar interested in the art forms of marginalized communities, or someone simply captivated by the beauty and depth of Chicano art, this book offers a window into a rich cultural tradition. Through its pages, we hope to honor the artistry and the voices of the Chicano community, illustrating how these tattoos symbolize a narrative of resistance, resilience, and celebration.

Dive into the "Chicano Tattoo Design Book" and discover the compelling narratives etched in ink—each design a reflection of a rich cultural heritage and a profound personal journey.

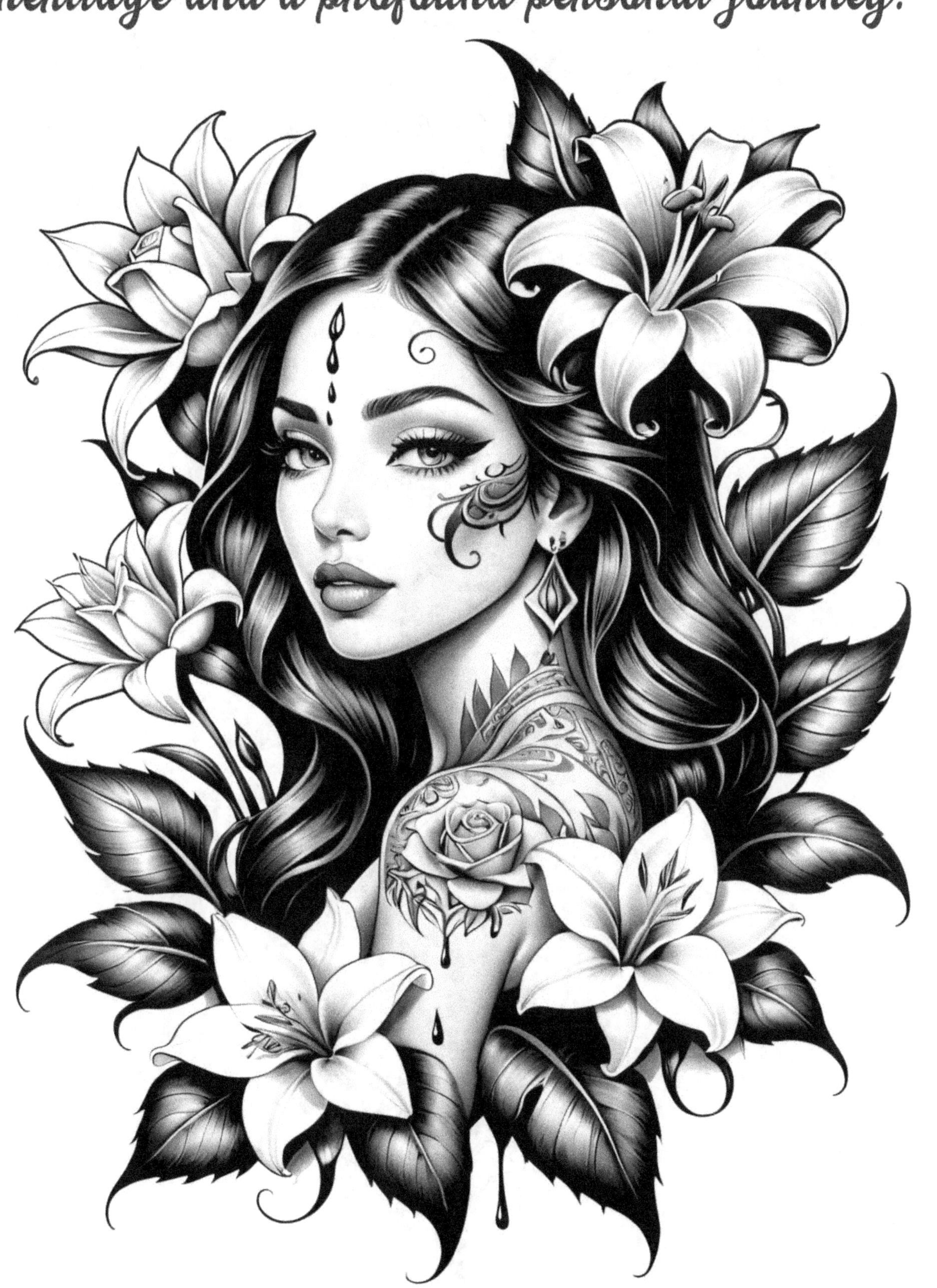

Heritage

Heritage in Chicano tattoos pays homage to historical and ancestral roots, particularly focusing on Aztec, Mayan, and indigenous symbols. Motifs like Aztec calendars, Mayan statues, and tribal masks connect wearers to their cultural history, emphasizing pride in their heritage and the continuity of their ancestors' traditions.

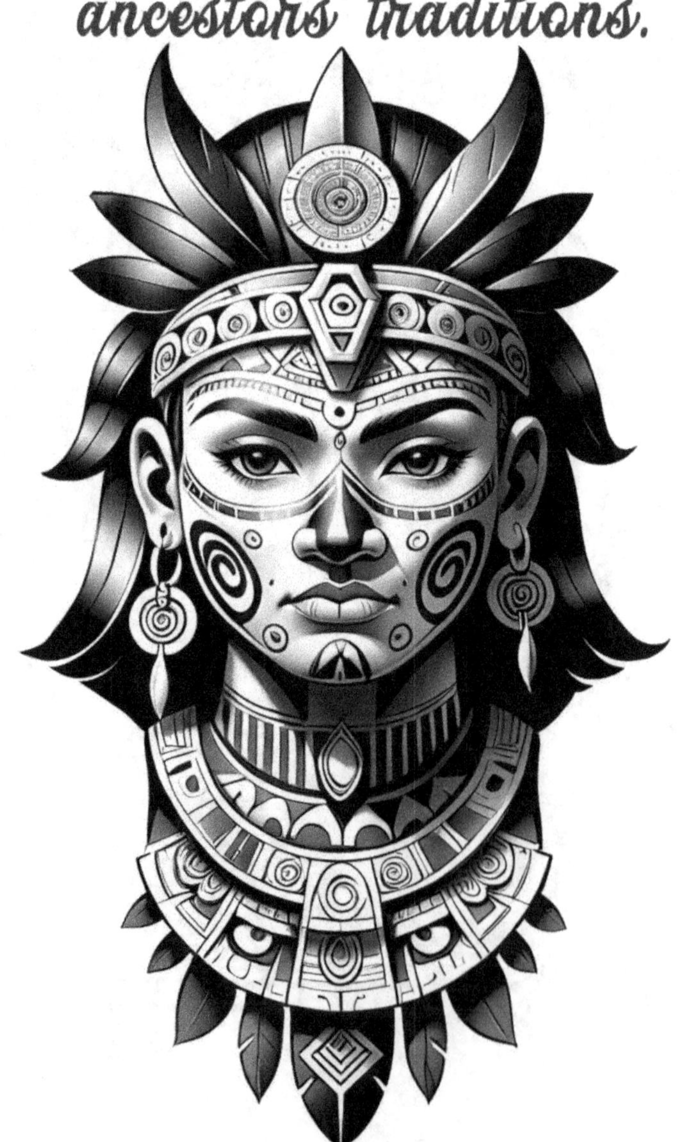

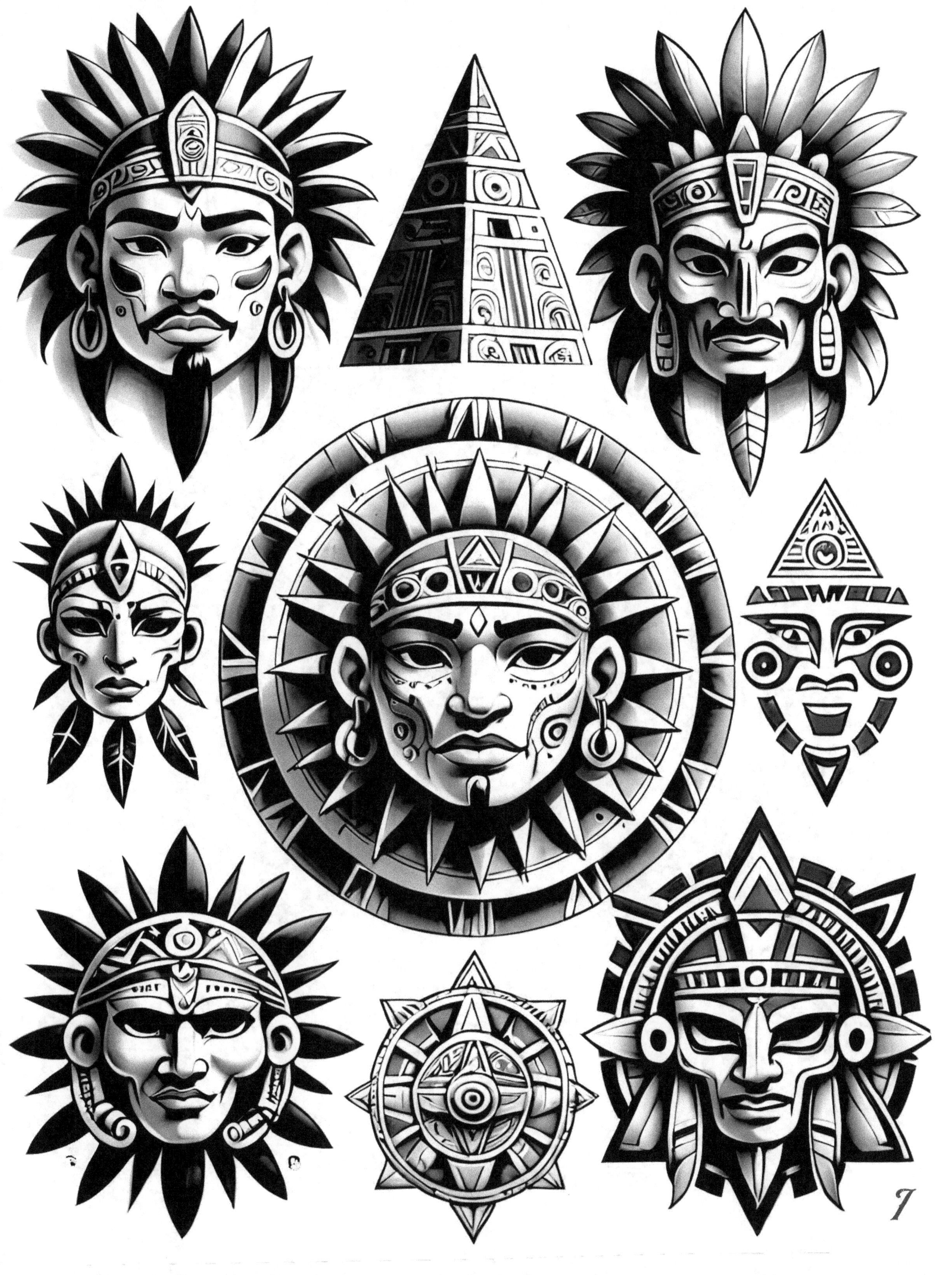

7

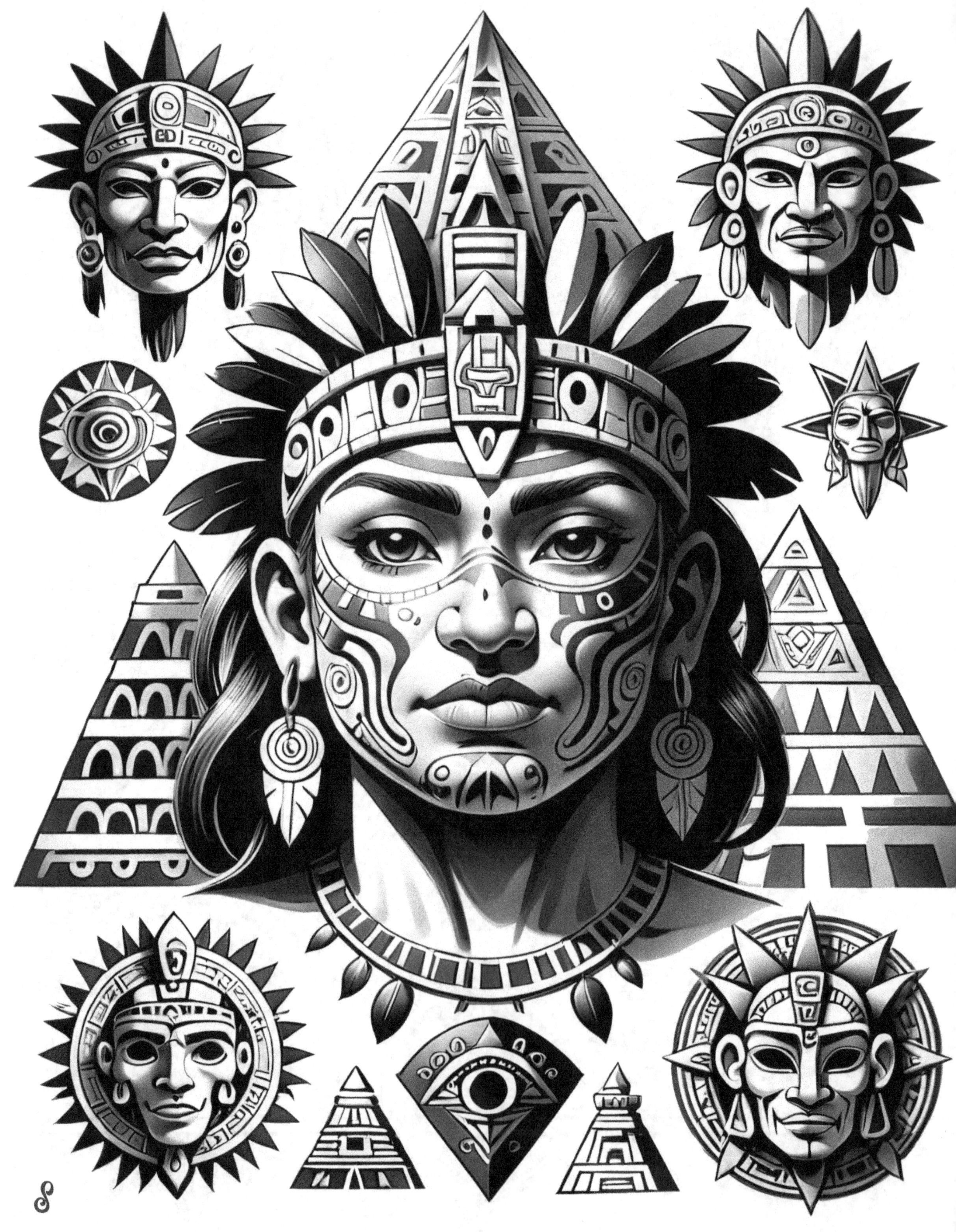

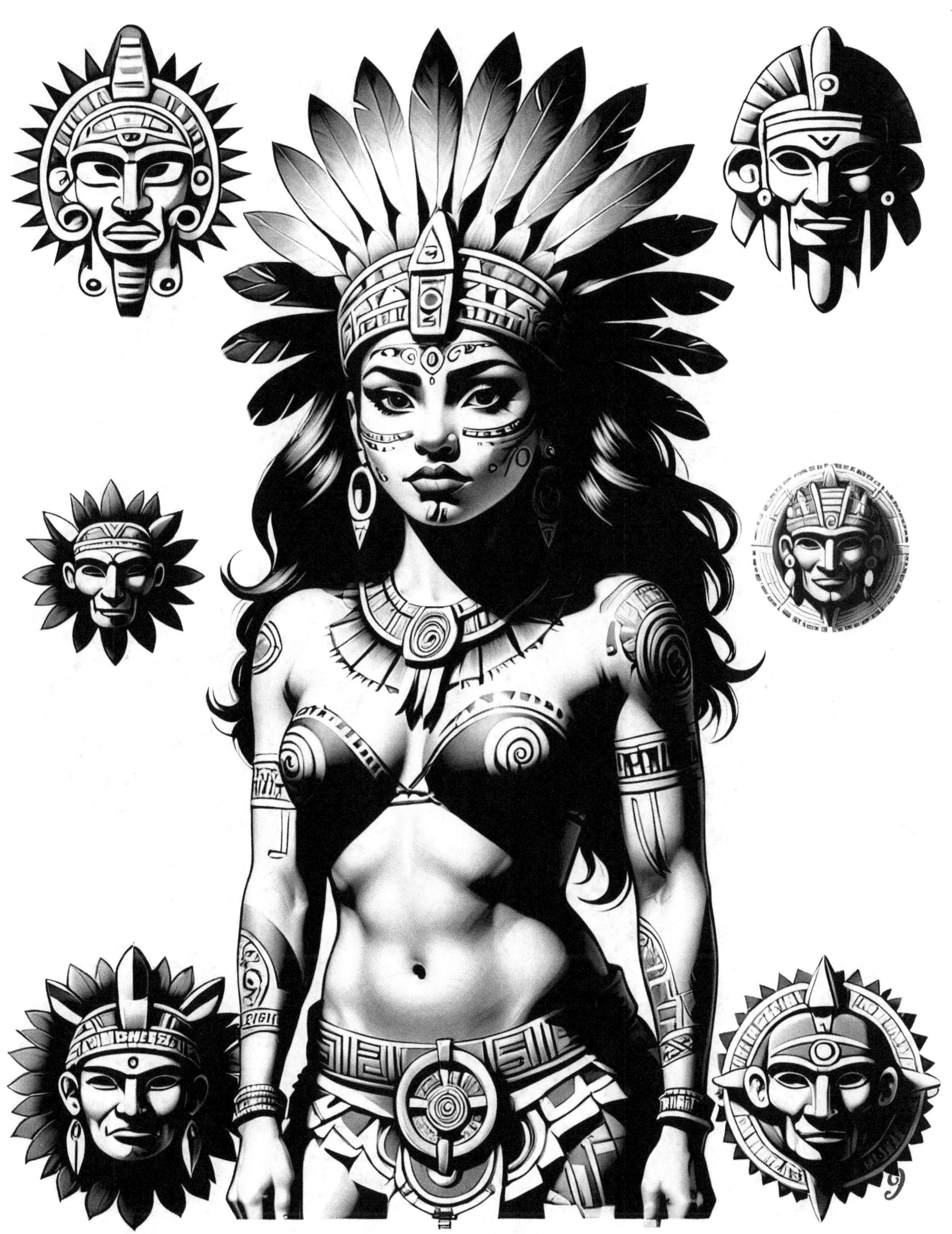

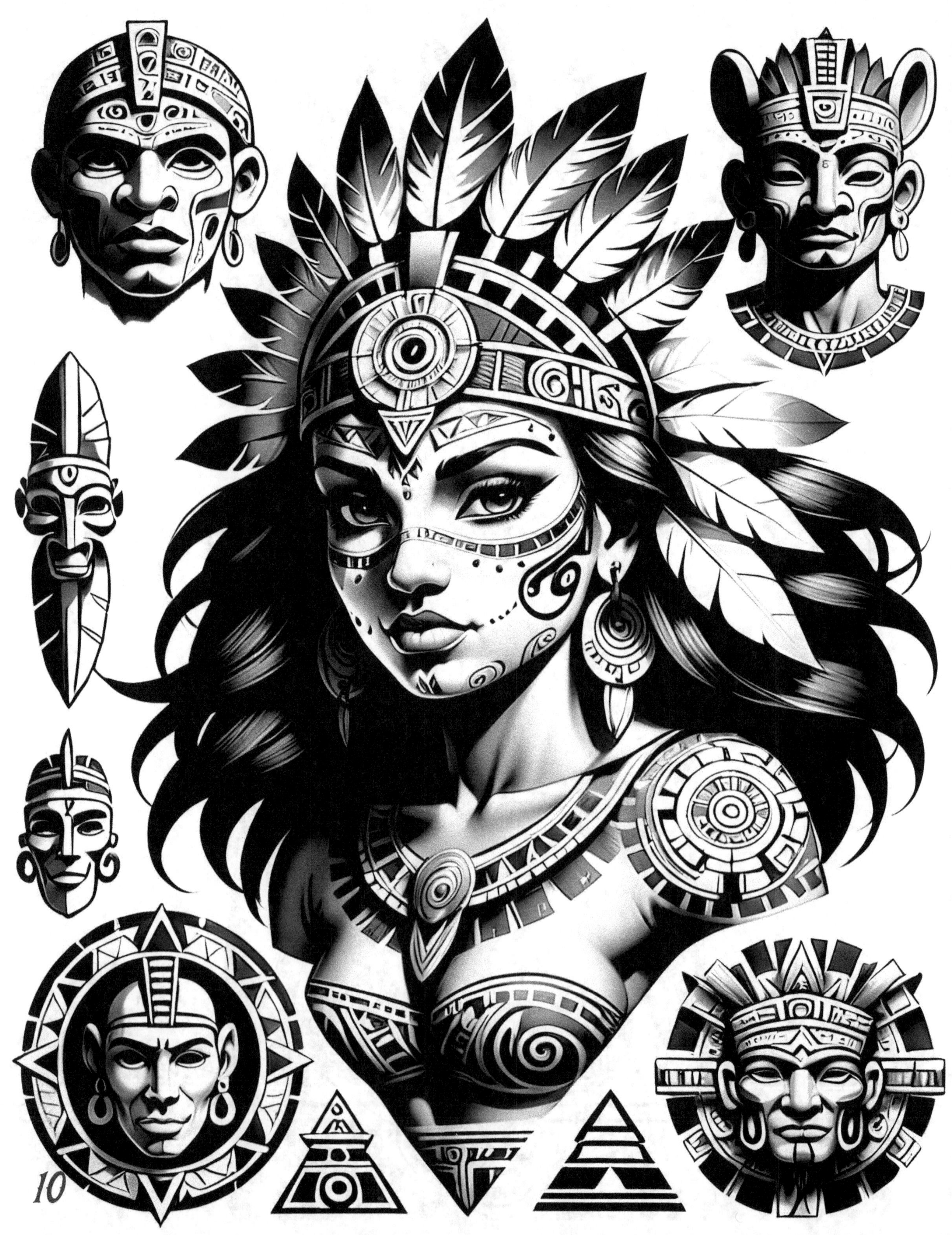

10

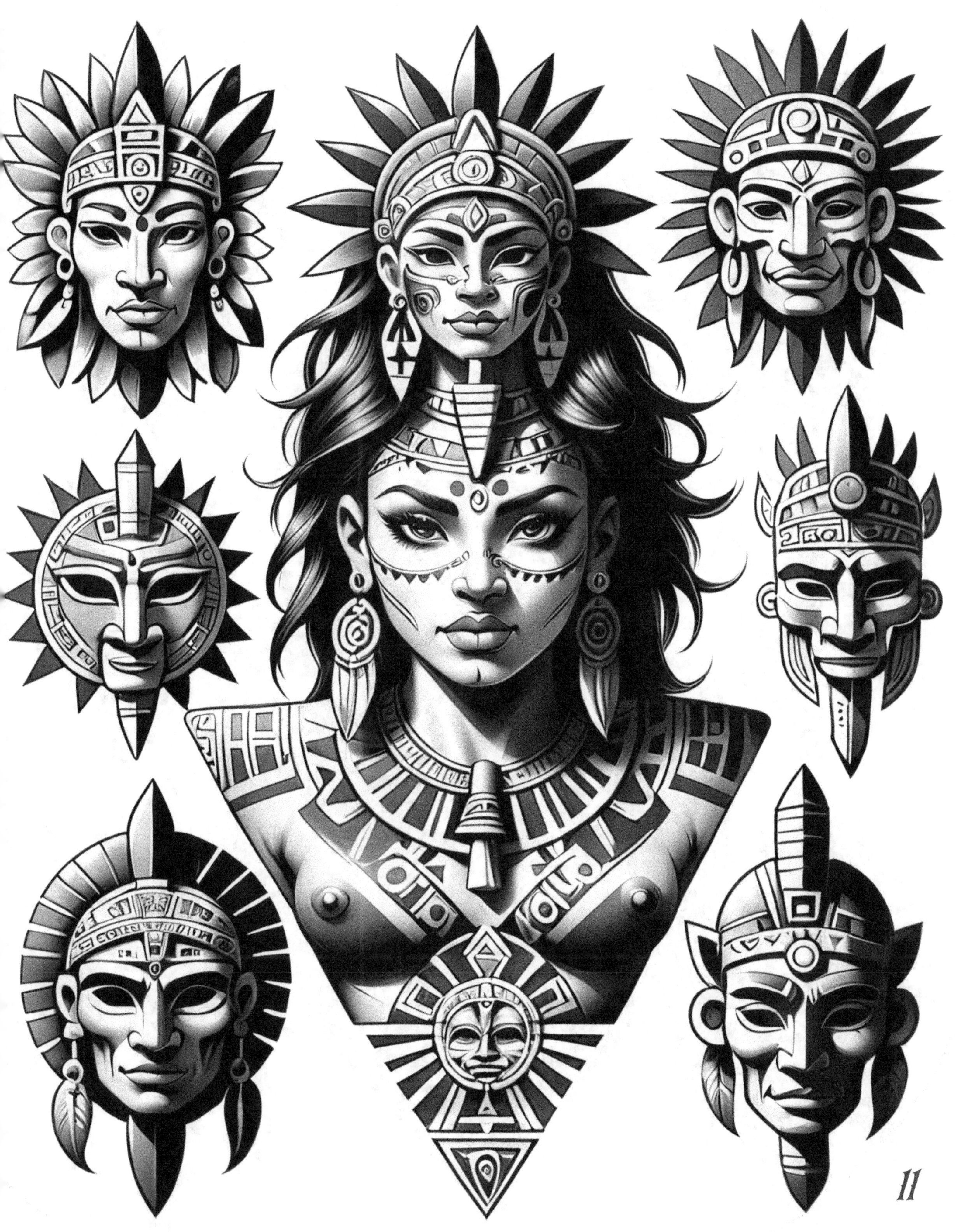

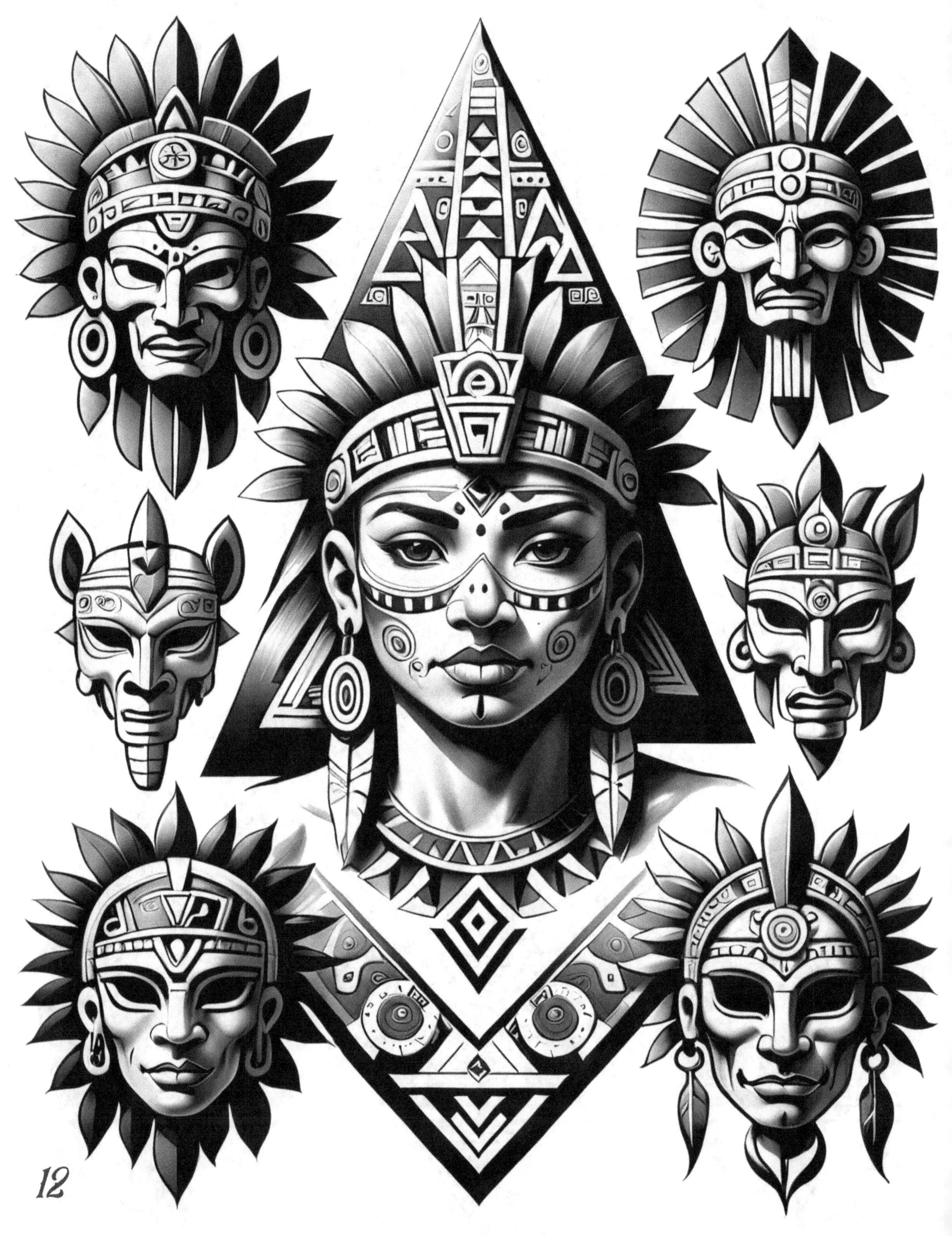
12

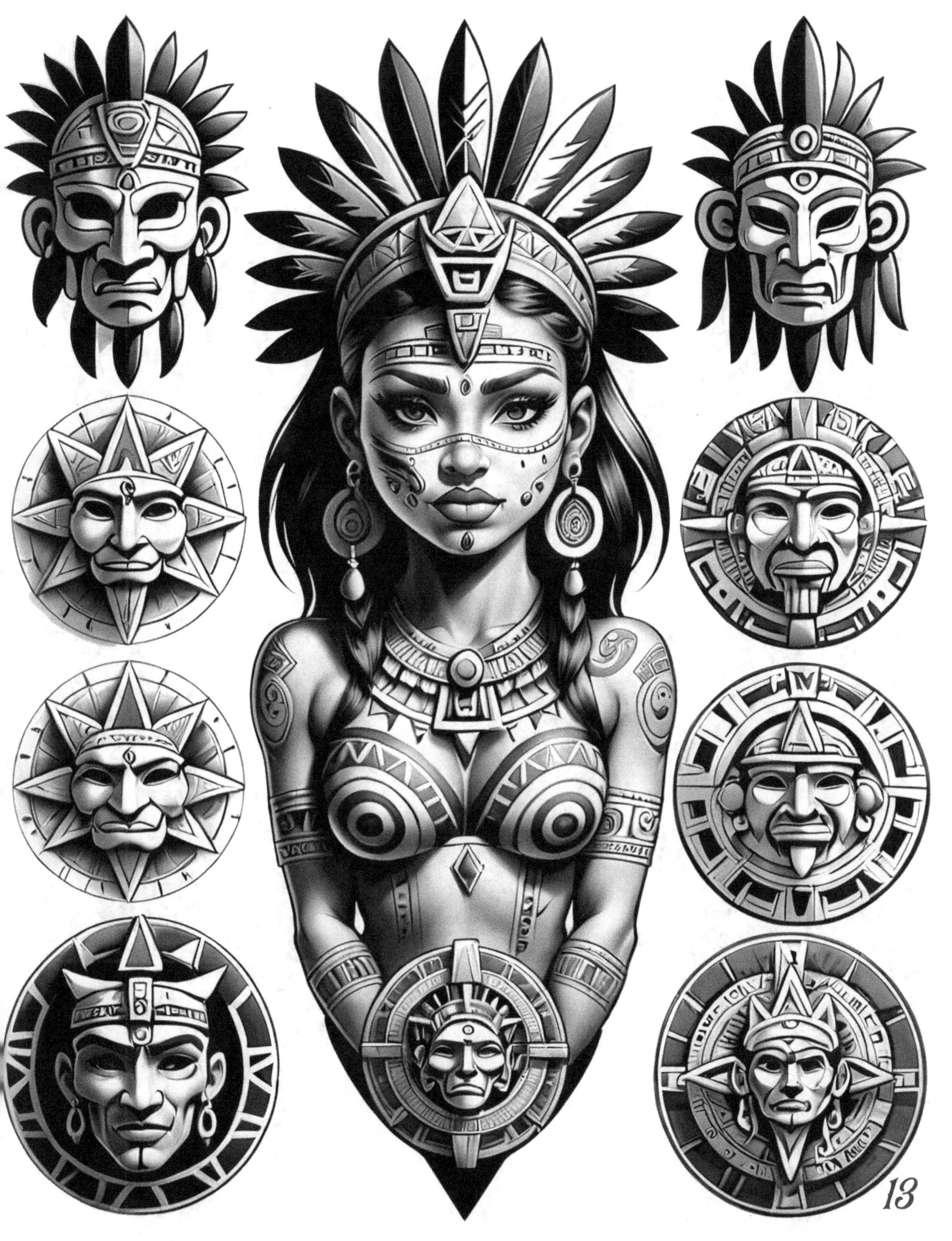

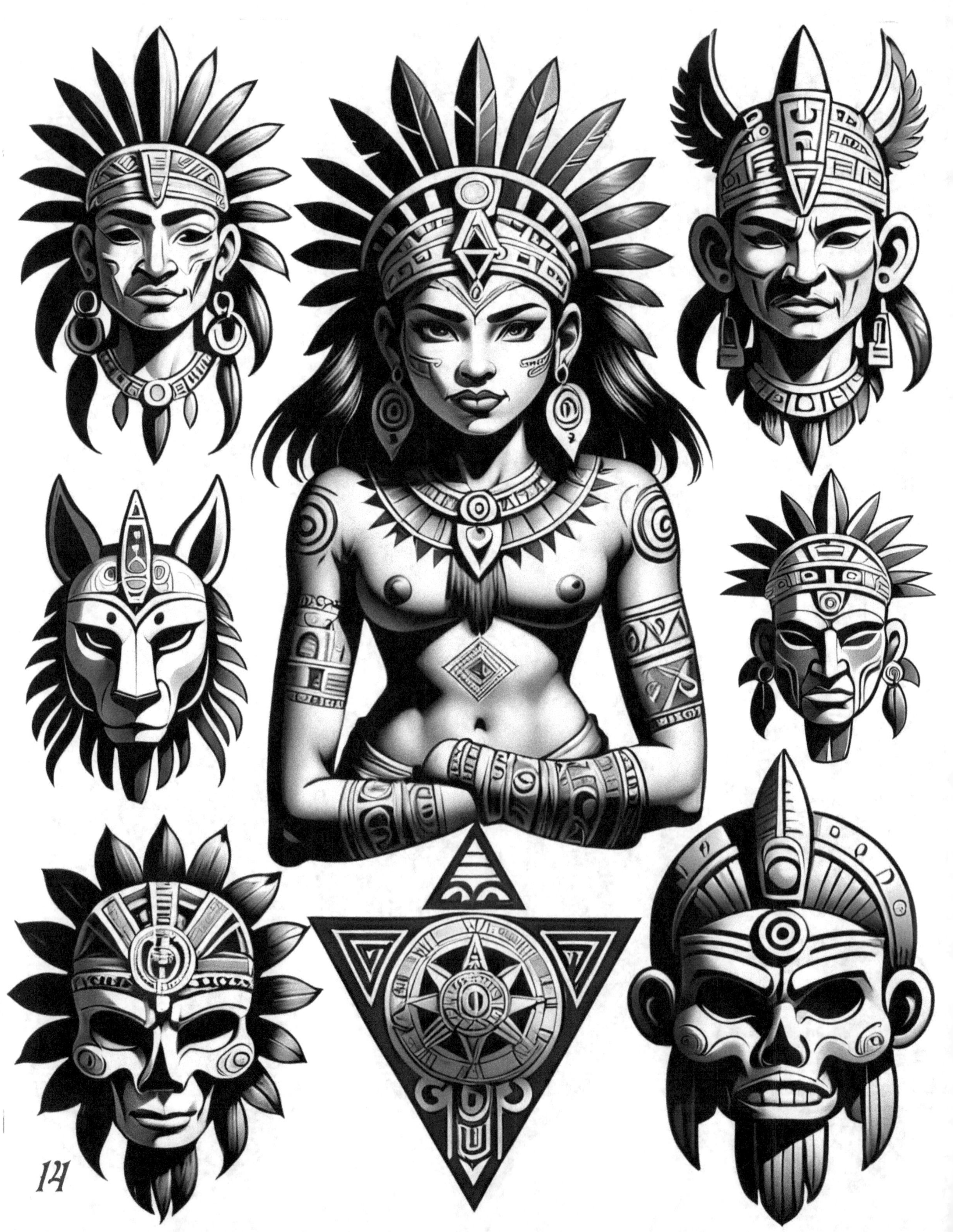

14

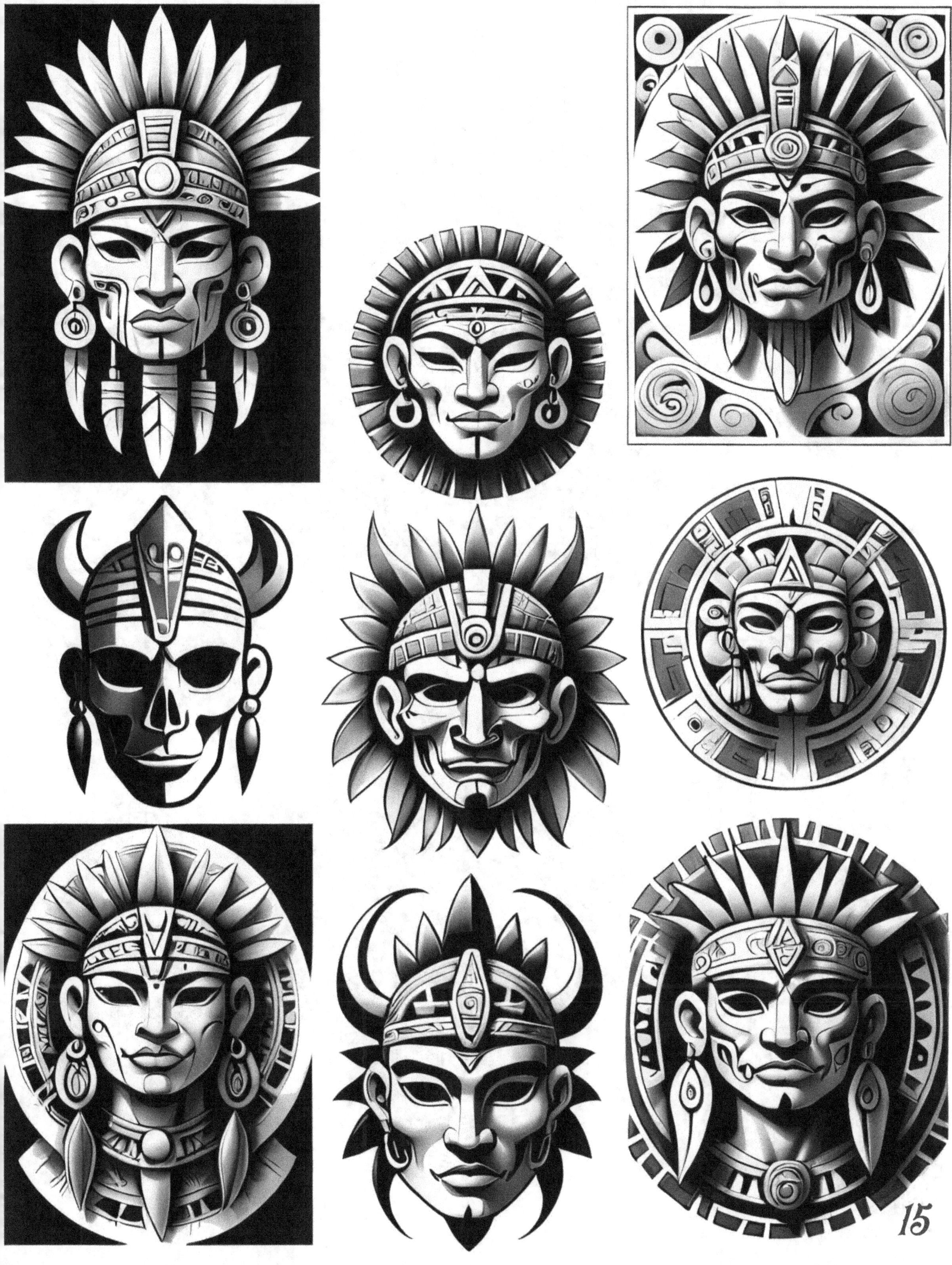

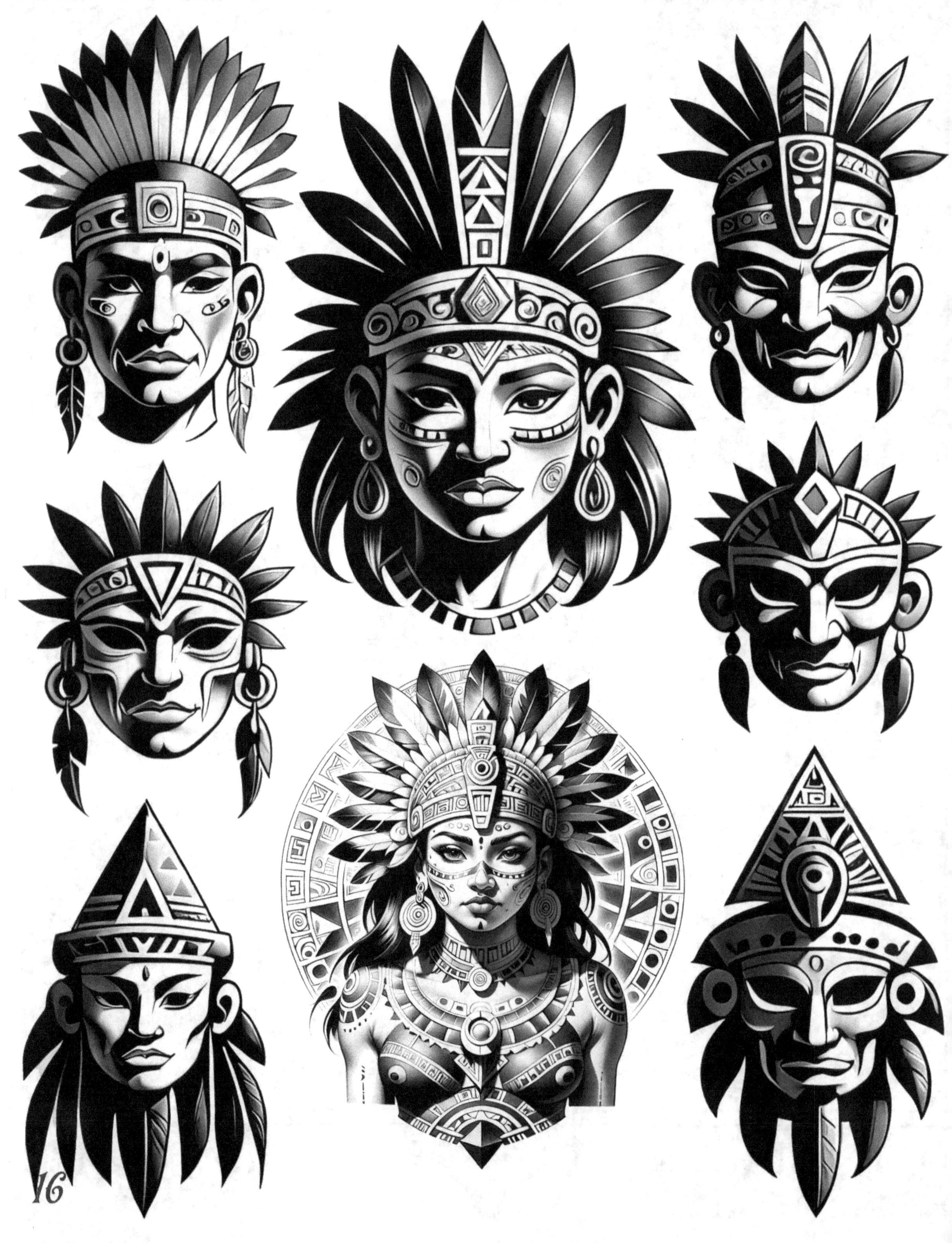

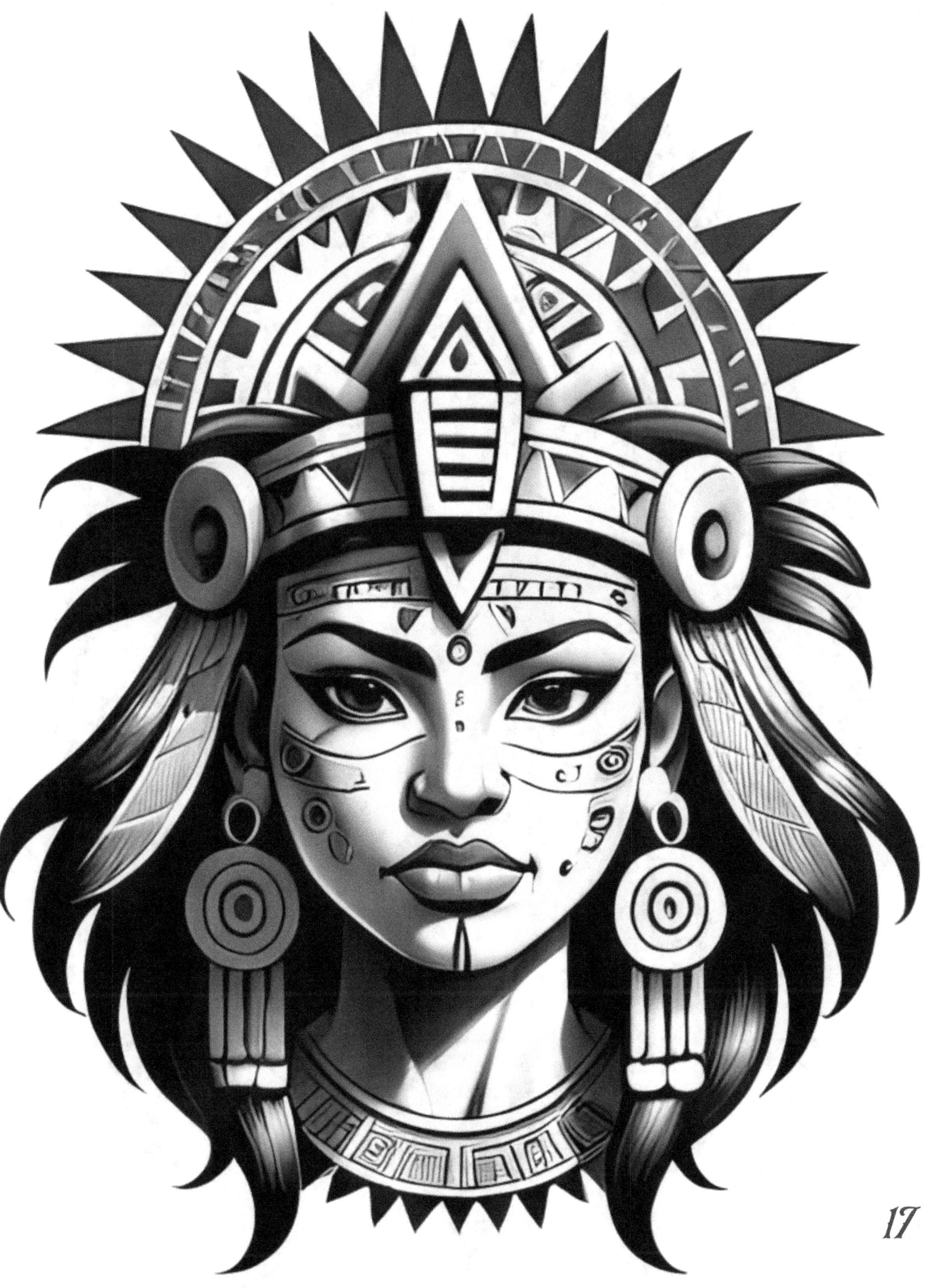

17

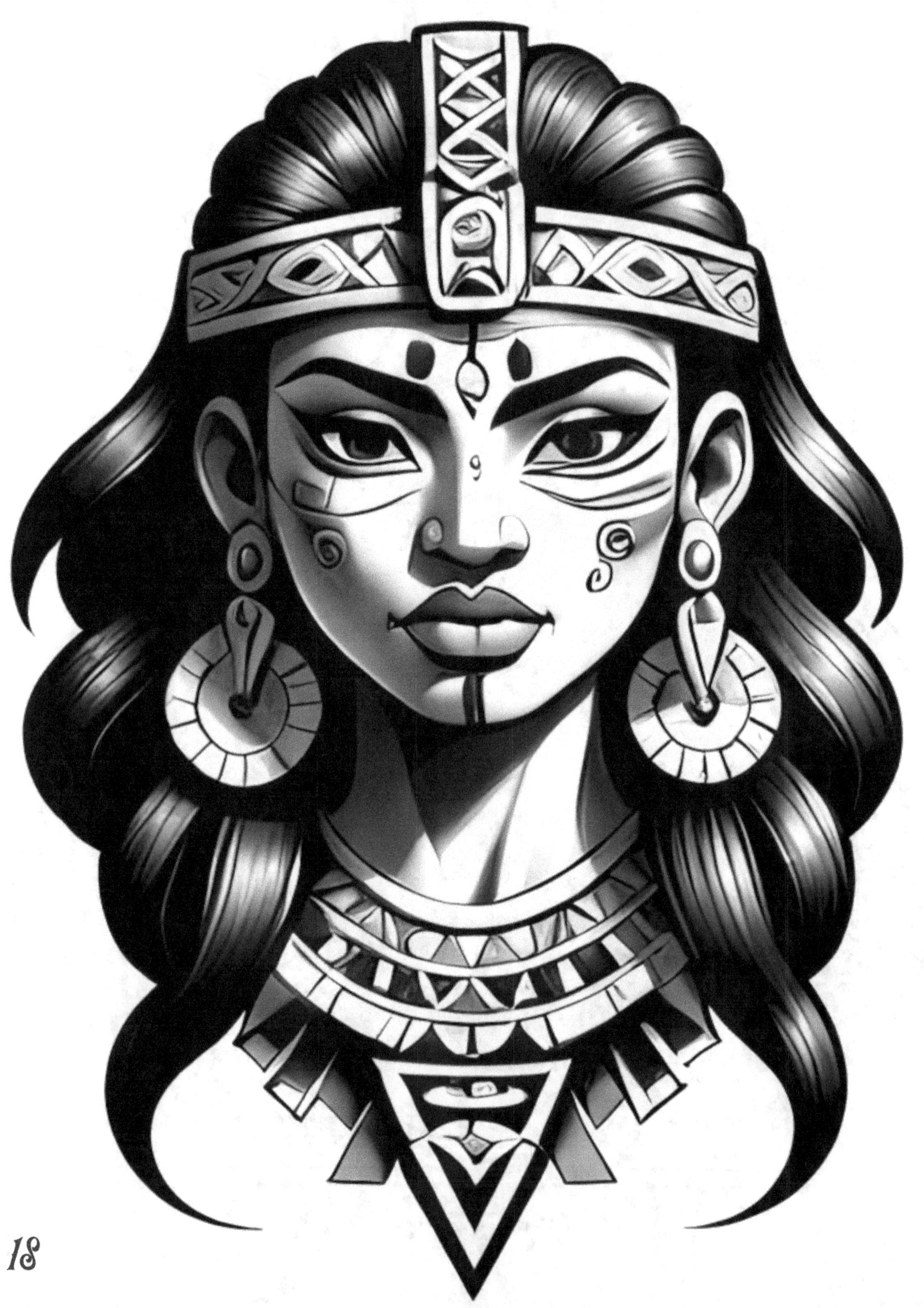

18

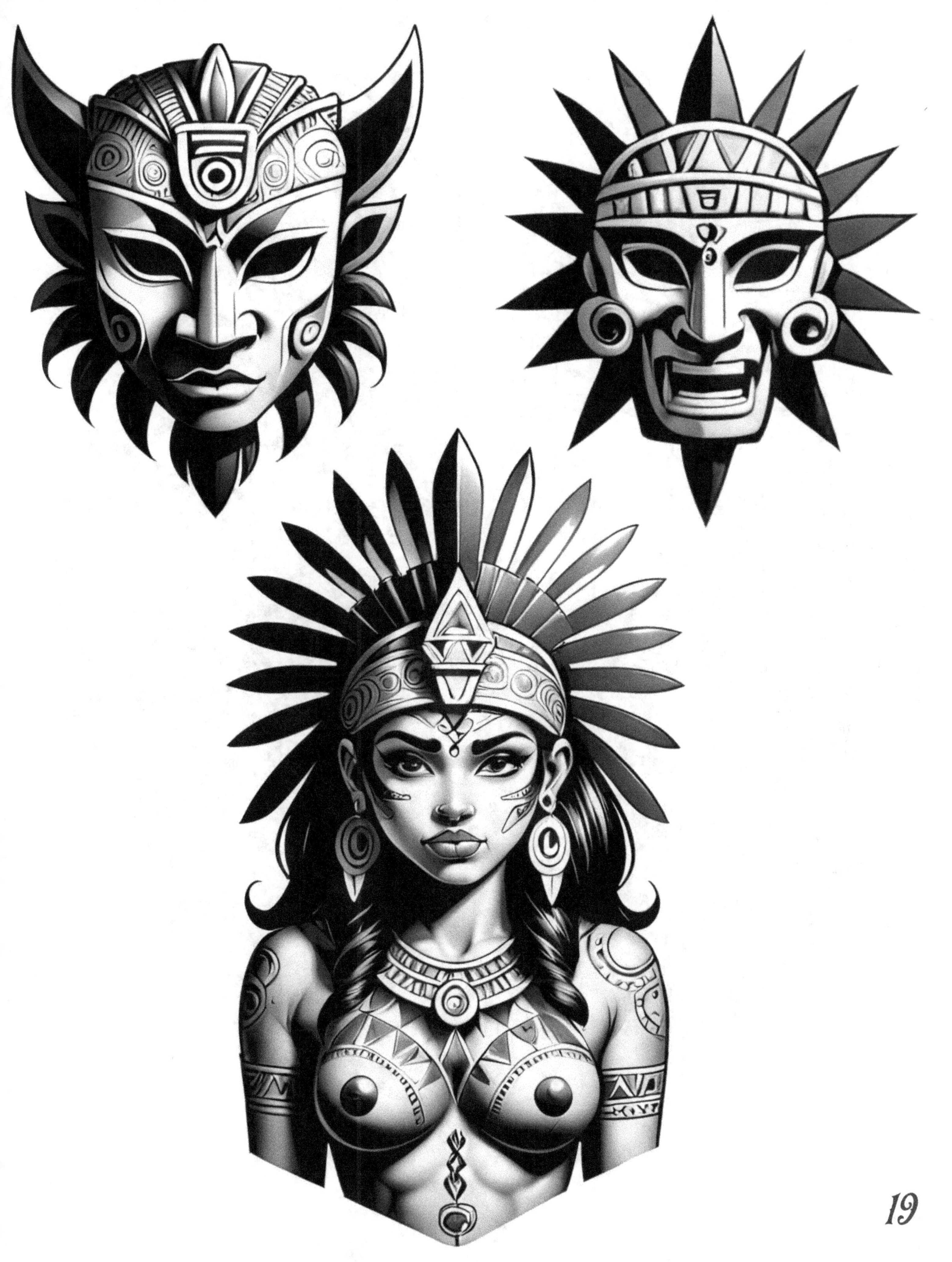

19

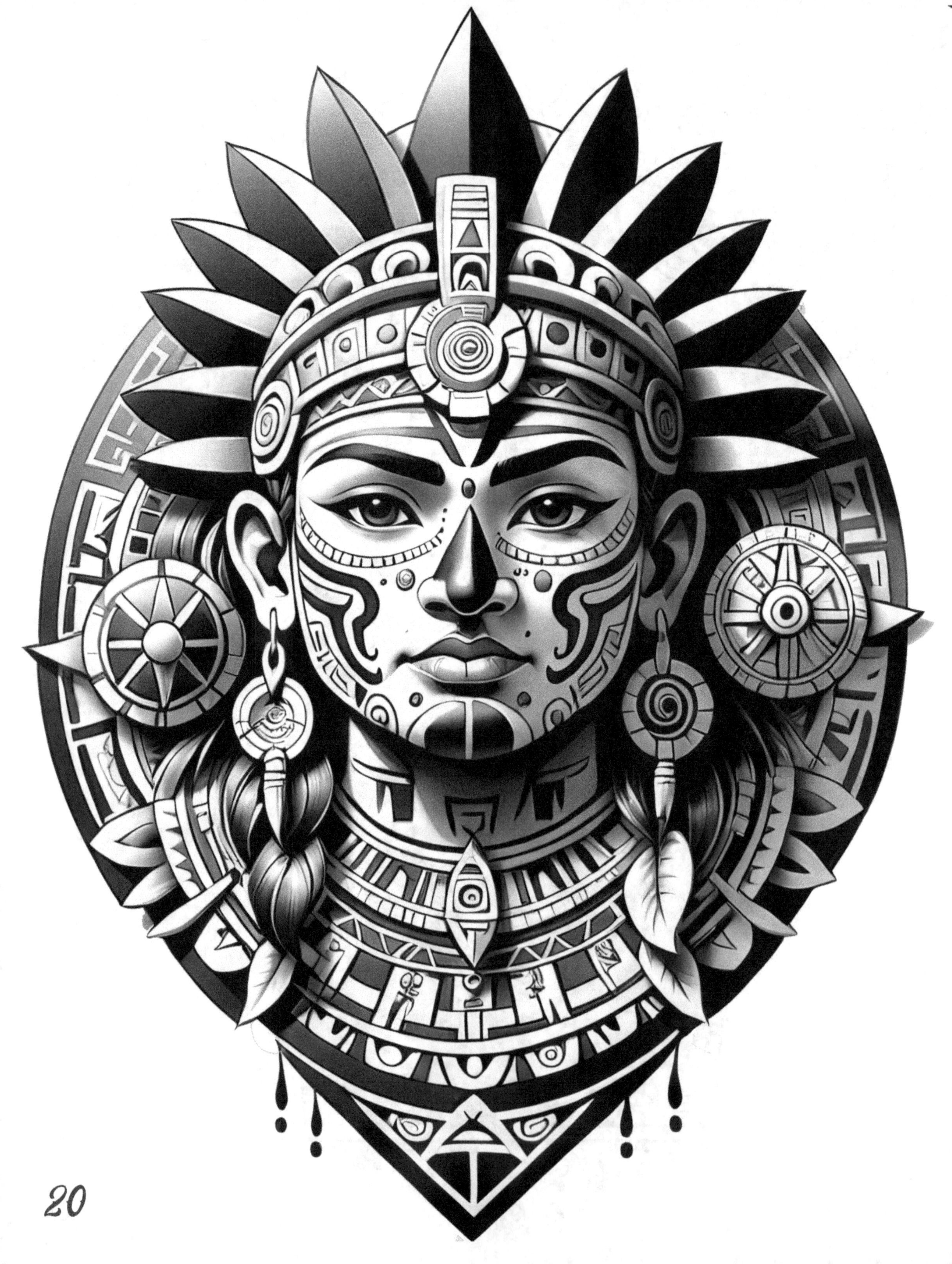

20

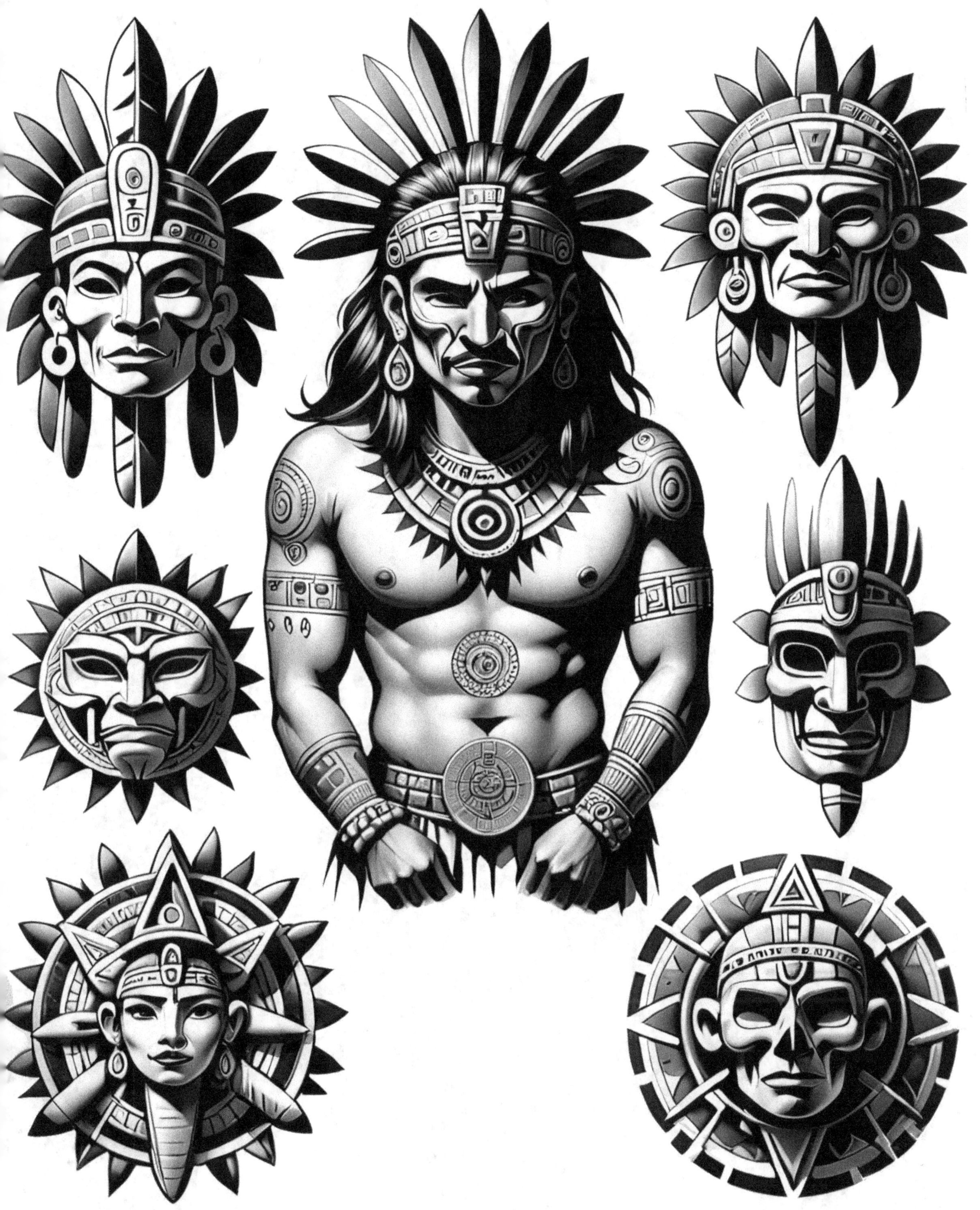

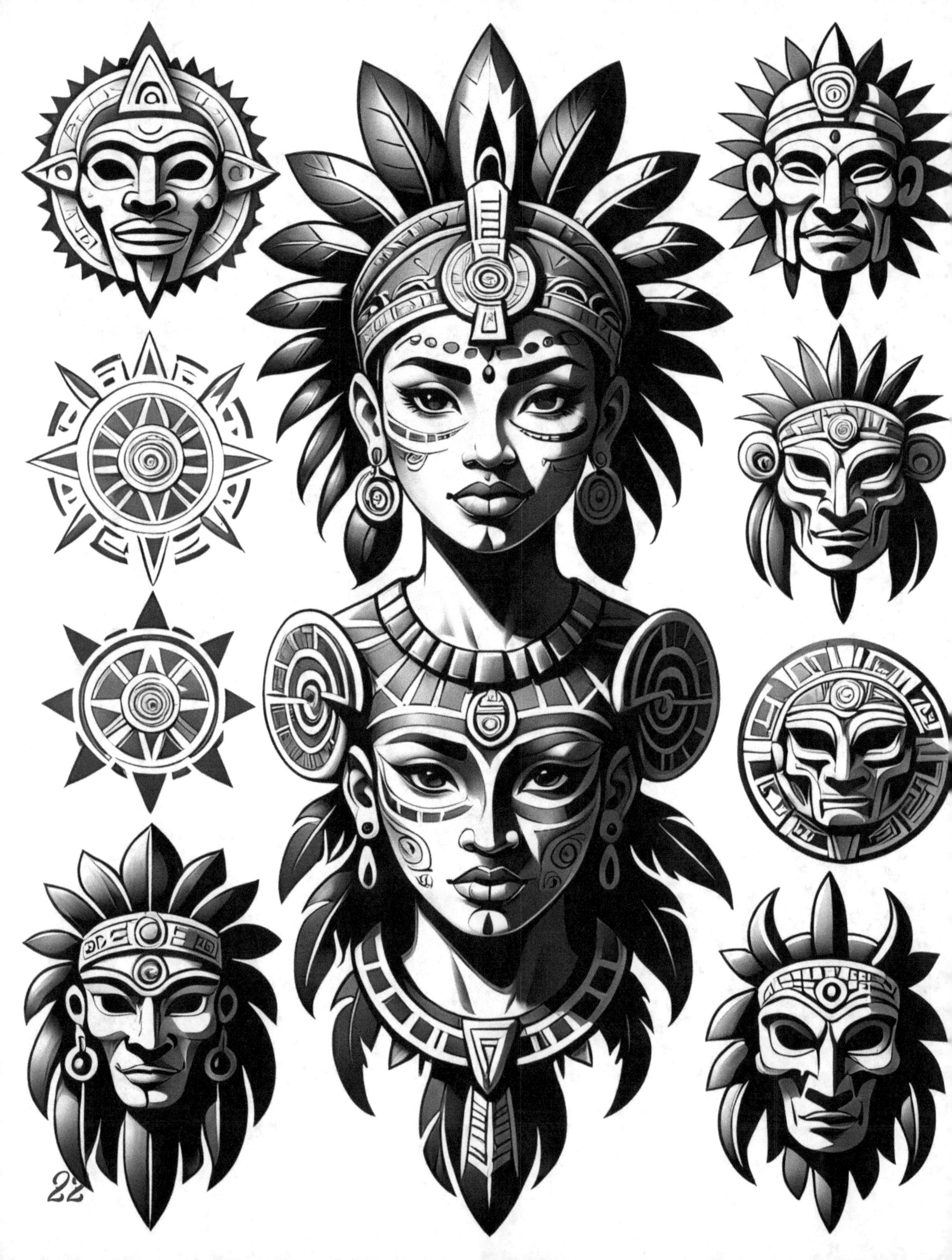

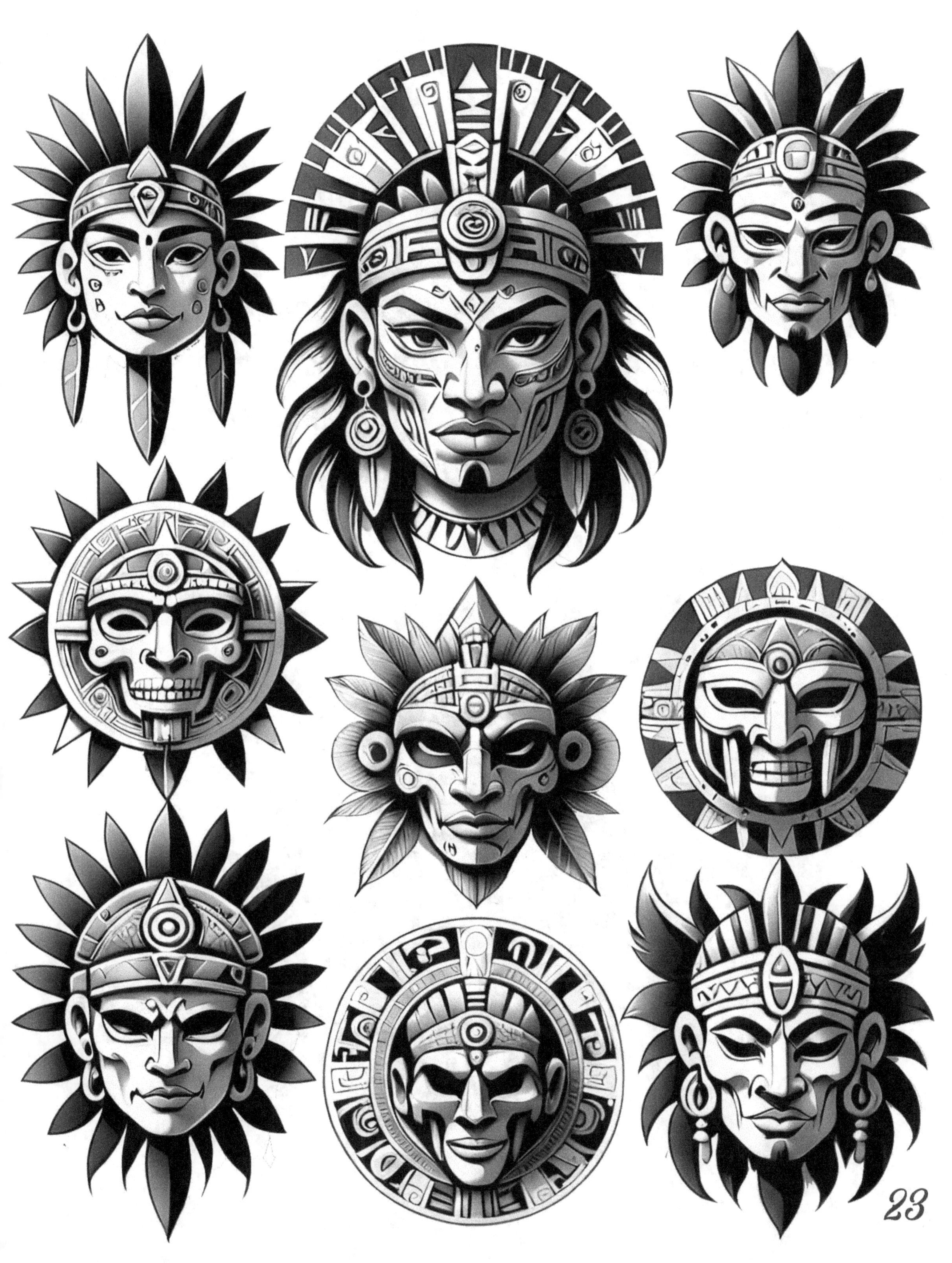

Honor

Honor in Chicano culture is often linked with family loyalty, respect, and personal integrity. Symbols like rosaries, crossed swords, or family crests represent deep commitments to personal codes and values, emphasizing the importance of honor and loyalty within the community.

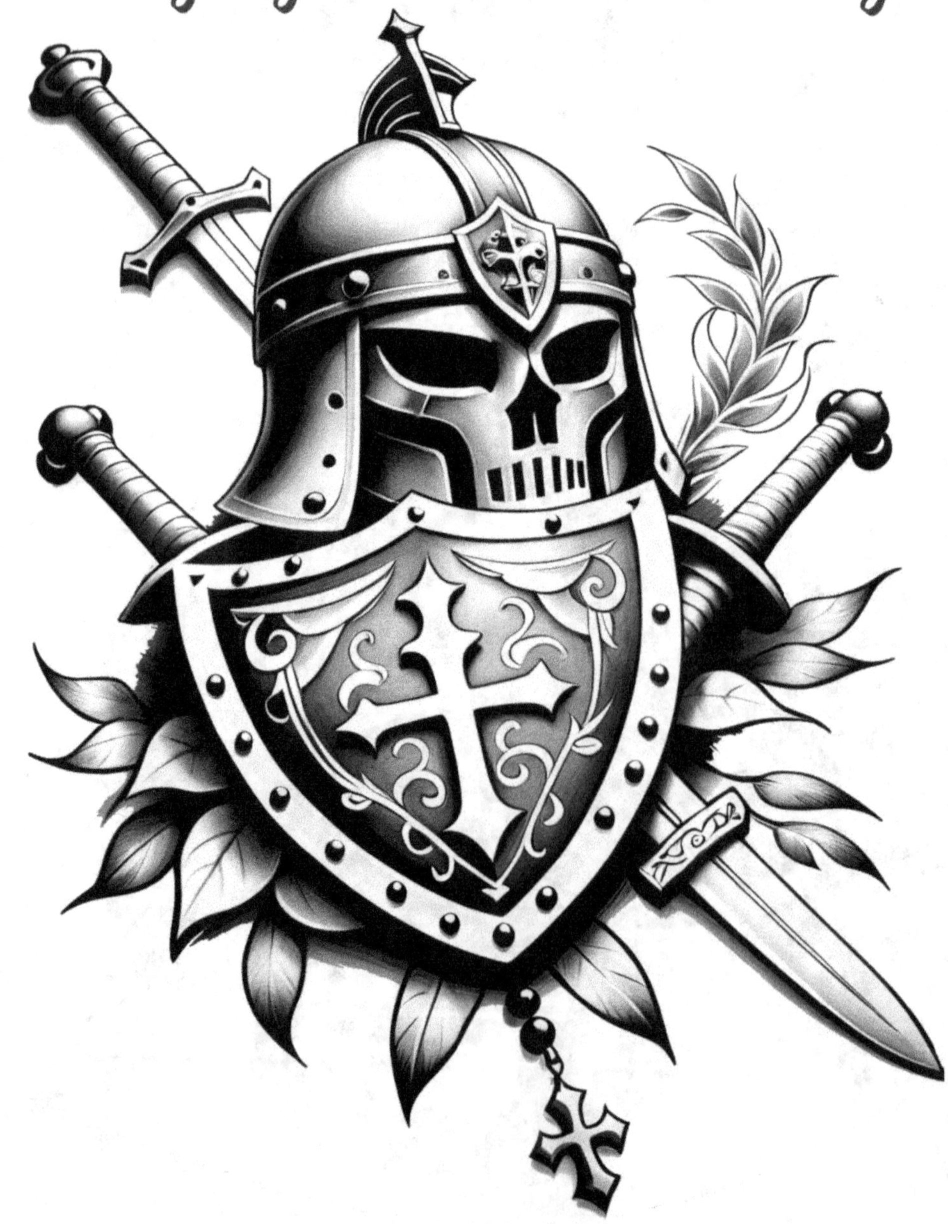

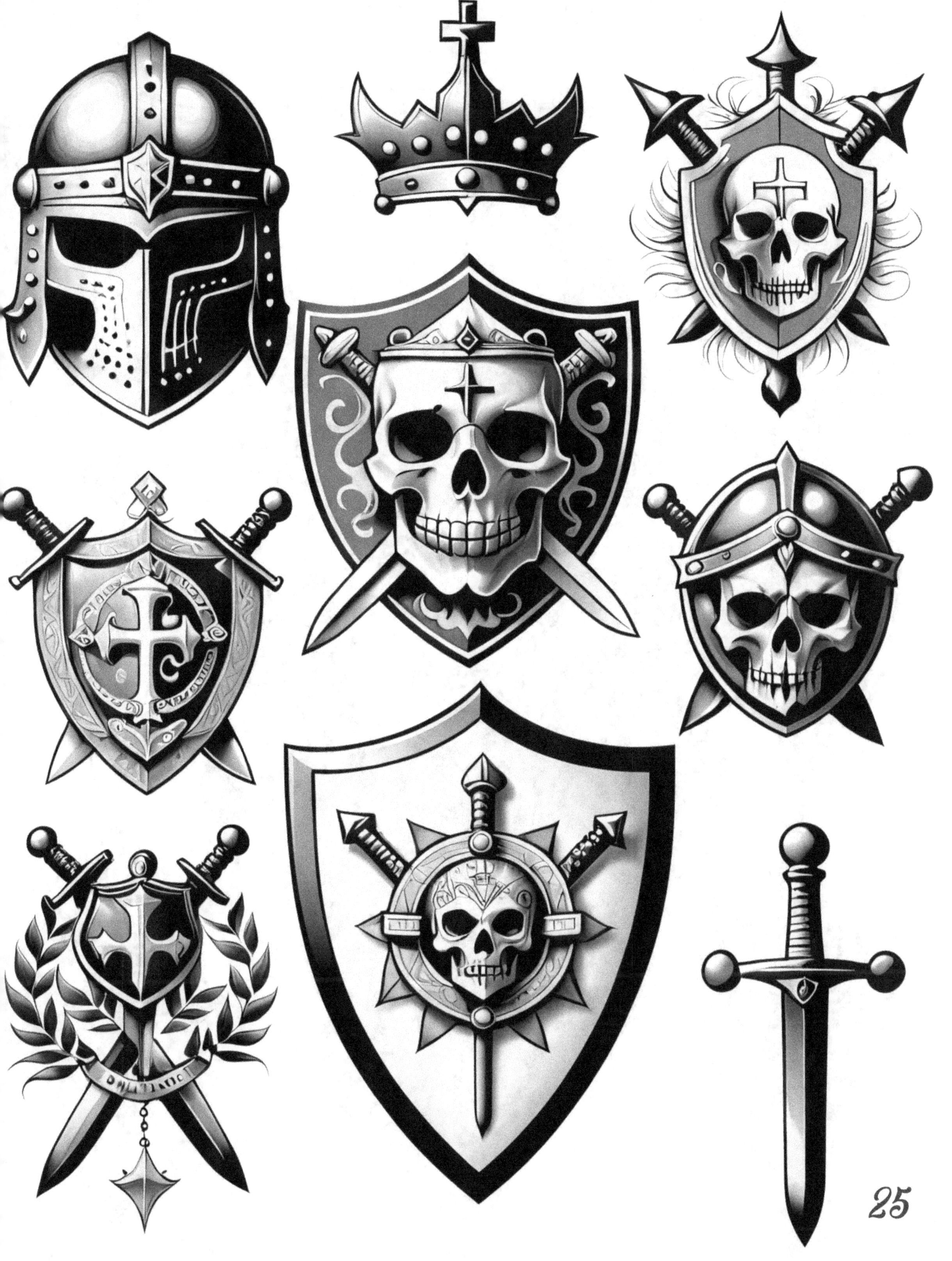

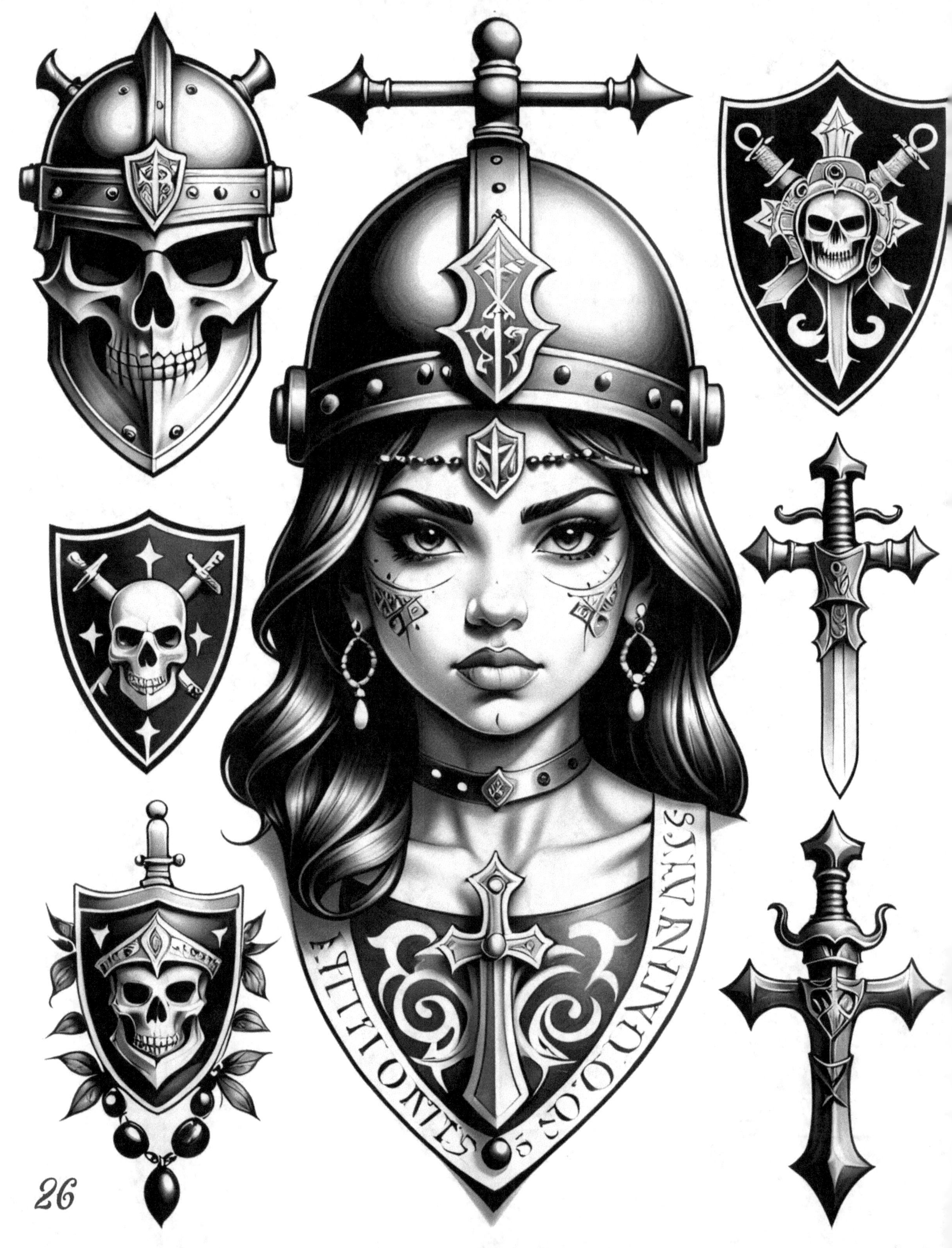

26

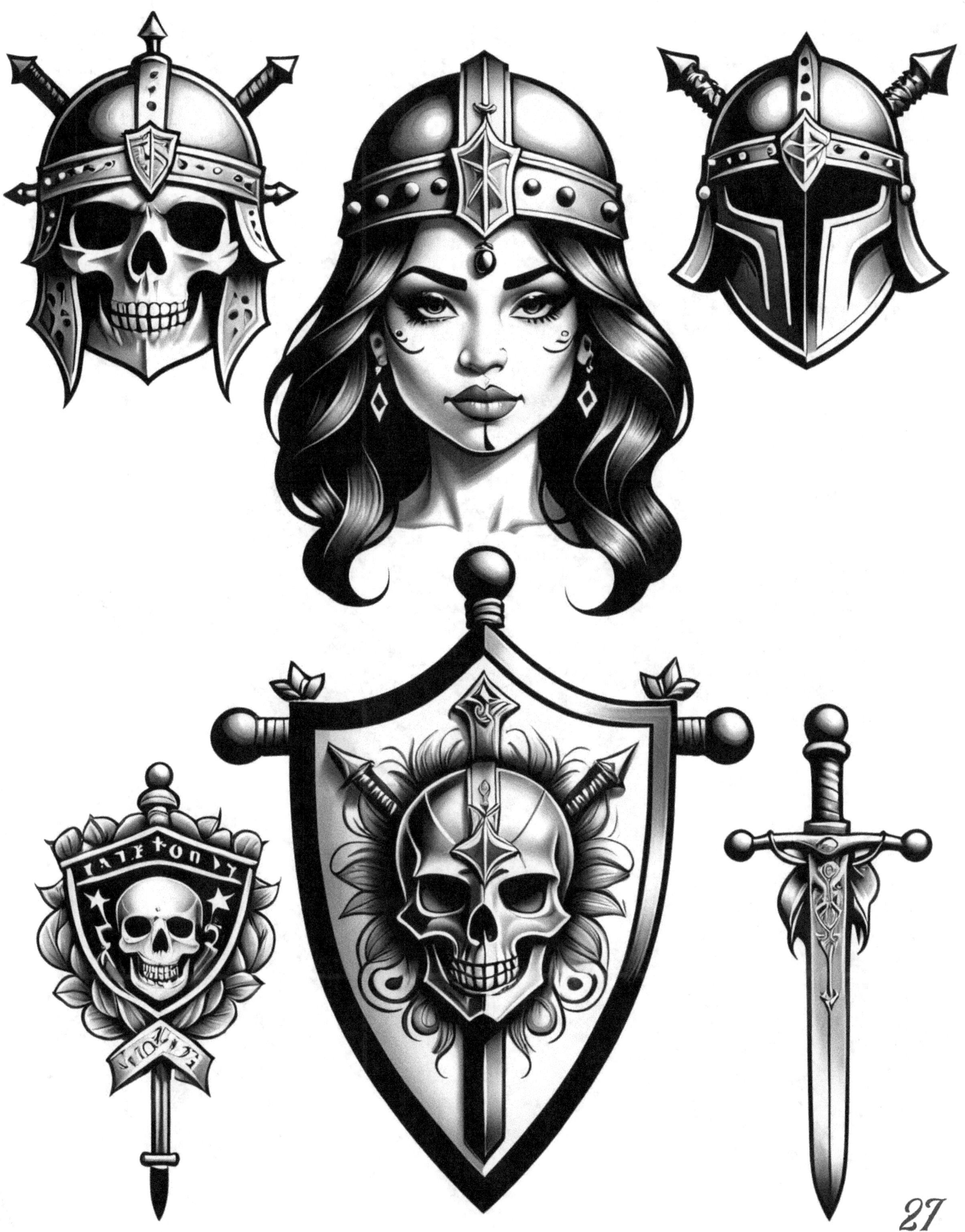

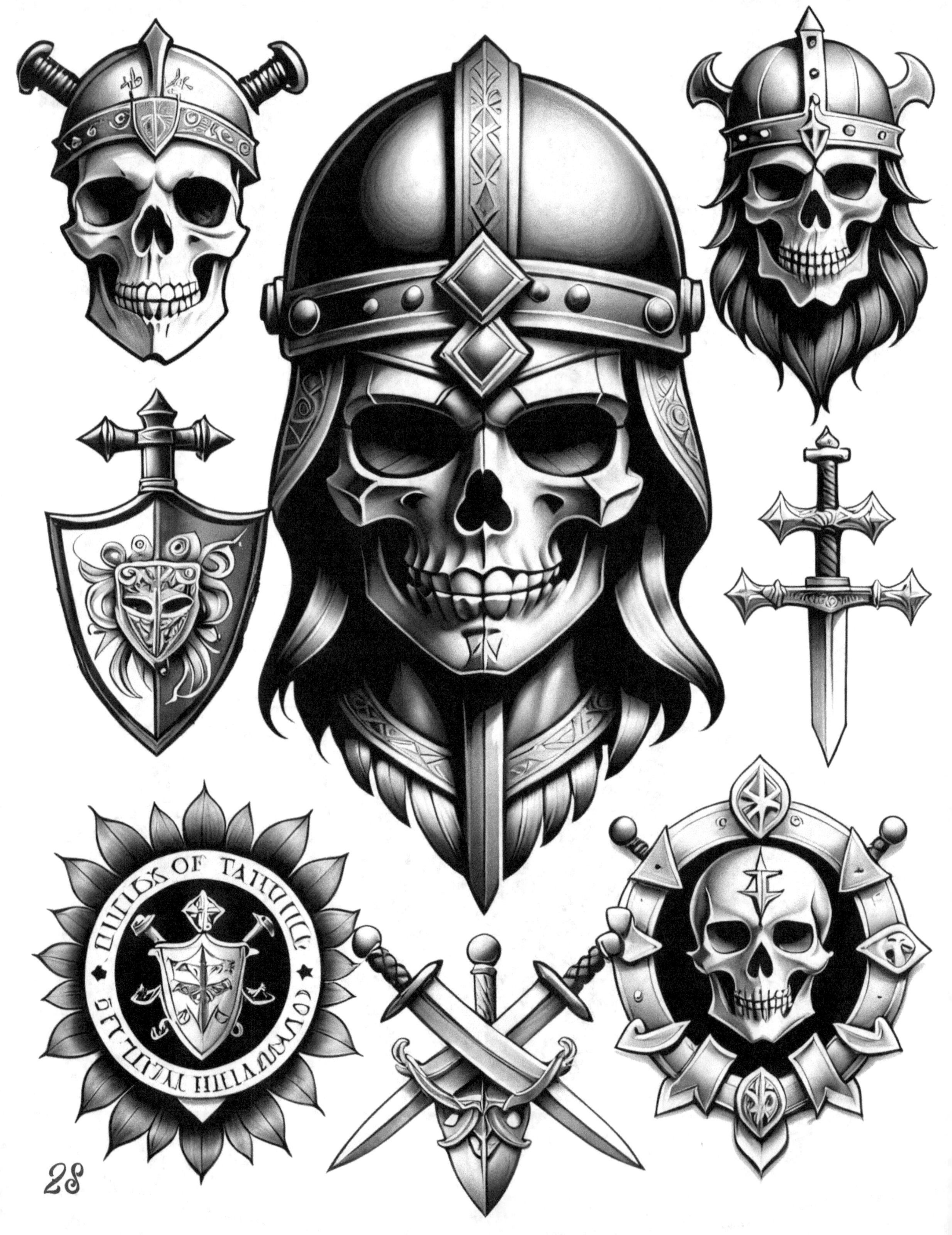

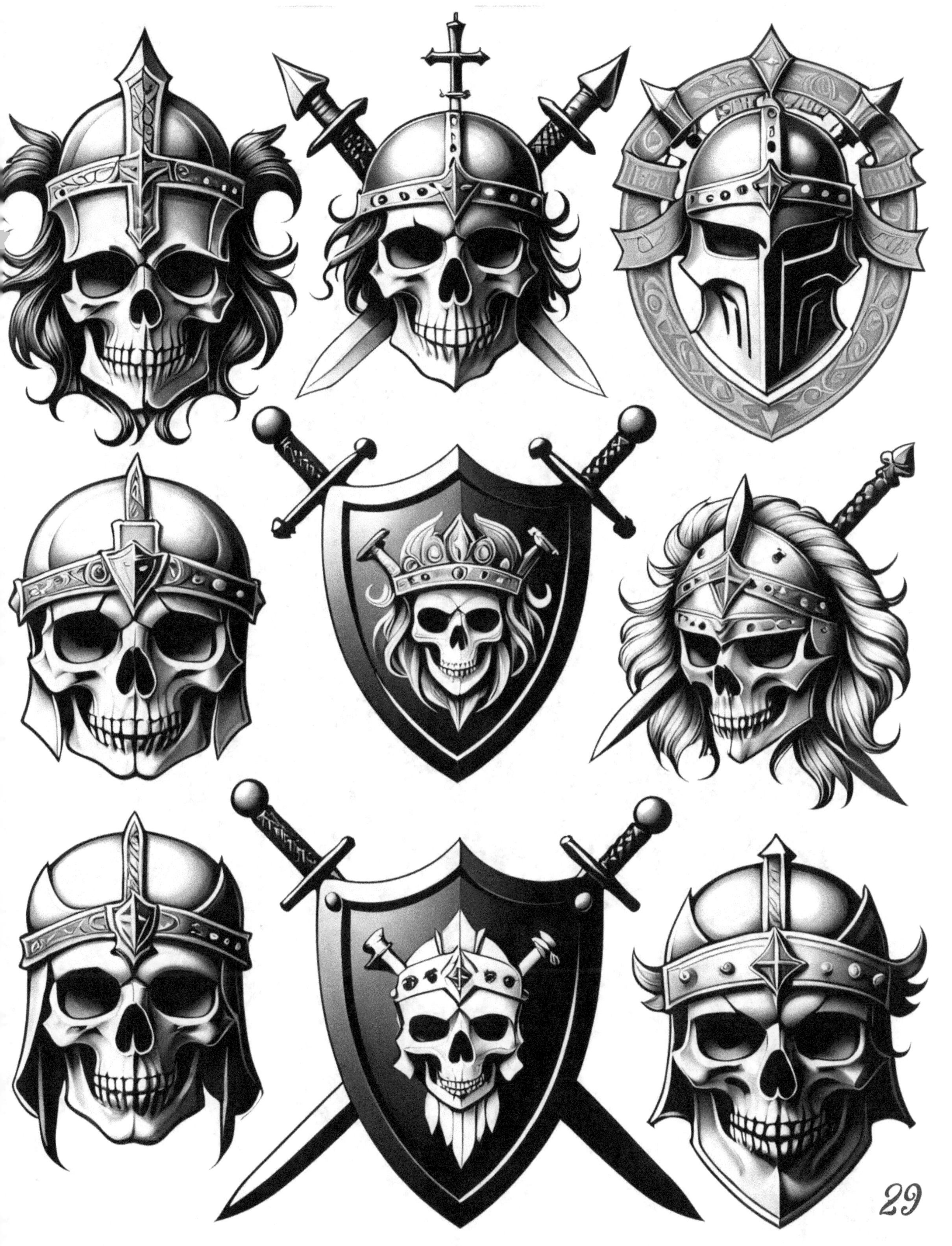

29

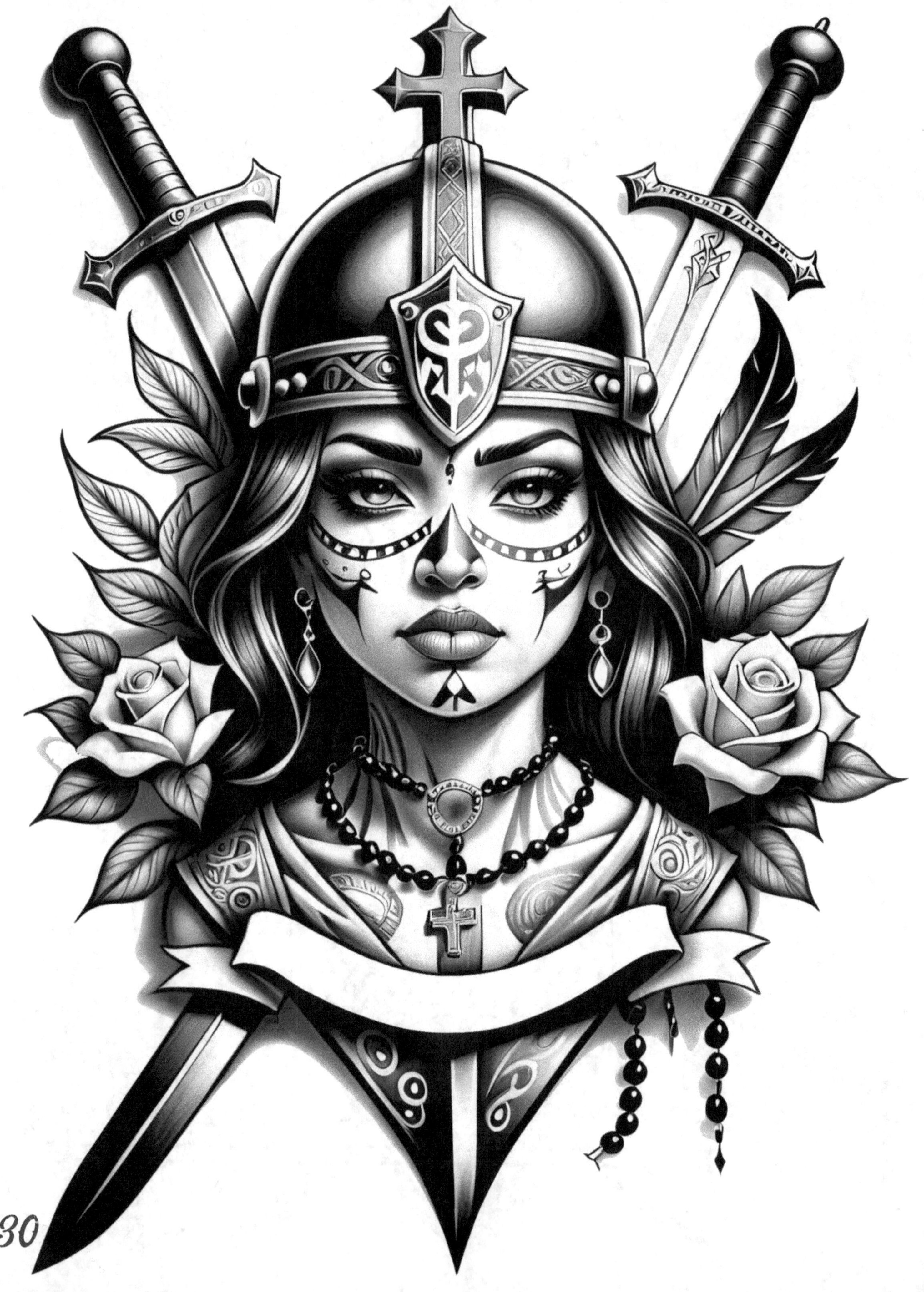

30

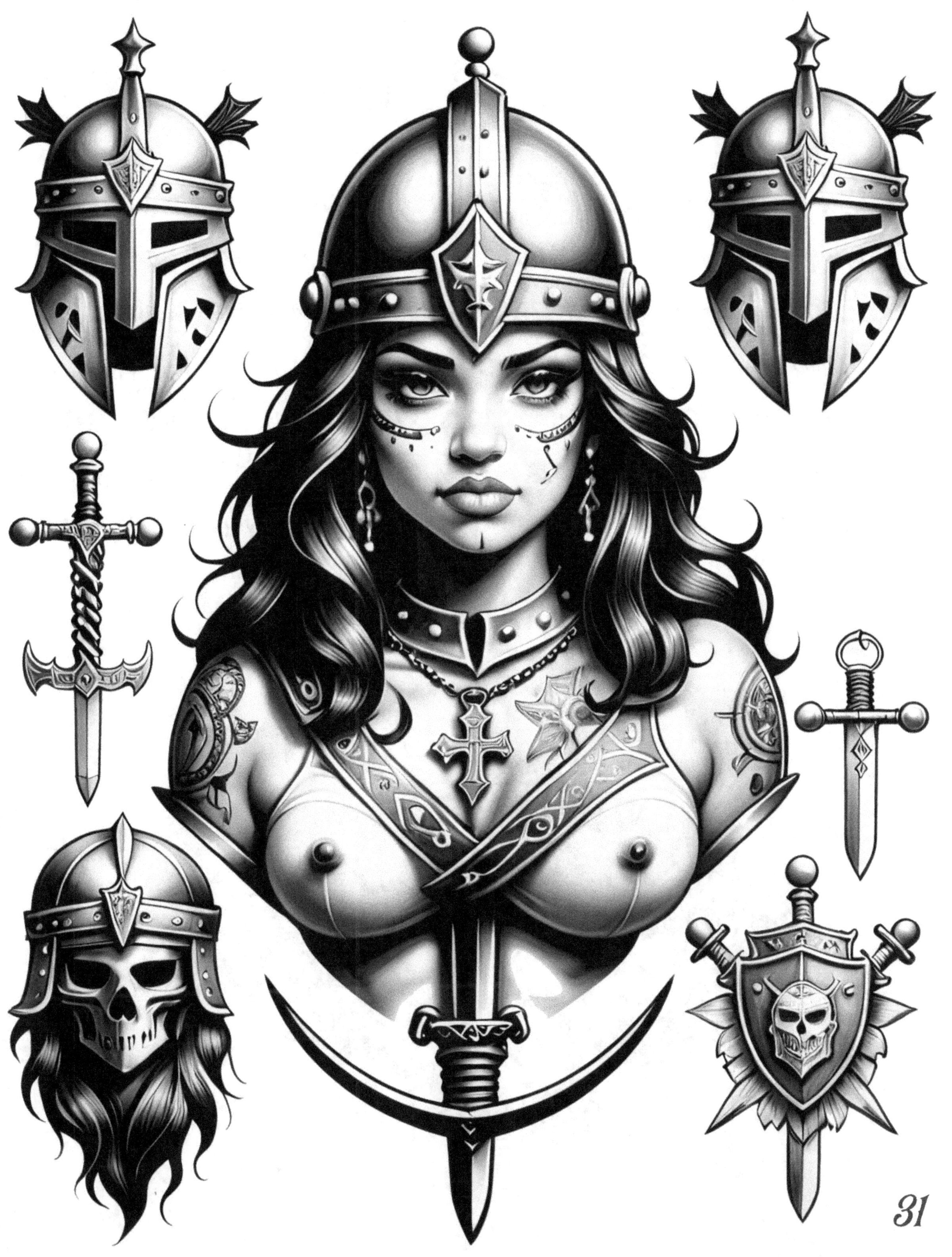

Cultural

Cultural motifs in Chicano tattoos celebrate the rich and diverse elements of Mexican and broader Latino heritage. Instruments like maracas and guitars, objects like sombreros and cacti, and symbols like the Mexican eagle proudly display cultural pride and connection. These tattoos often serve as a vibrant expression of cultural identity and a celebration of heritage.

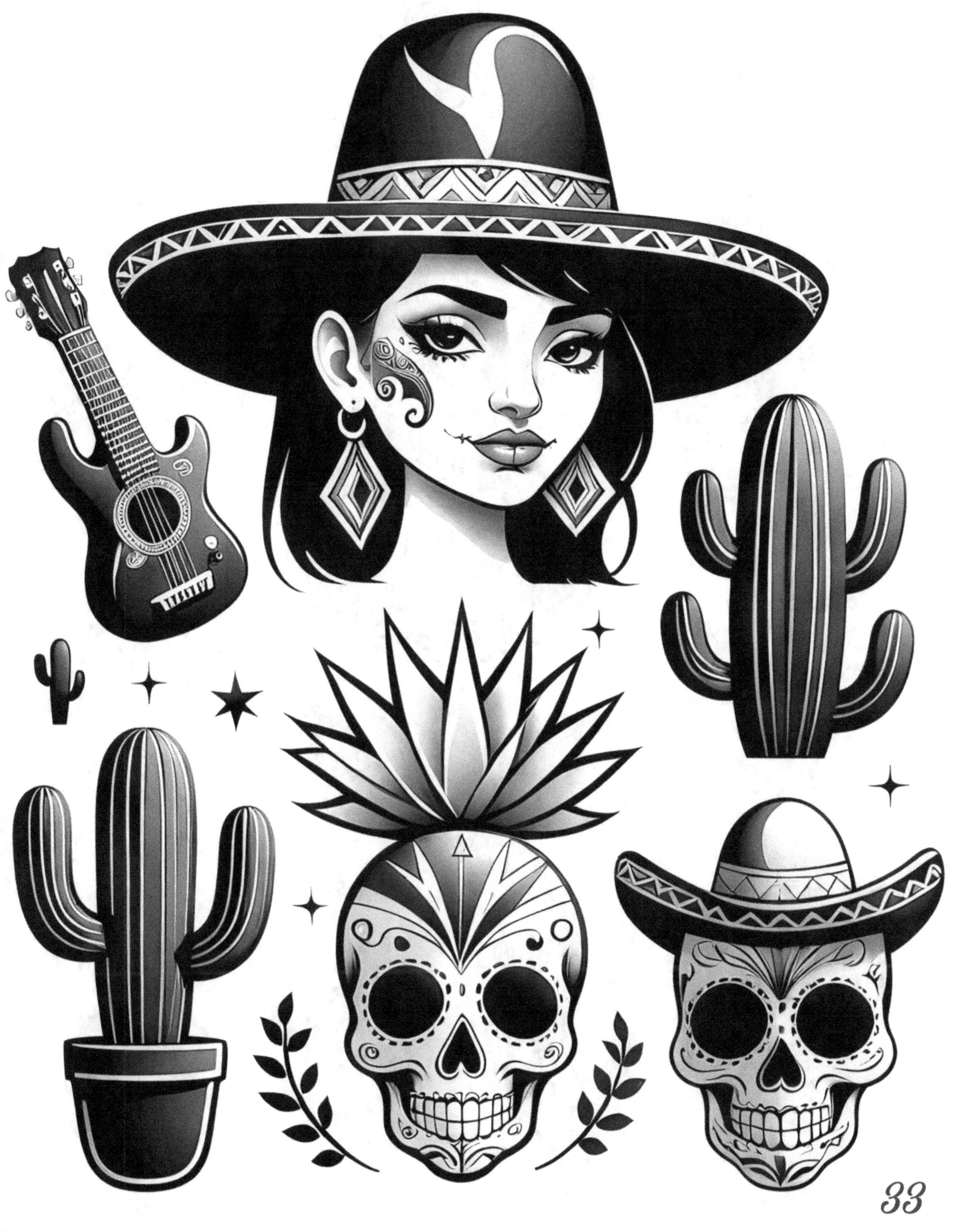

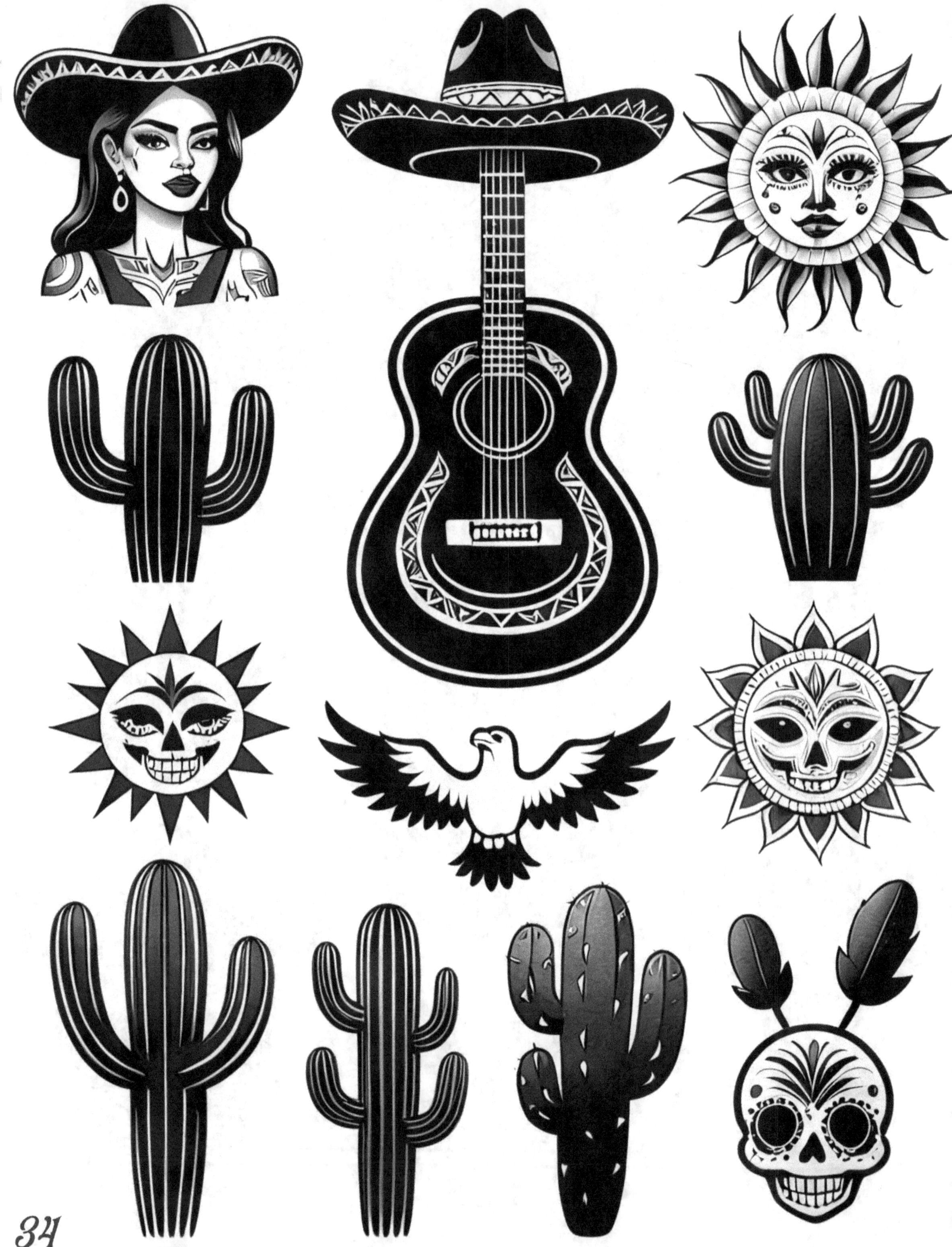

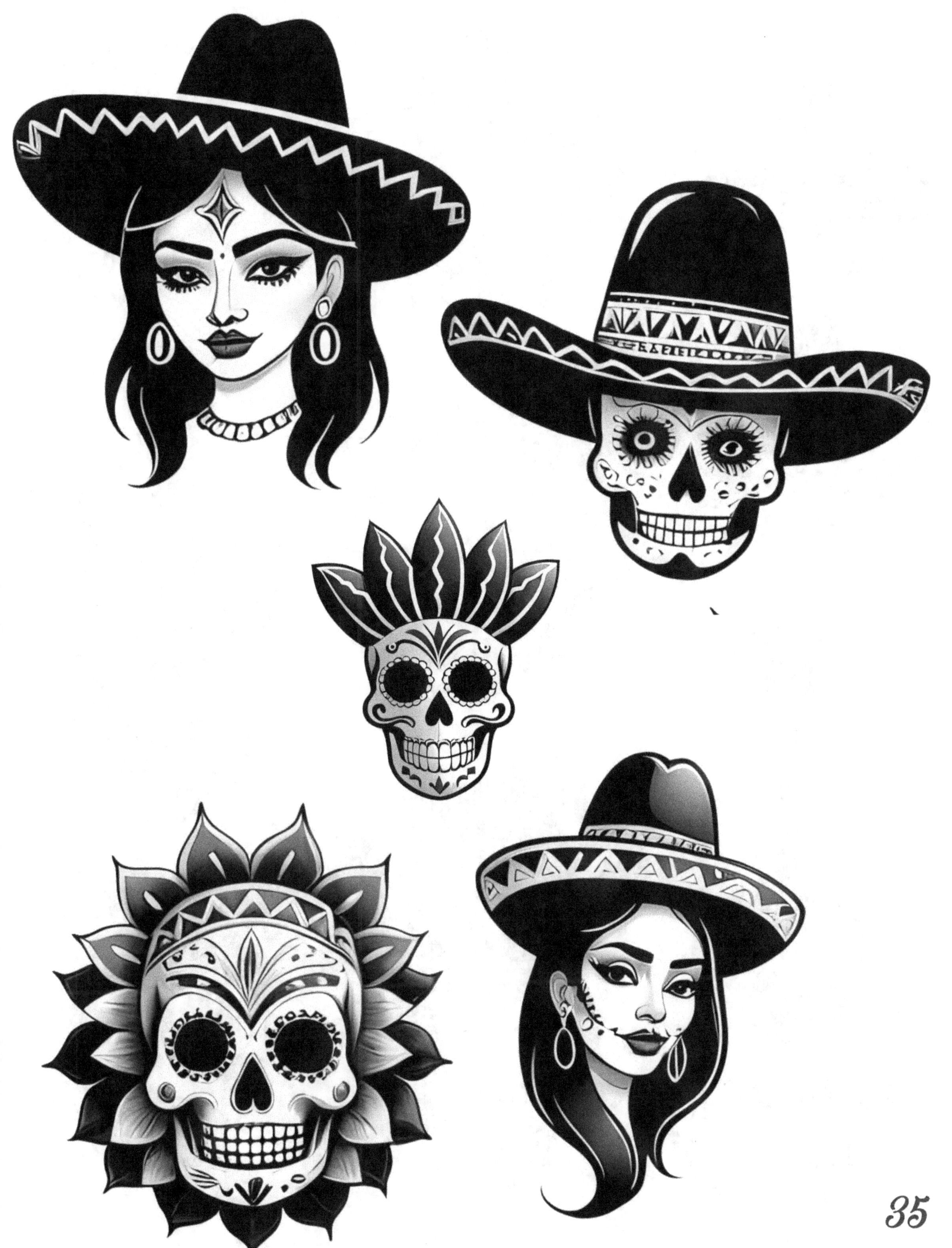

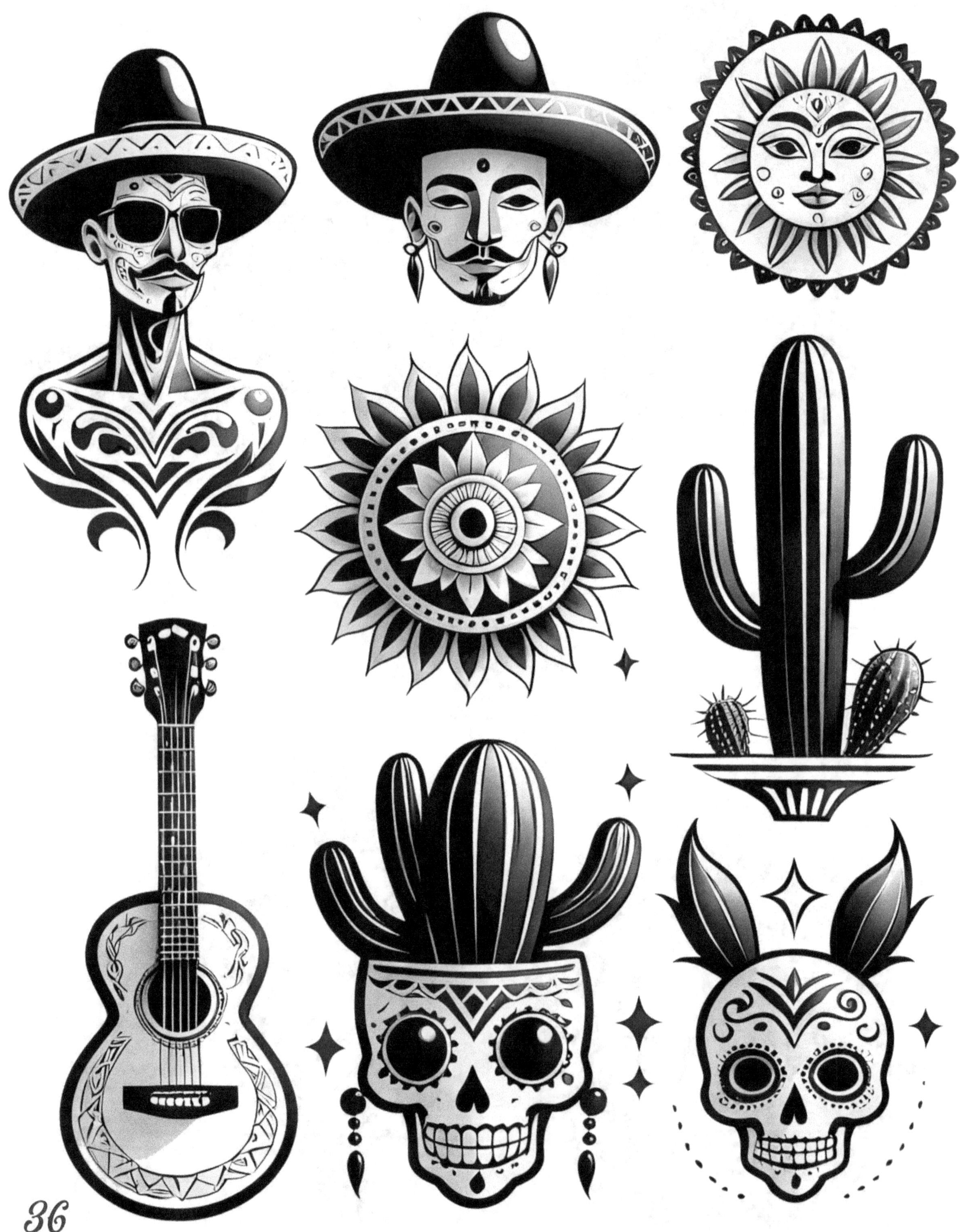

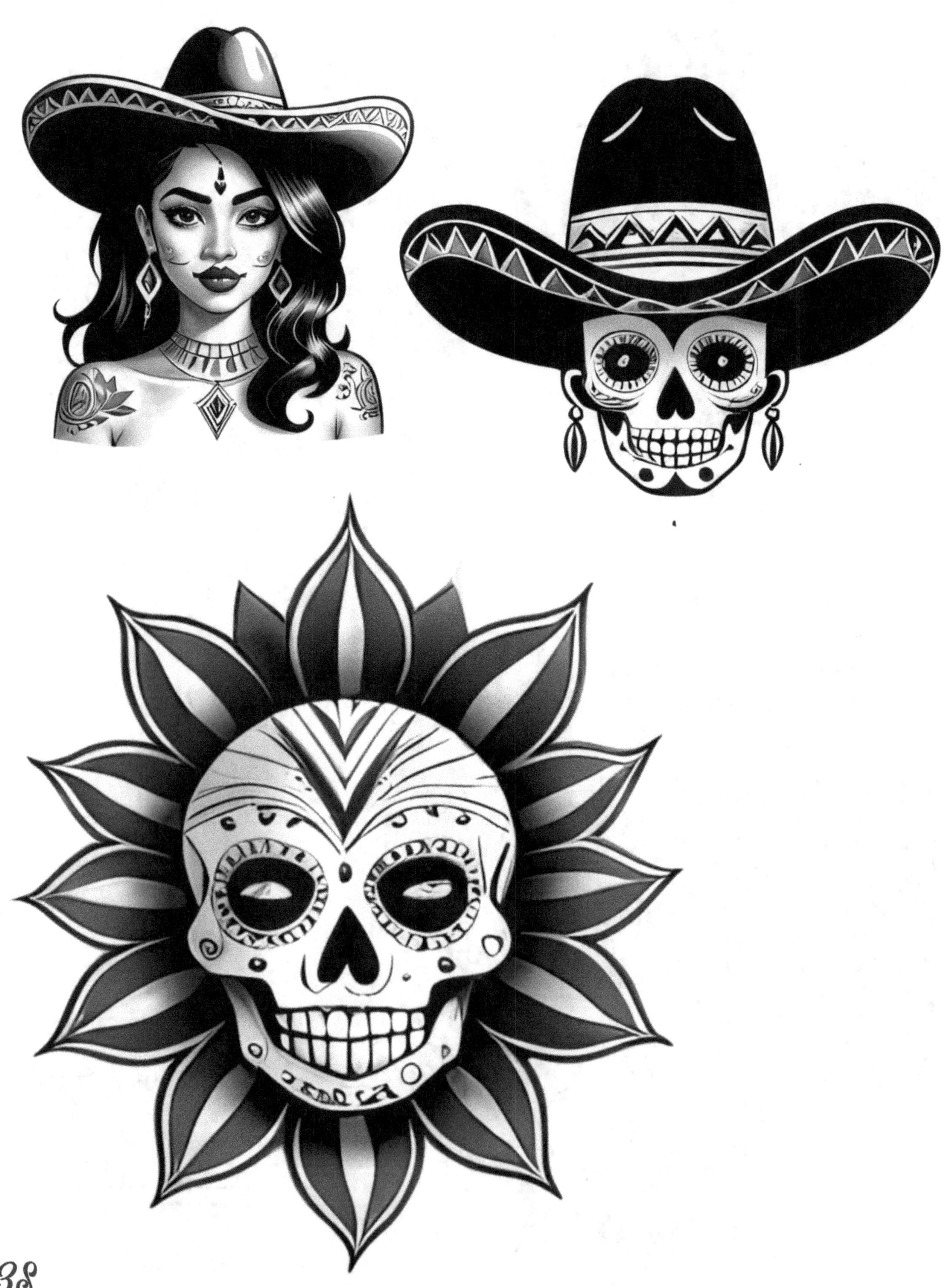

38

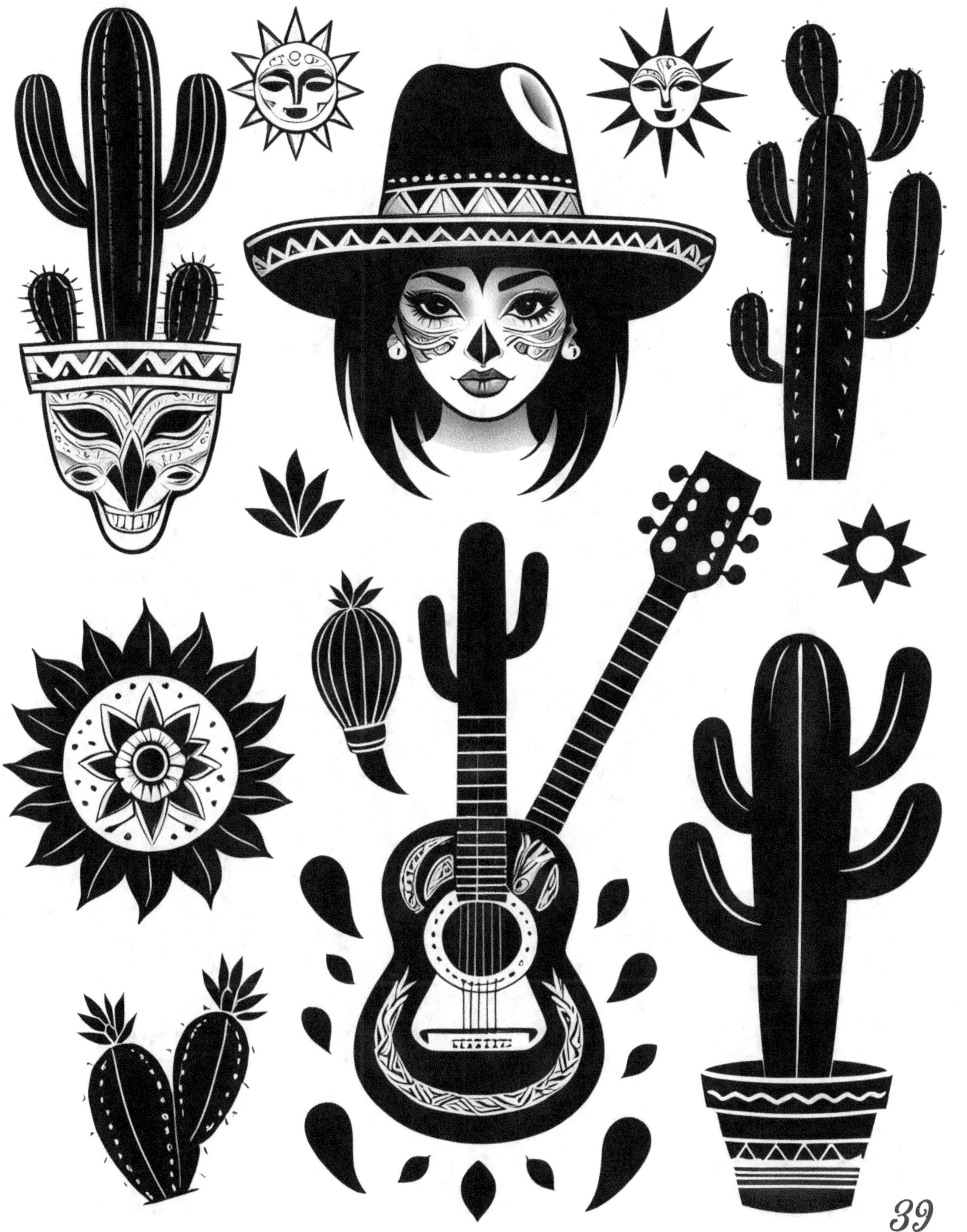

39

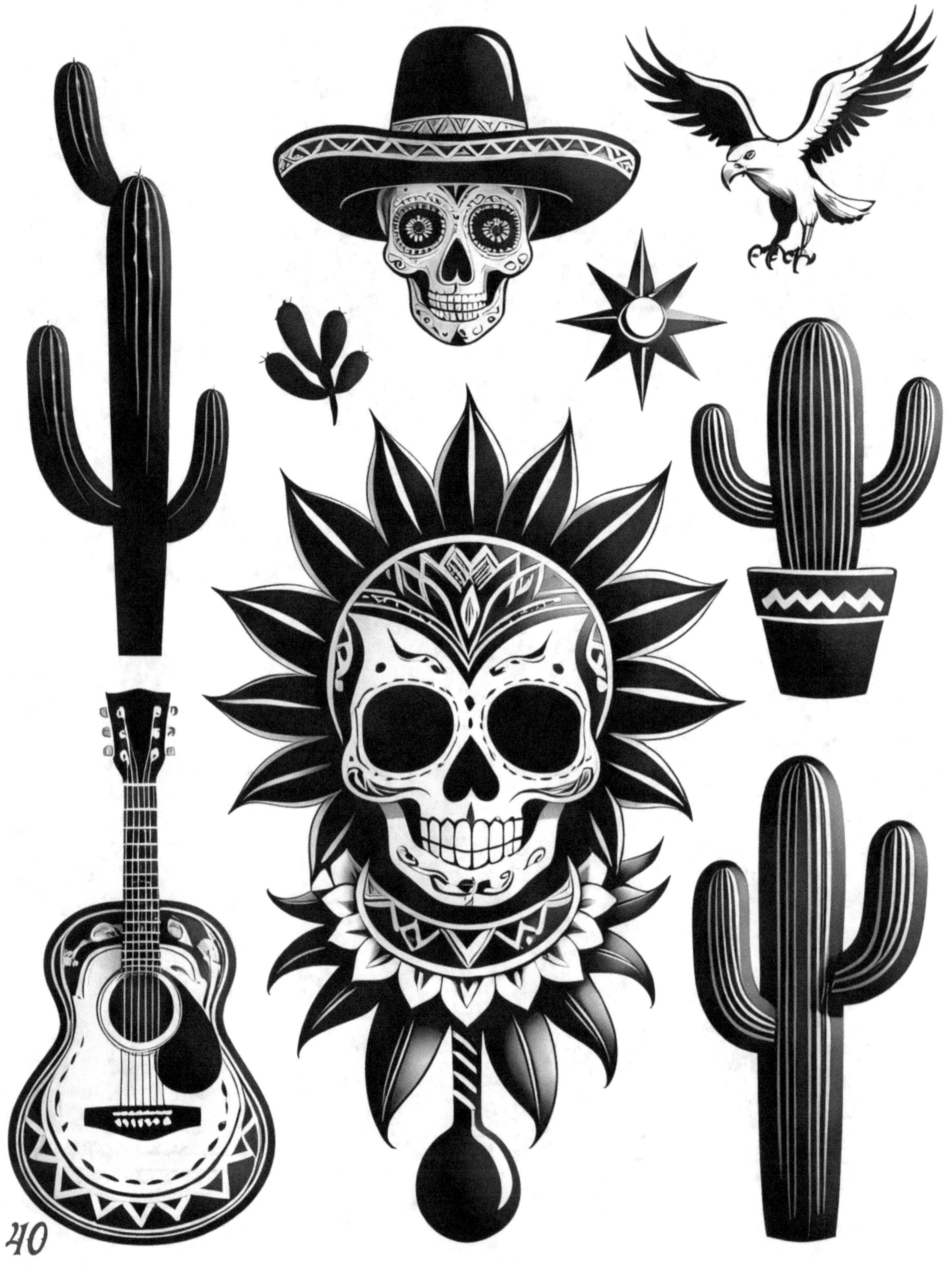

40

Loss

Loss is a profound theme in Chicano tattoos, often depicted through symbols like wilted roses, teardrops, and tombstones. These designs commemorate loved ones, reflect personal sorrow, and honor memories, providing a permanent tribute to those who have passed away and the impact they had on the wearer's life

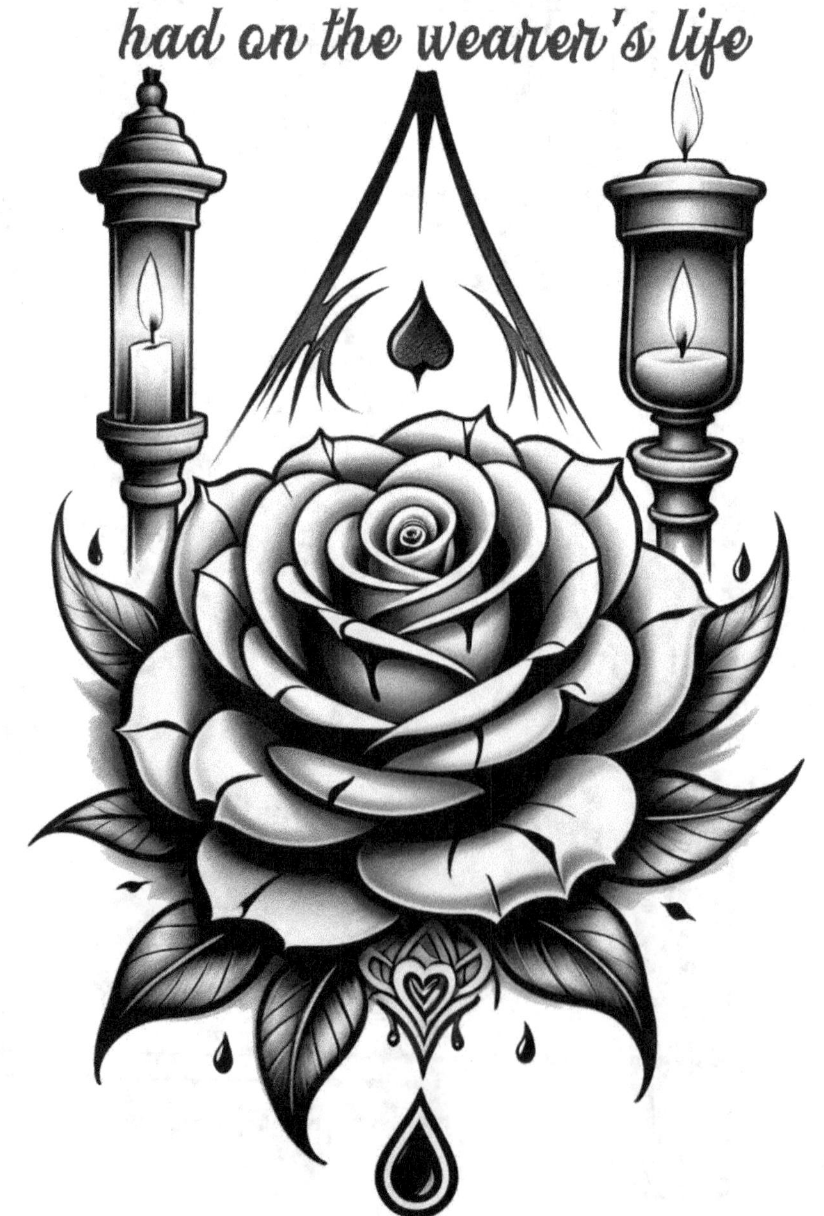

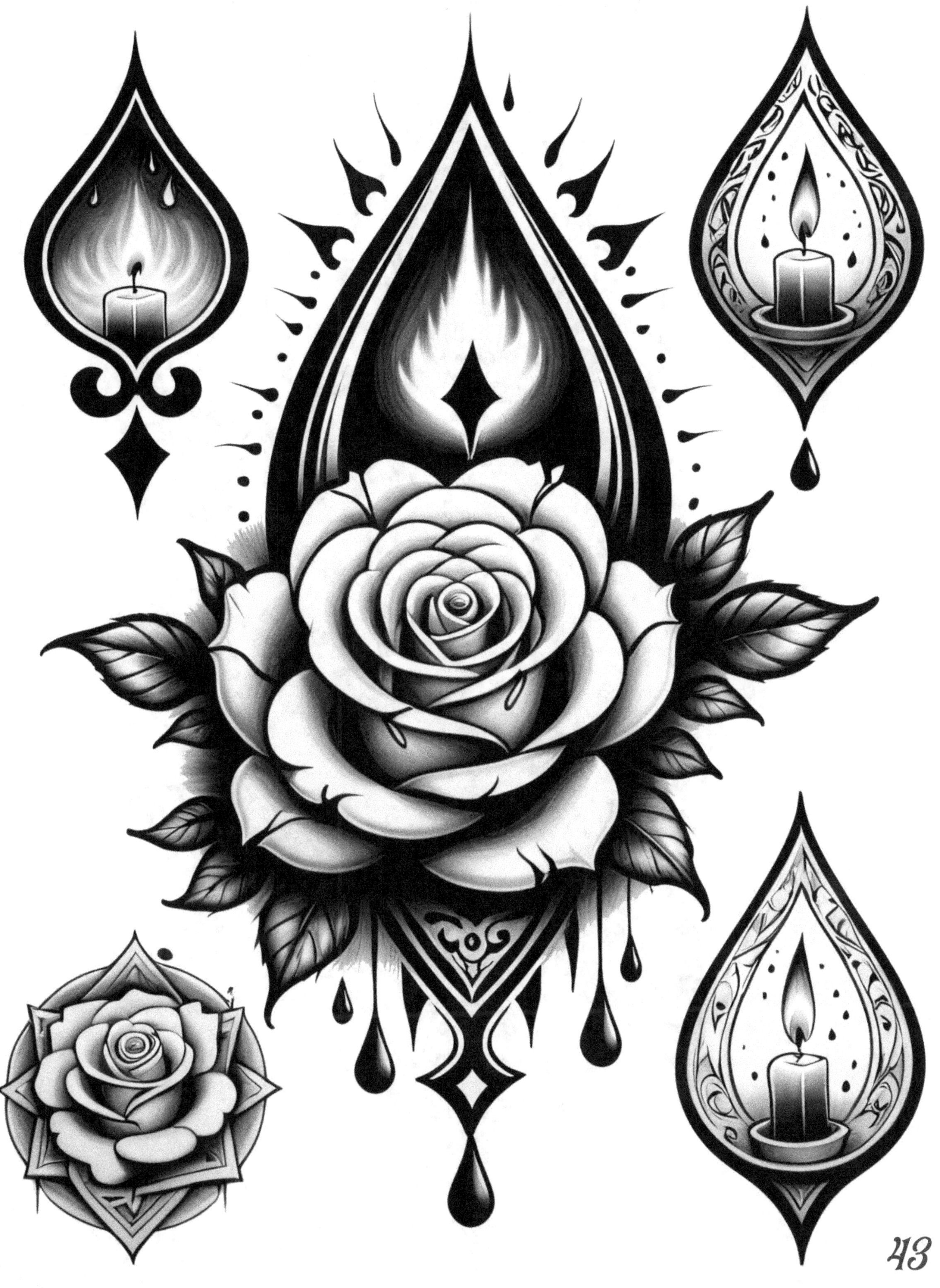

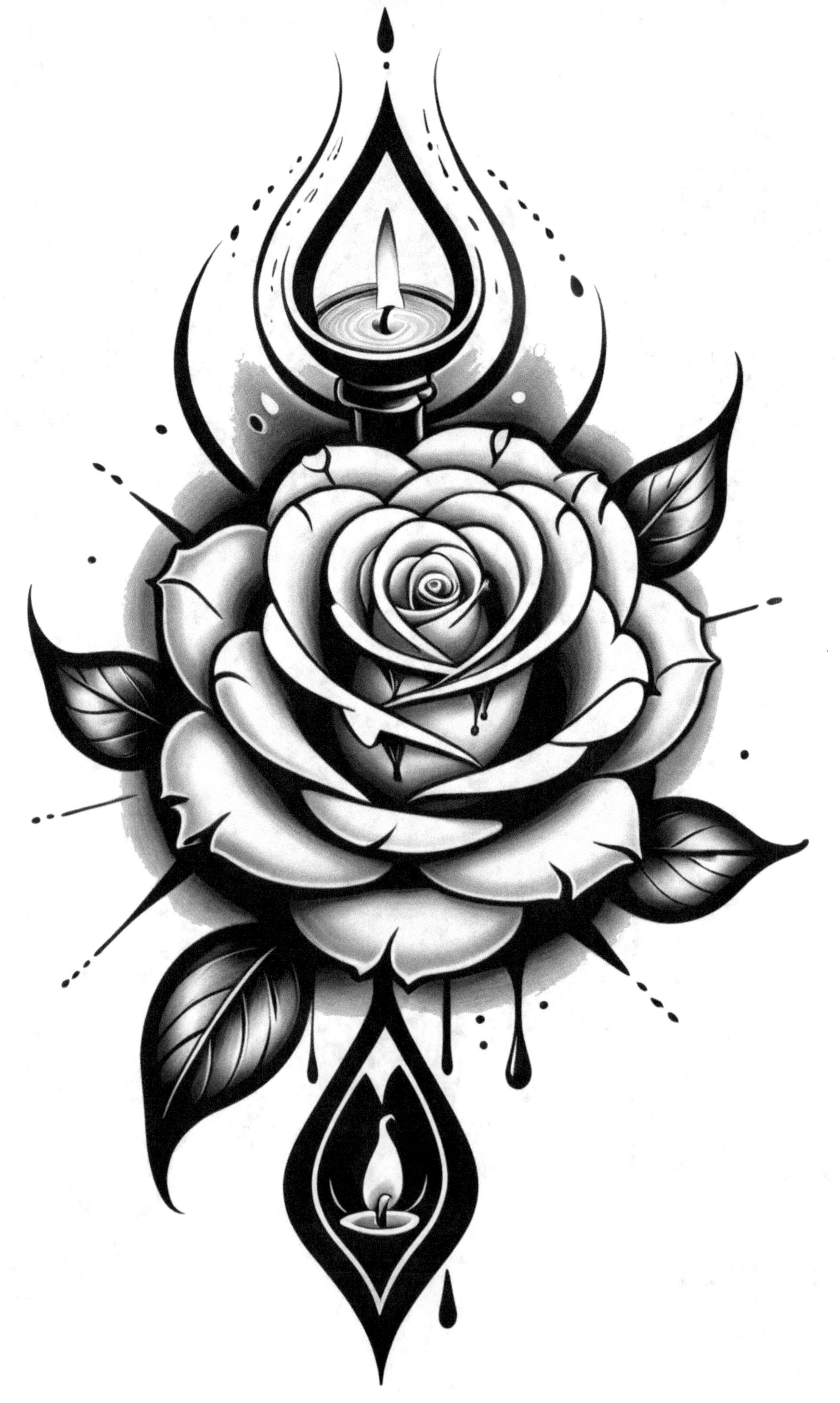

44

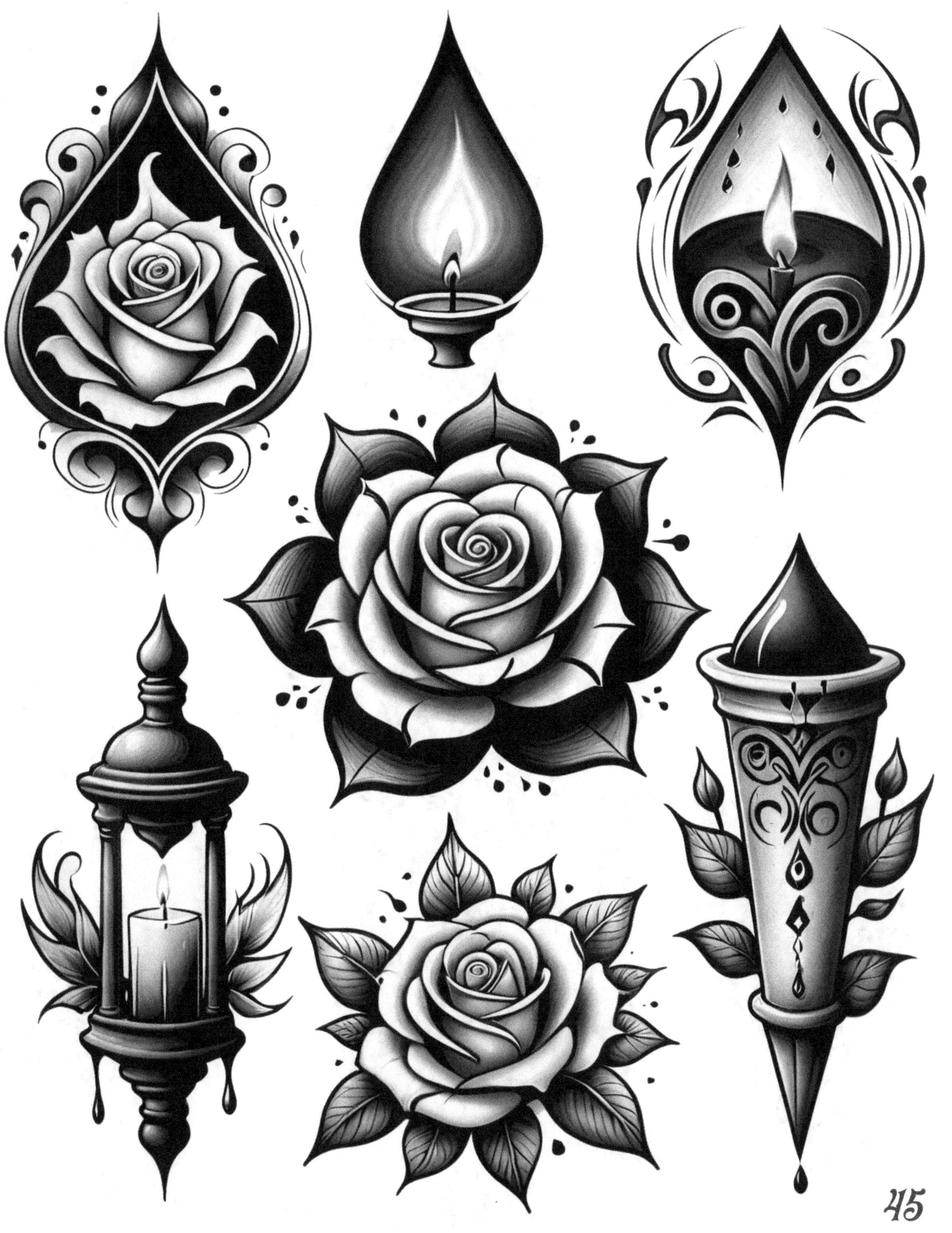

45

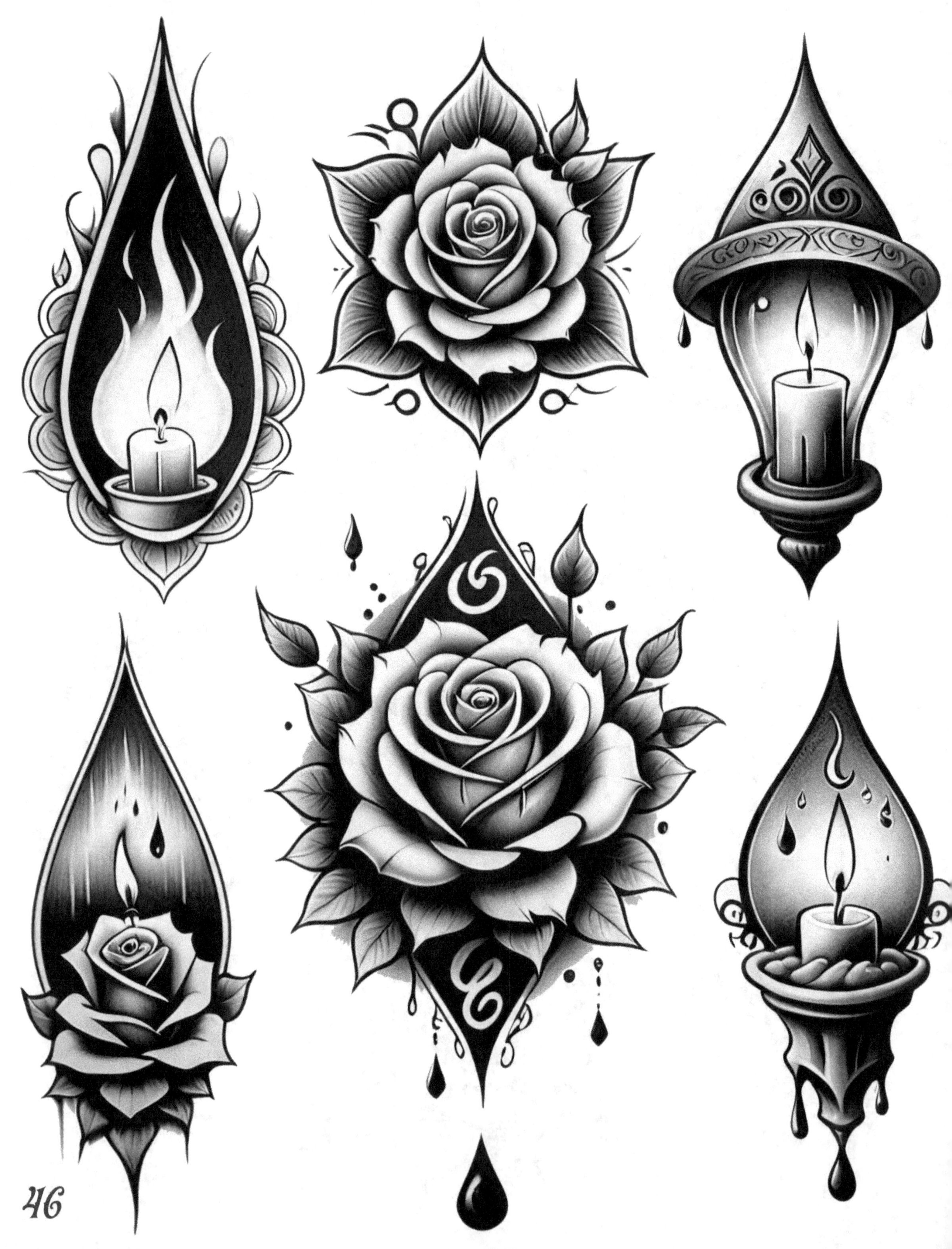

46

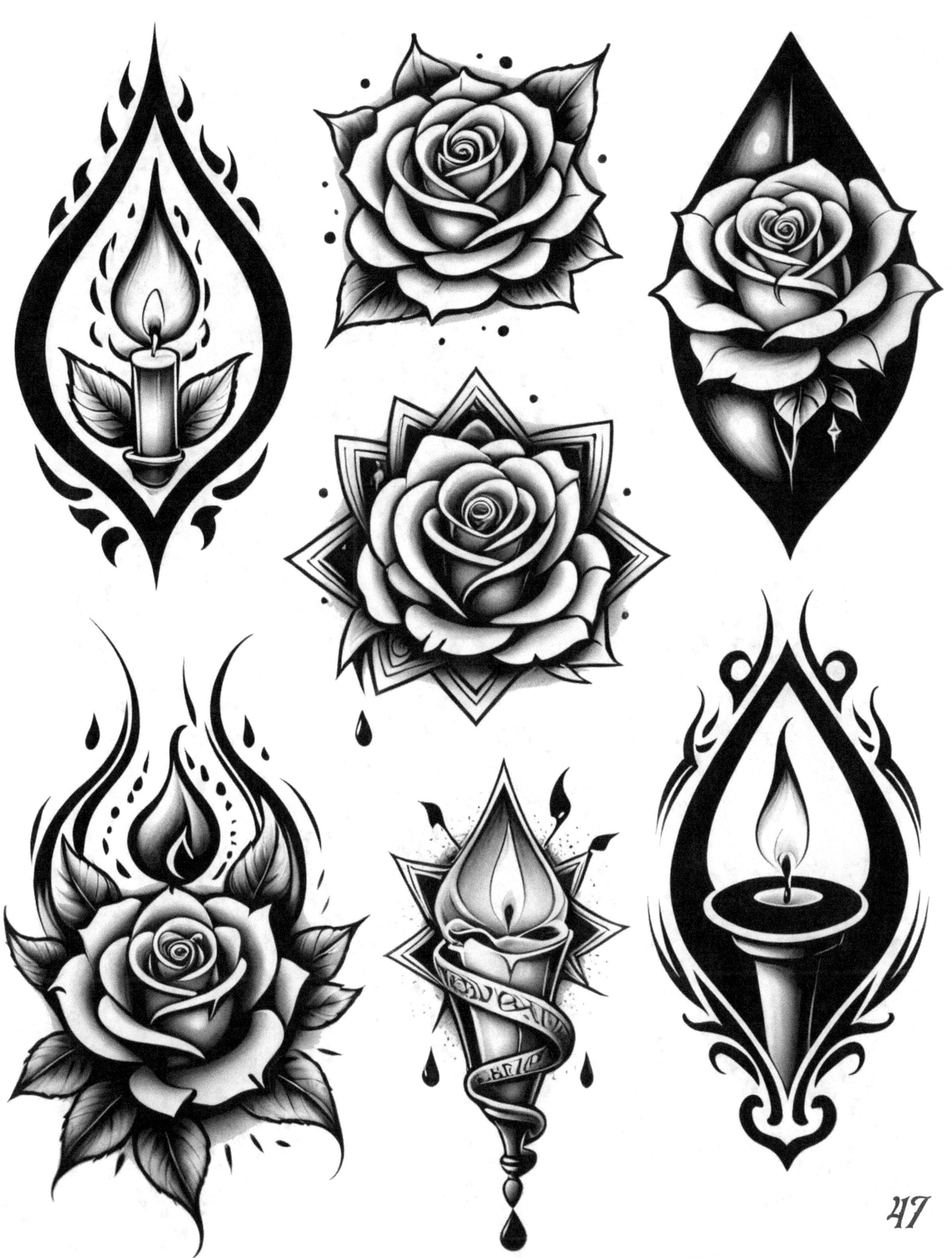

47

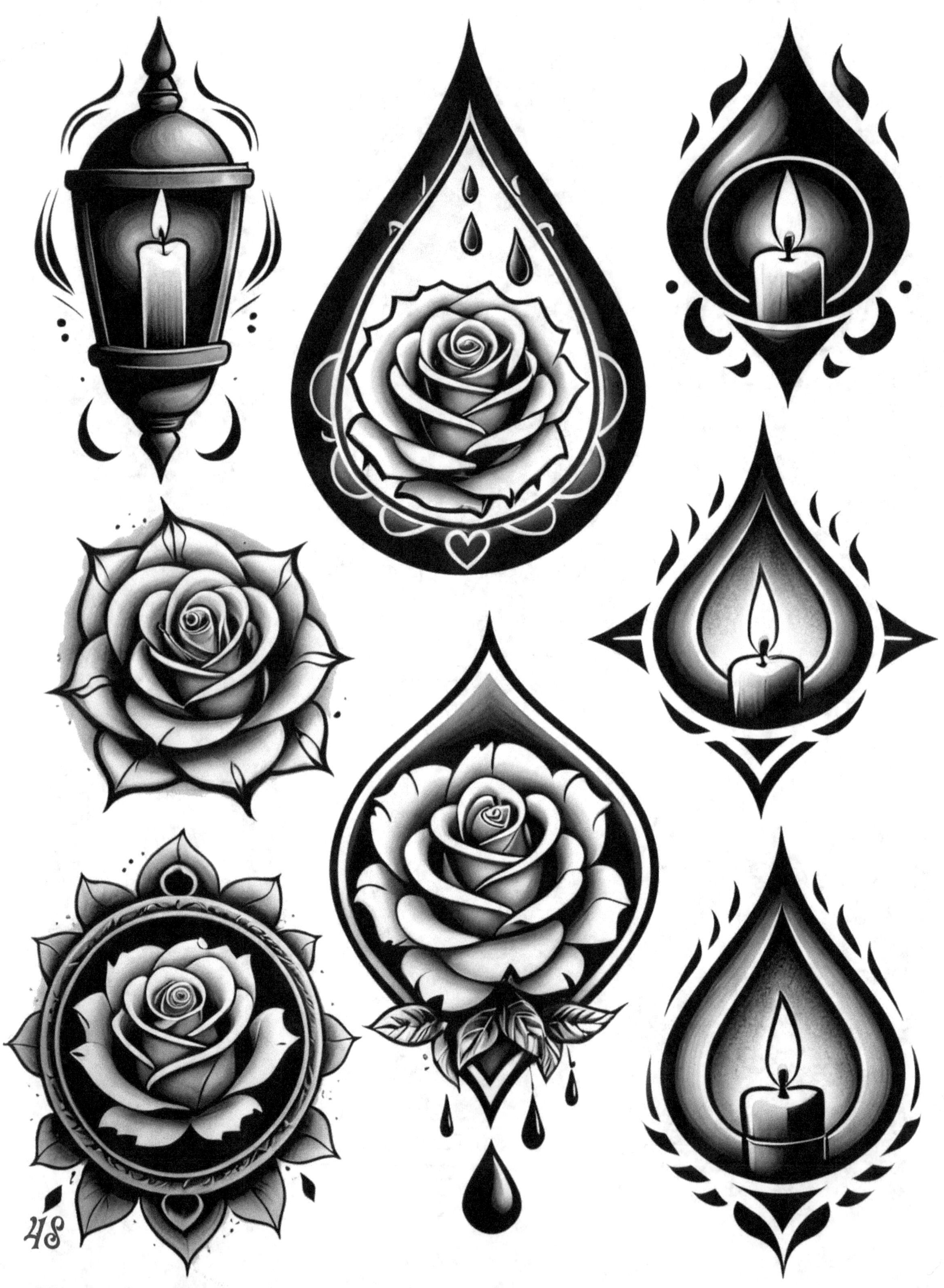

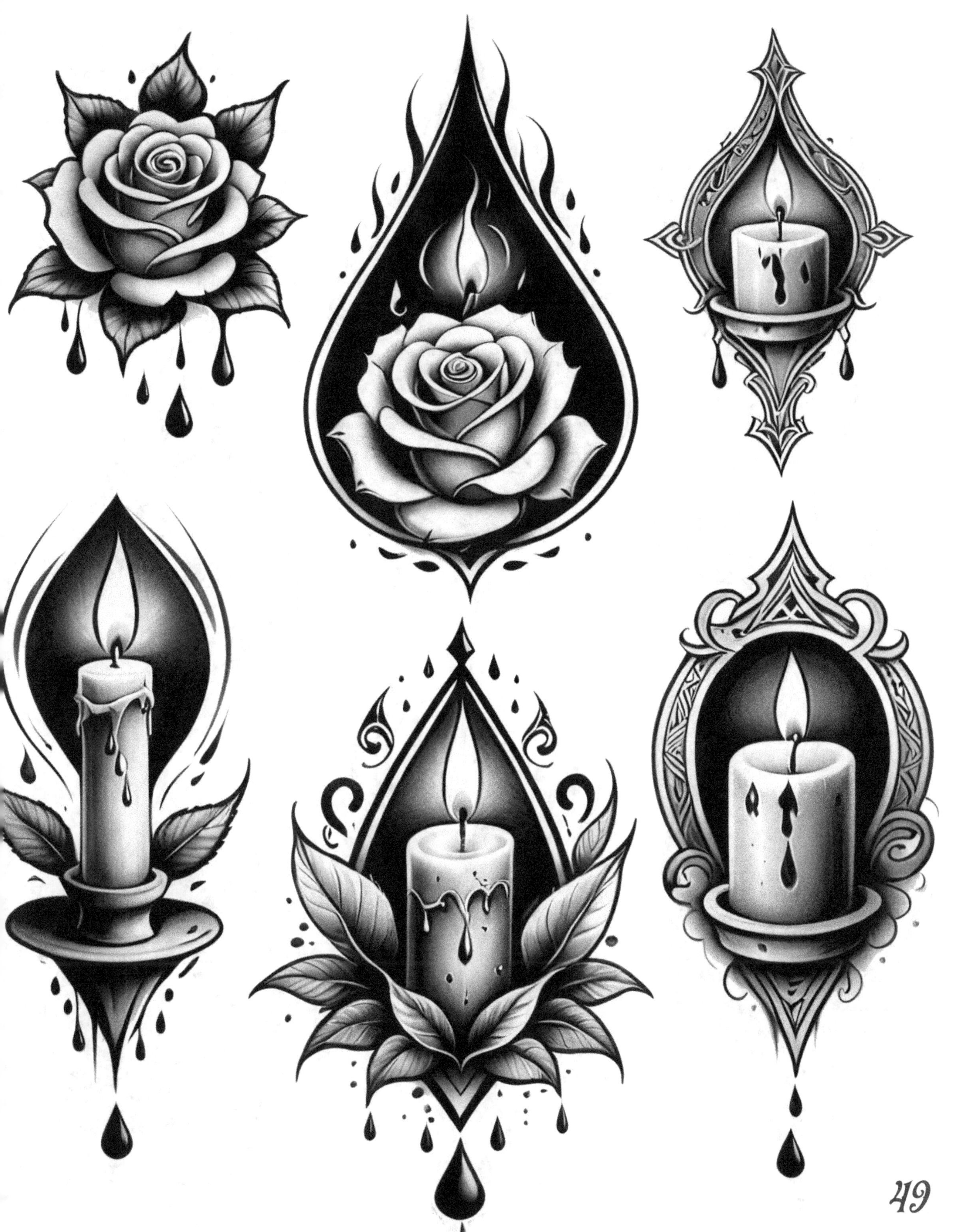

49

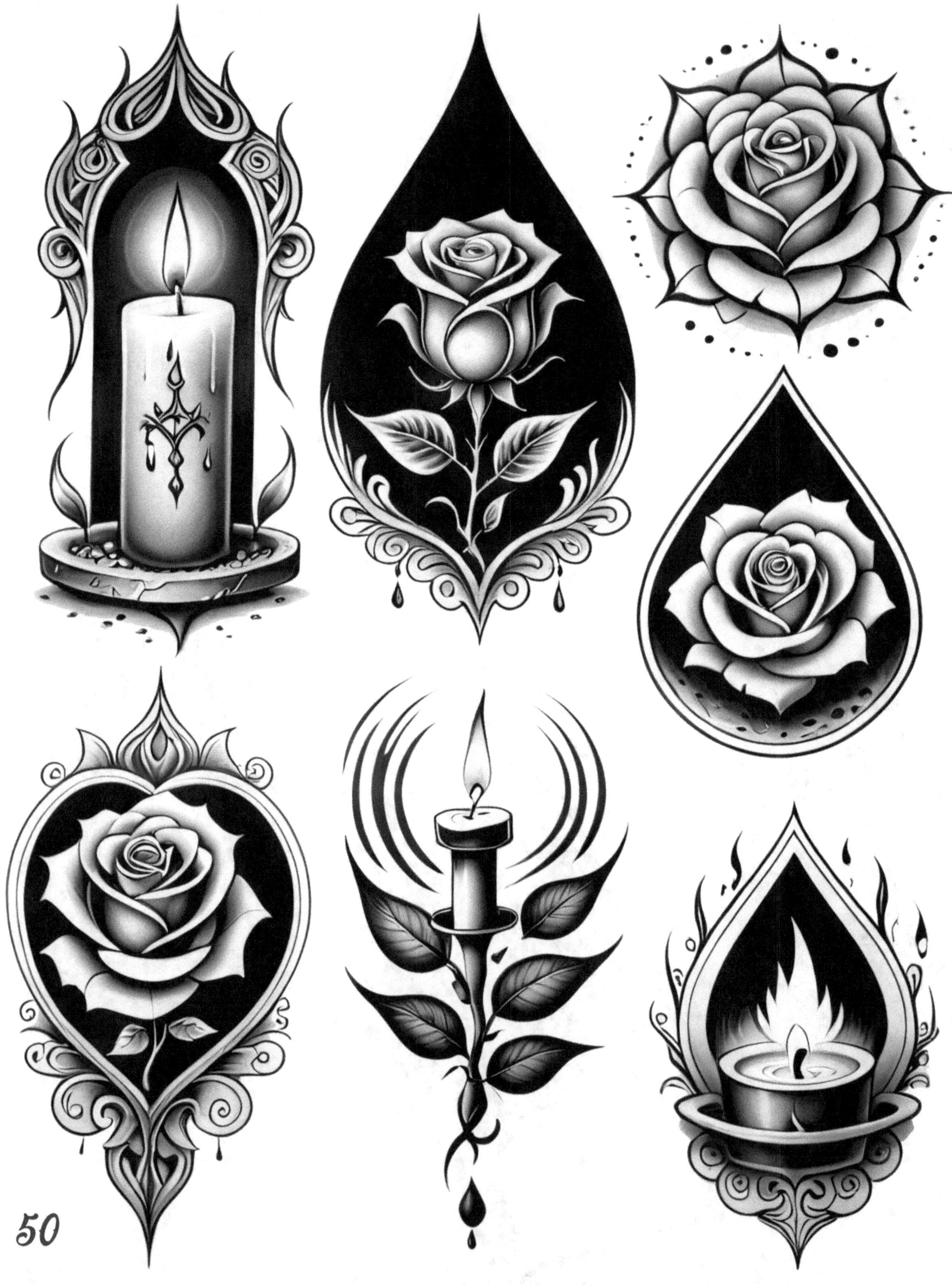

50

The music

The music theme in Chicano tattoos captures the cultural importance of music as a form of expression and connection. Designs featuring musical instruments like guitars or saxophones, vinyl records, and notes celebrate the influence of music genres pivotal to Chicano identity, such as Mariachi, Ranchera, and even elements of Hip-Hop.

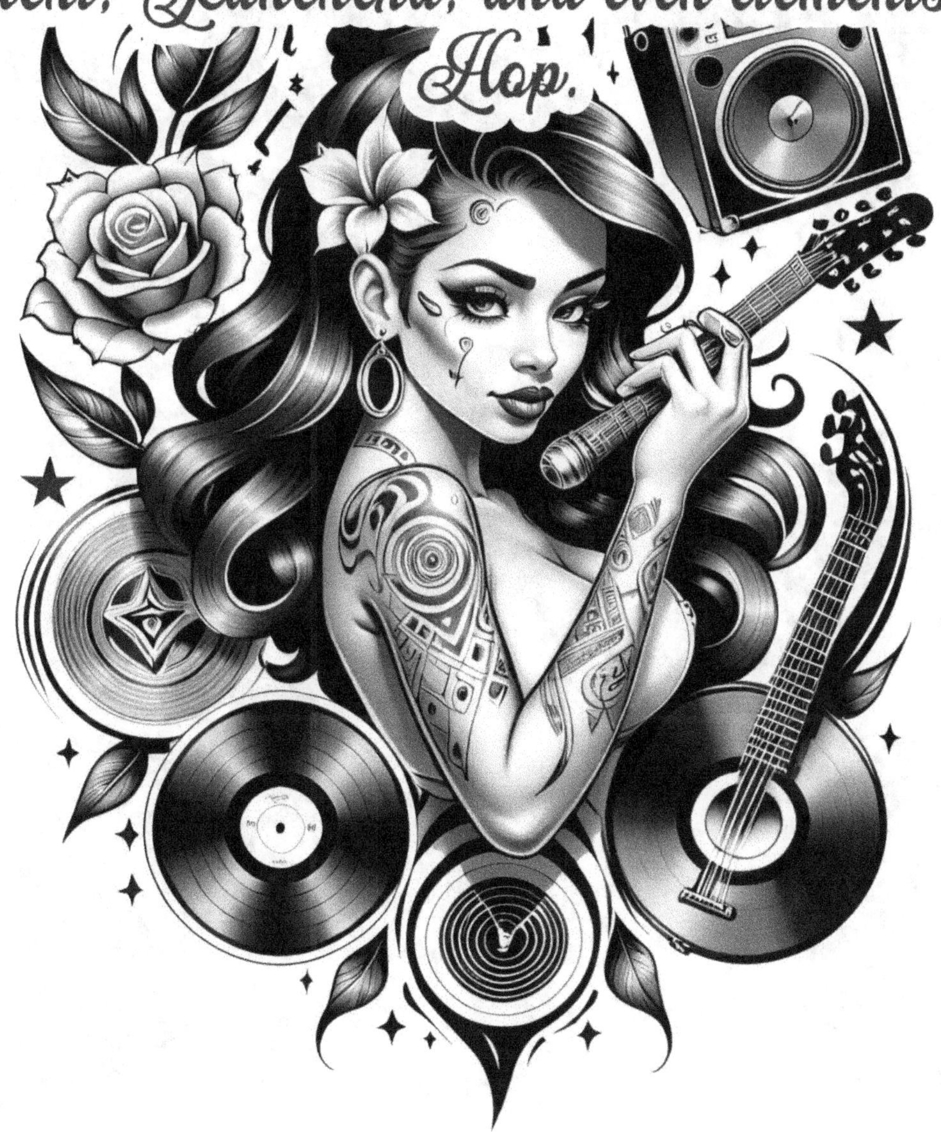

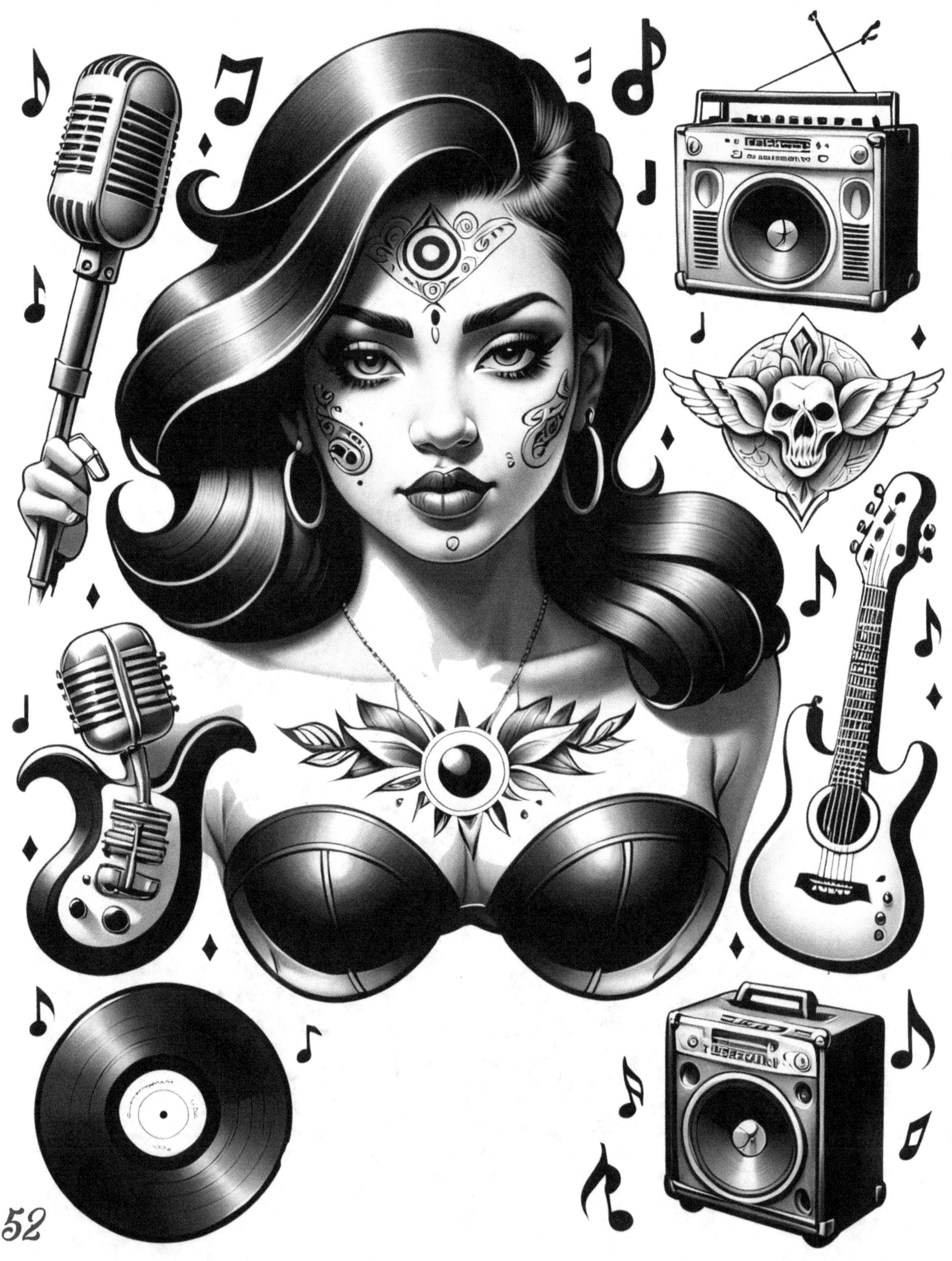

52

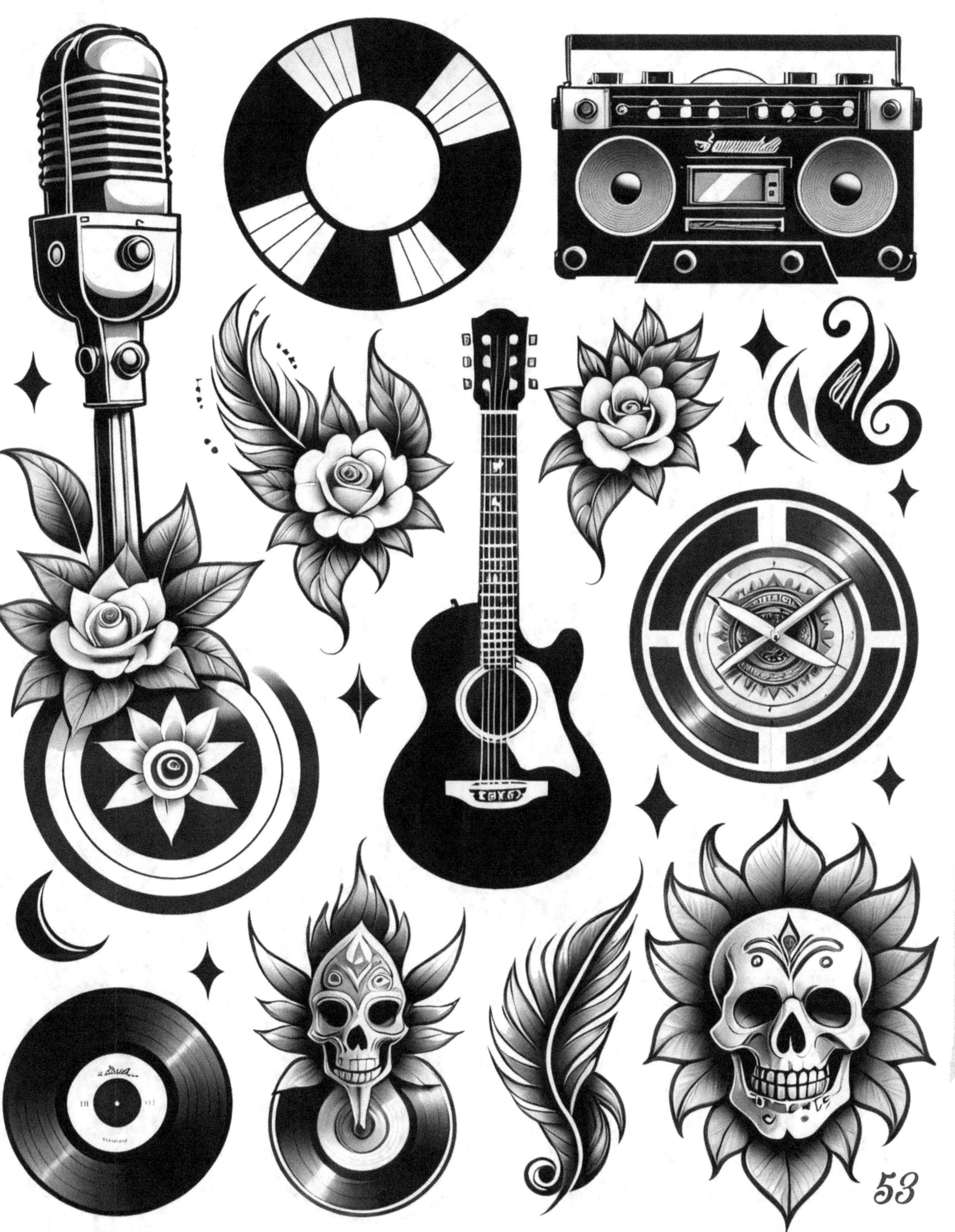

53

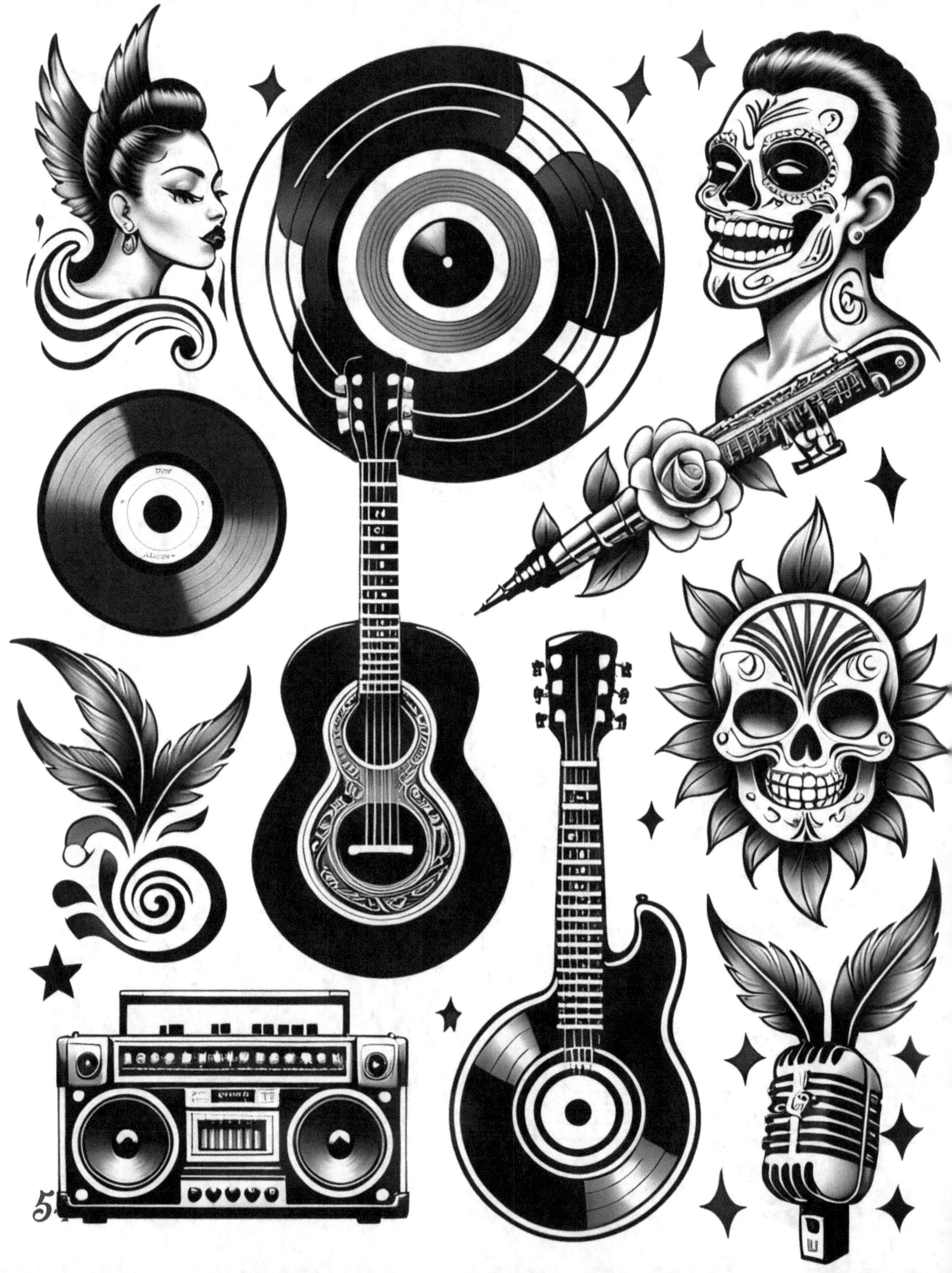

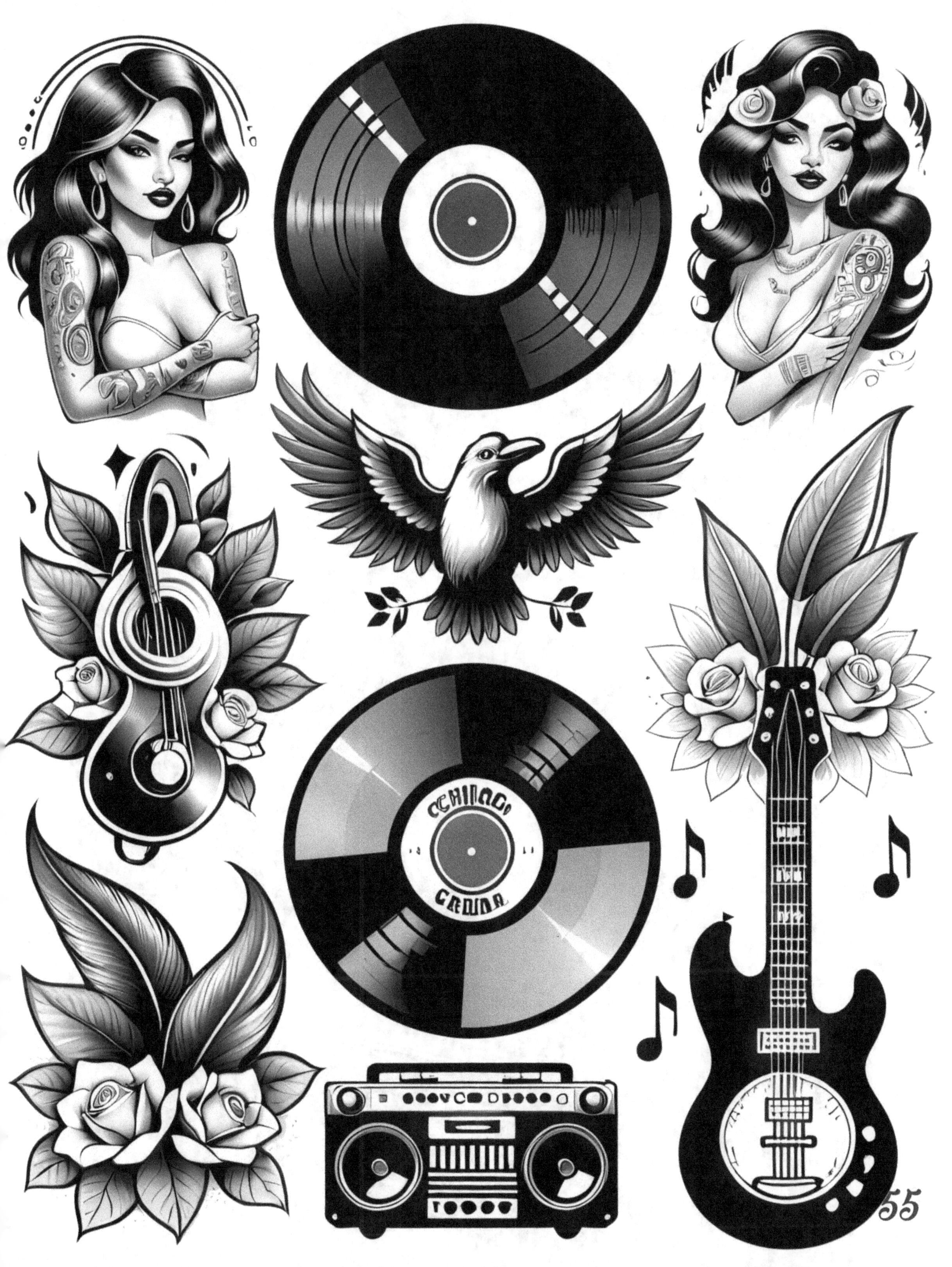

55

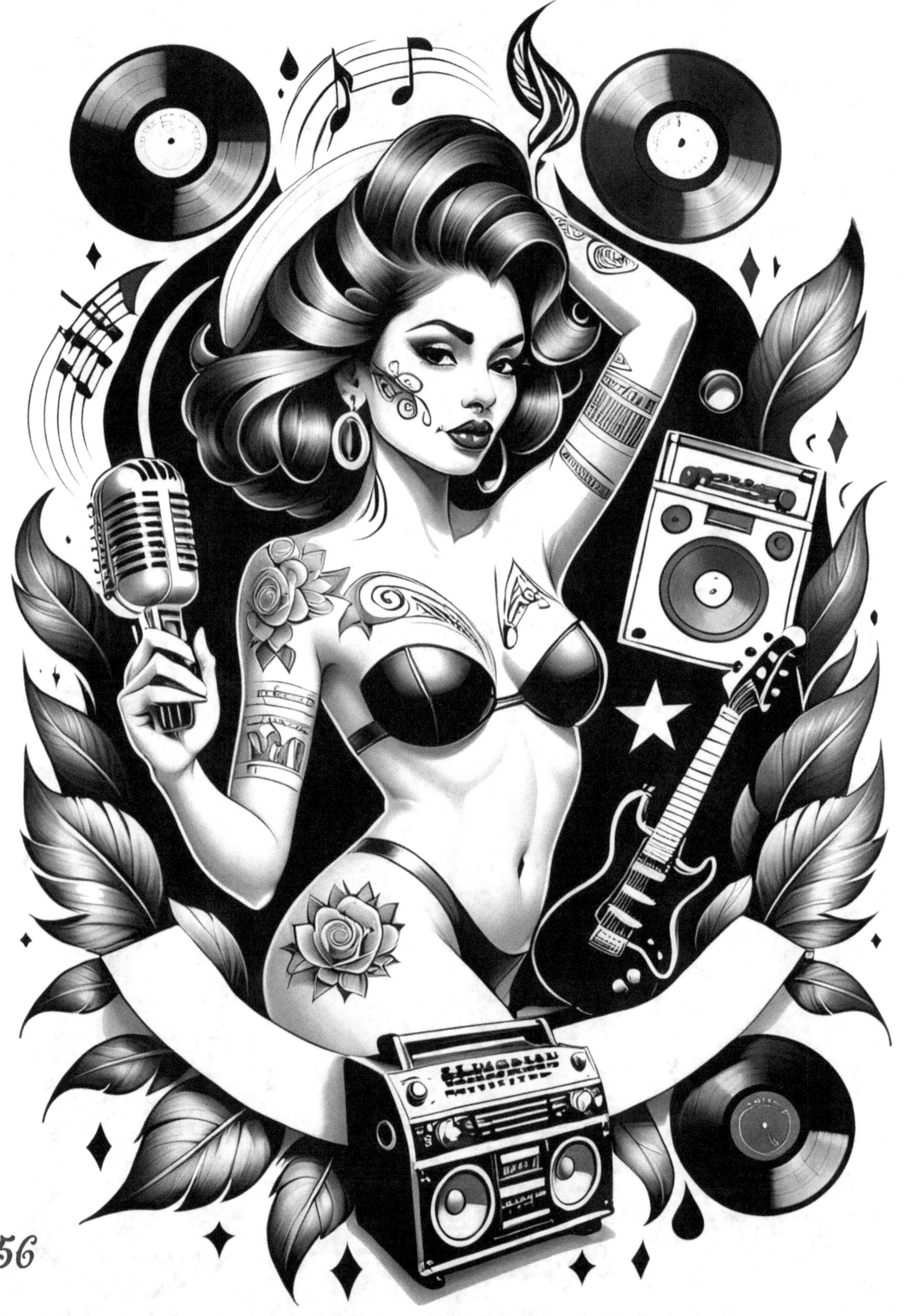

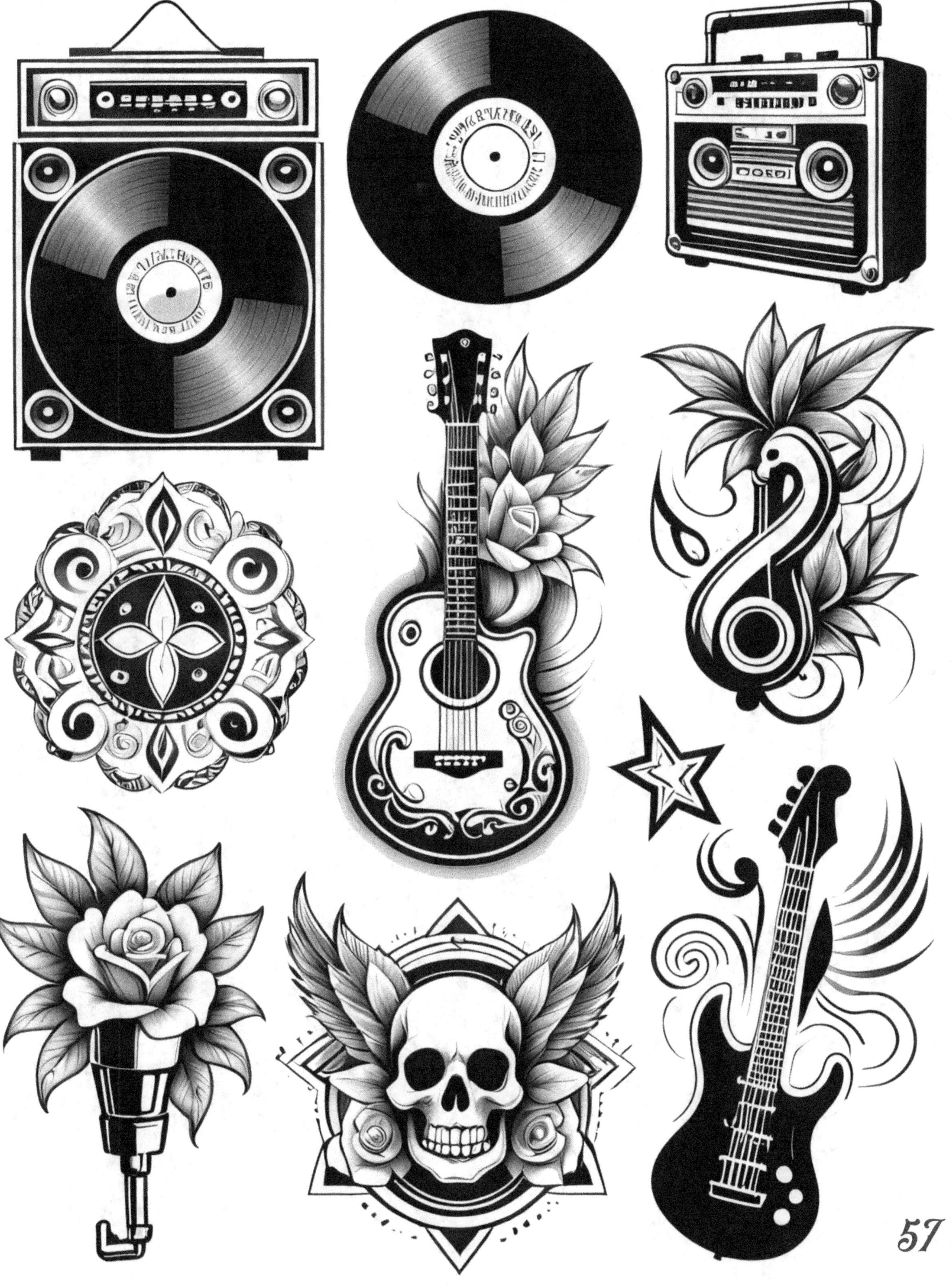

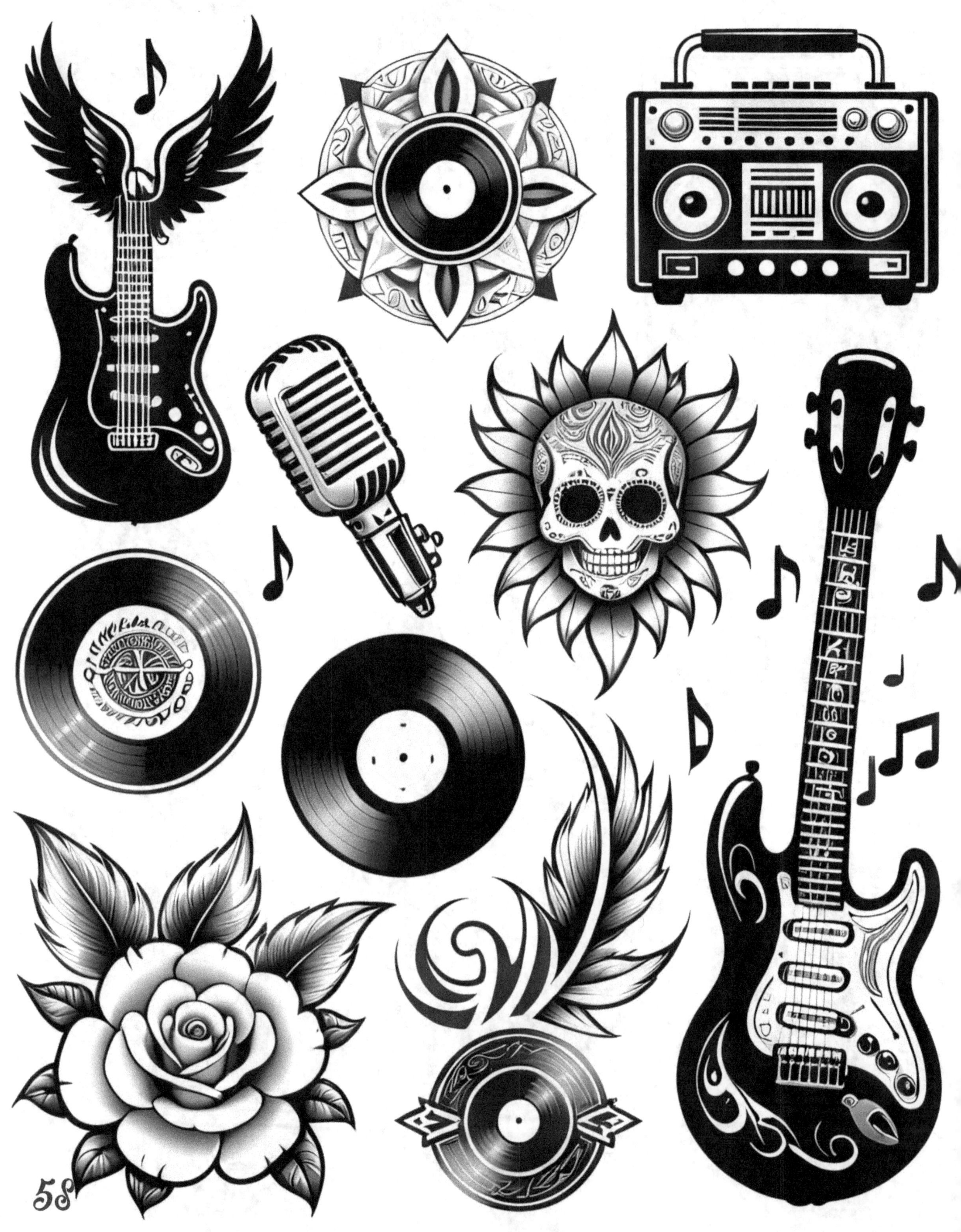

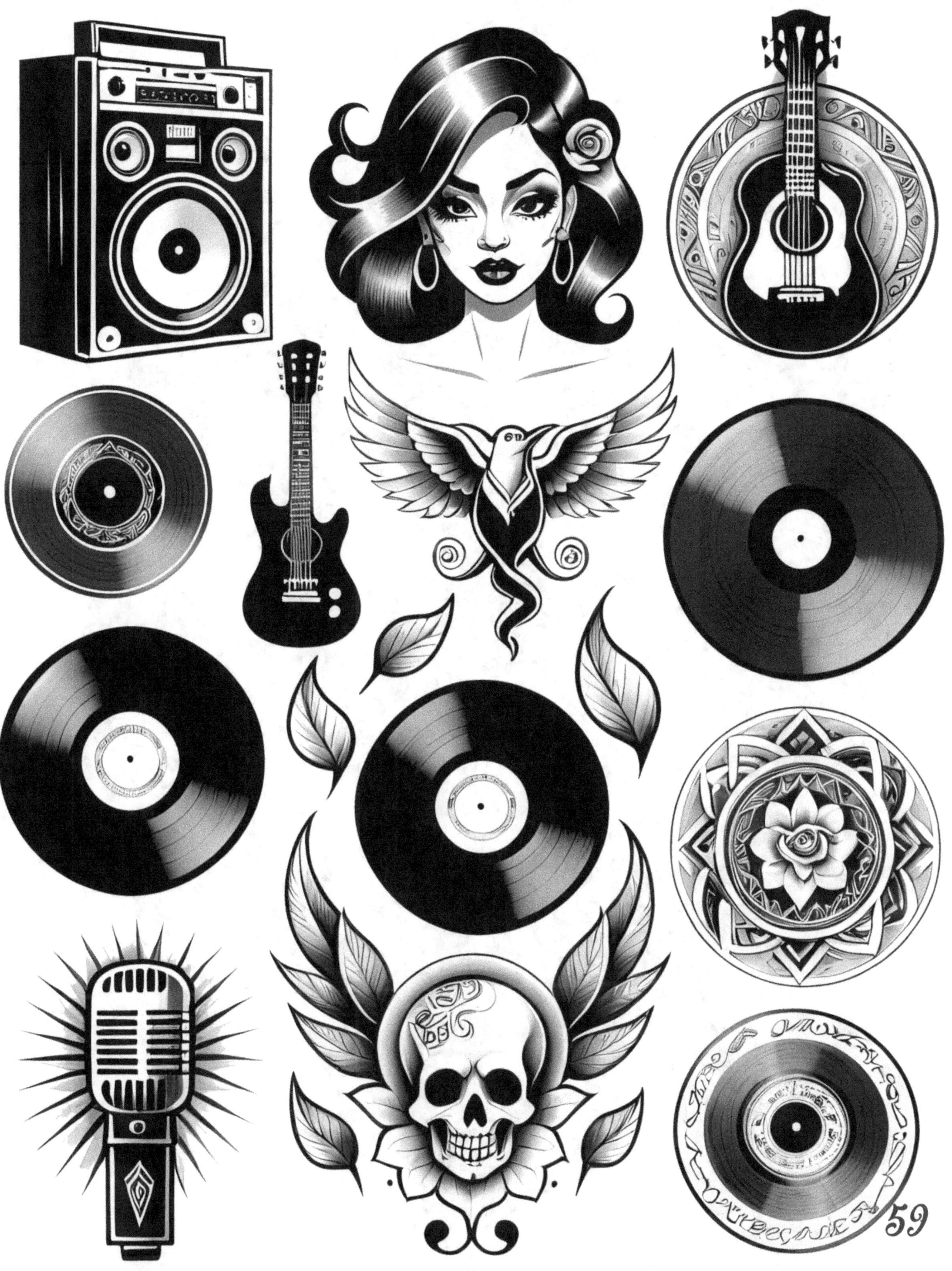

59

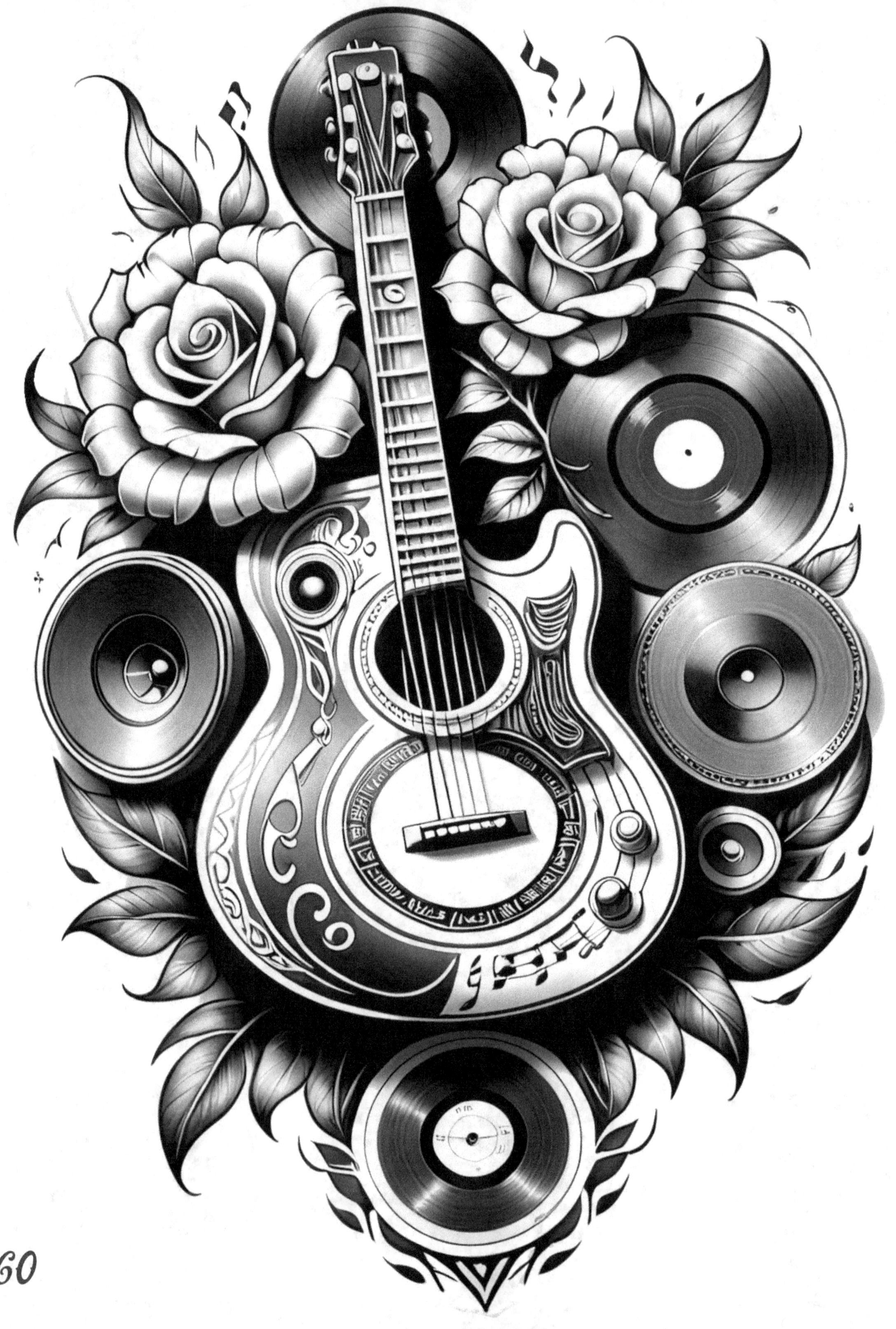

60

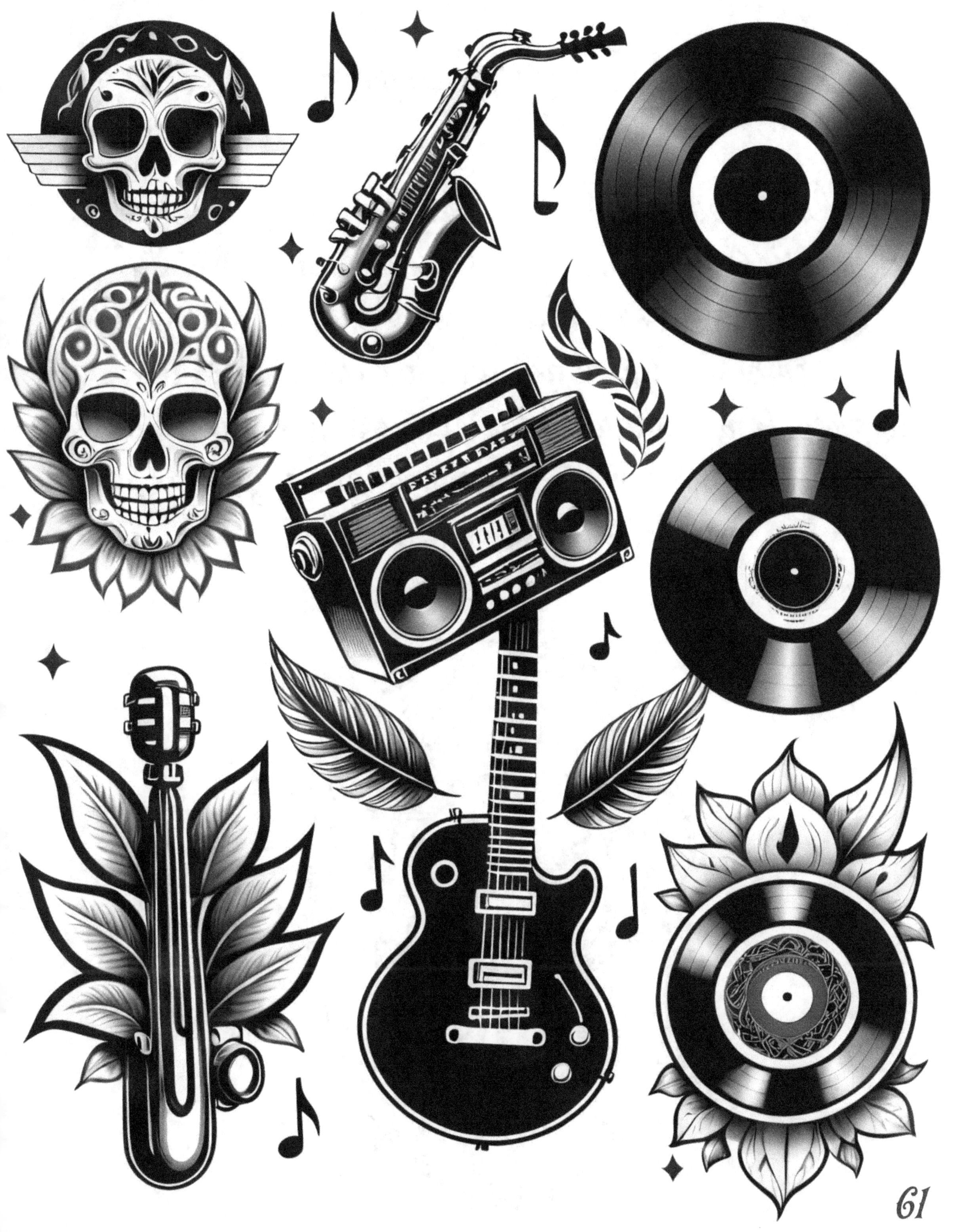

Rebellion

Rebellion in Chicano tattoos often signifies a resistance to societal norms and authority. Symbols such as raised fists, flames, and graffiti embody a defiance and a protest against oppression, capturing the spirit of resistance that is deeply rooted in the history and struggles of the Chicano community.

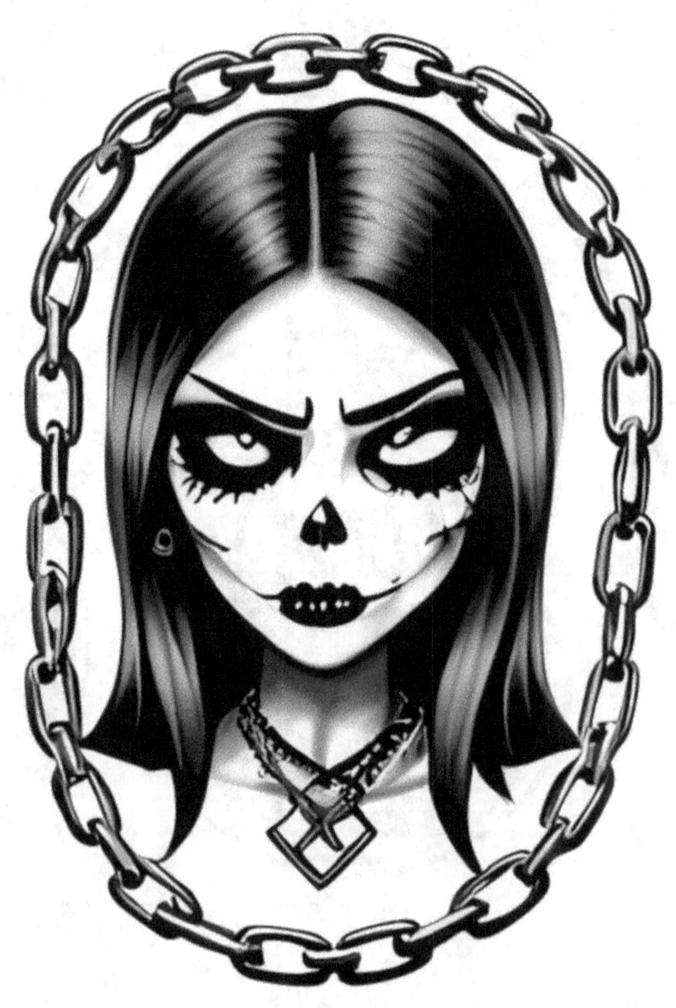

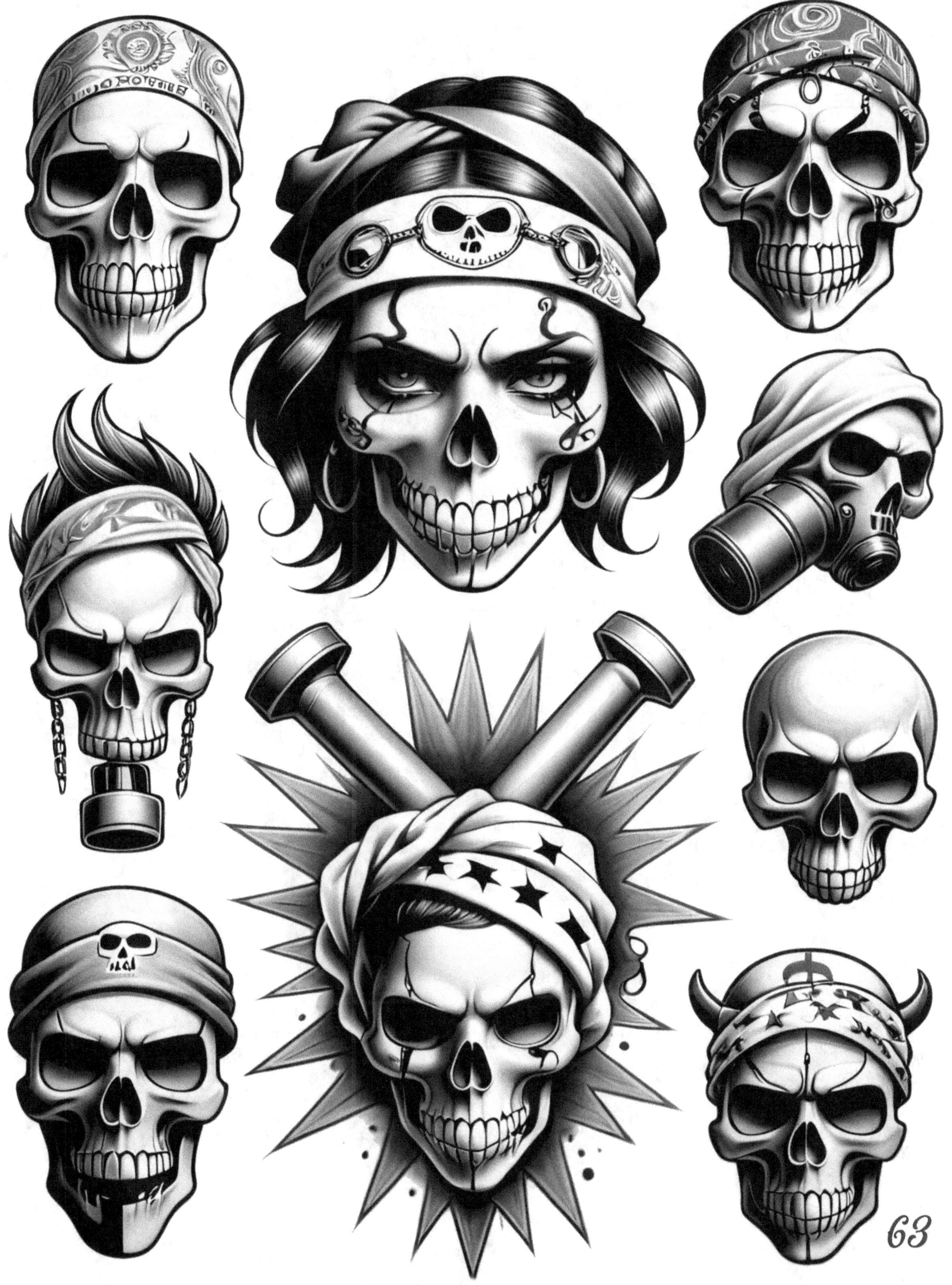

63

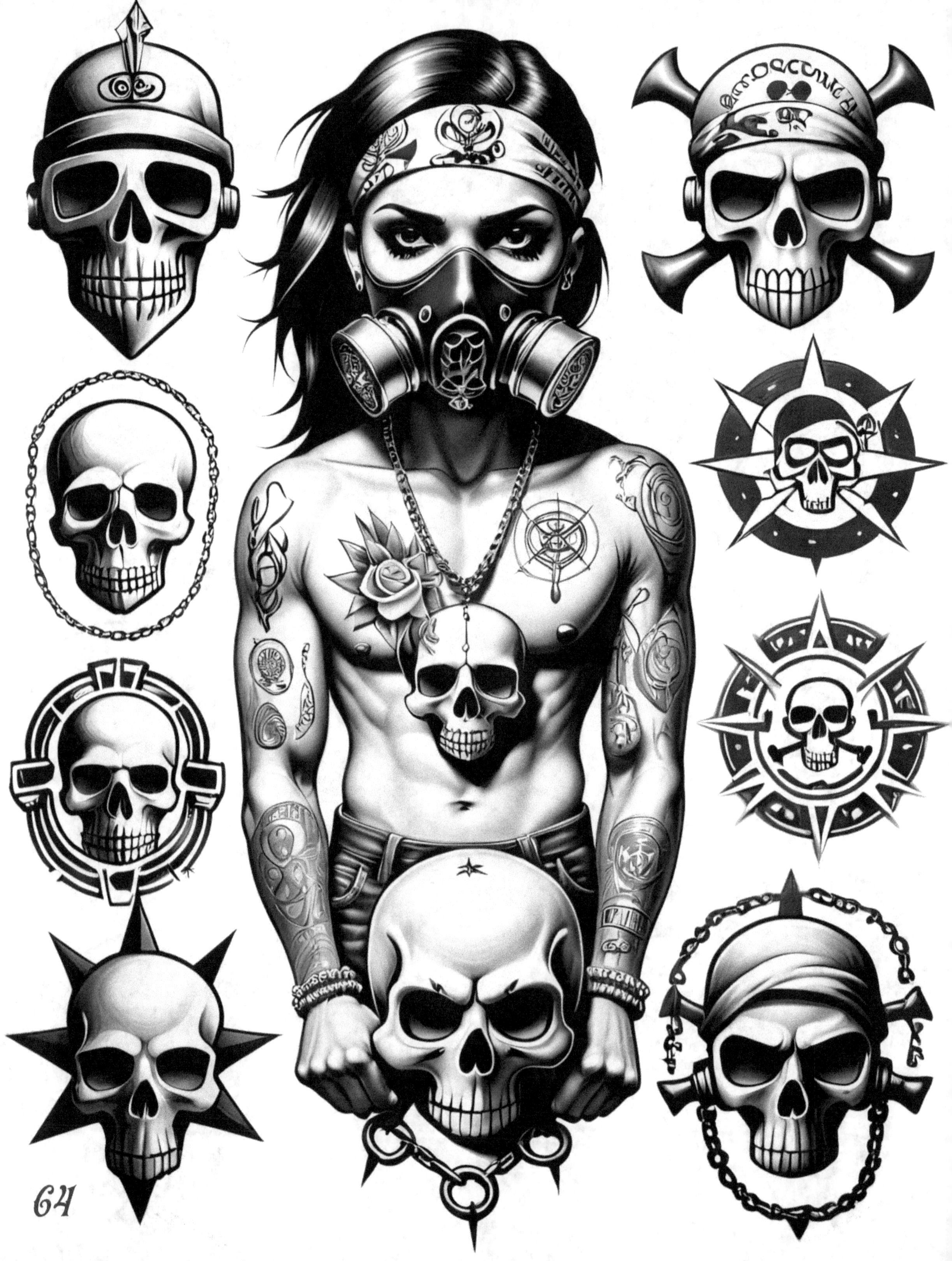

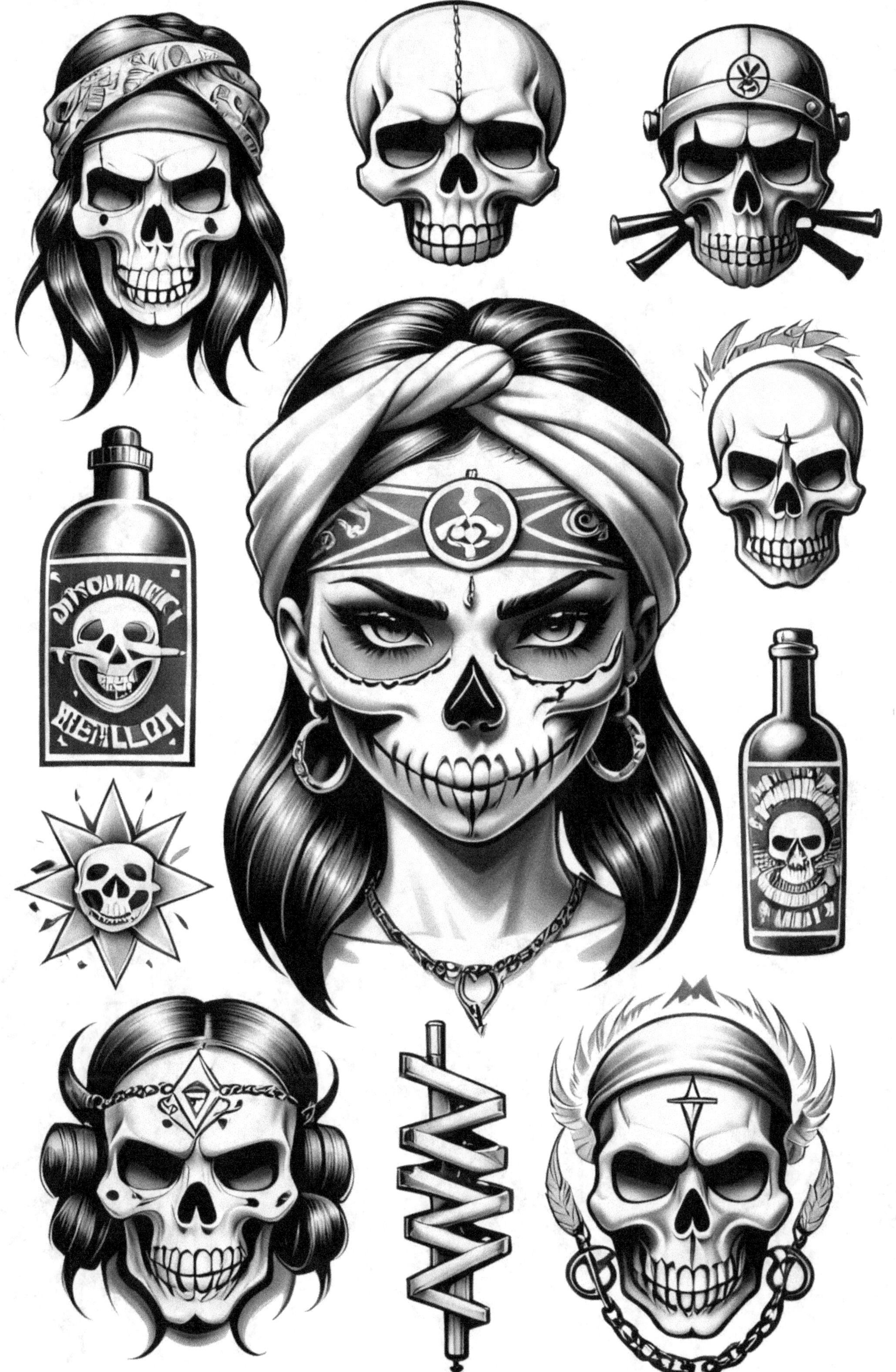

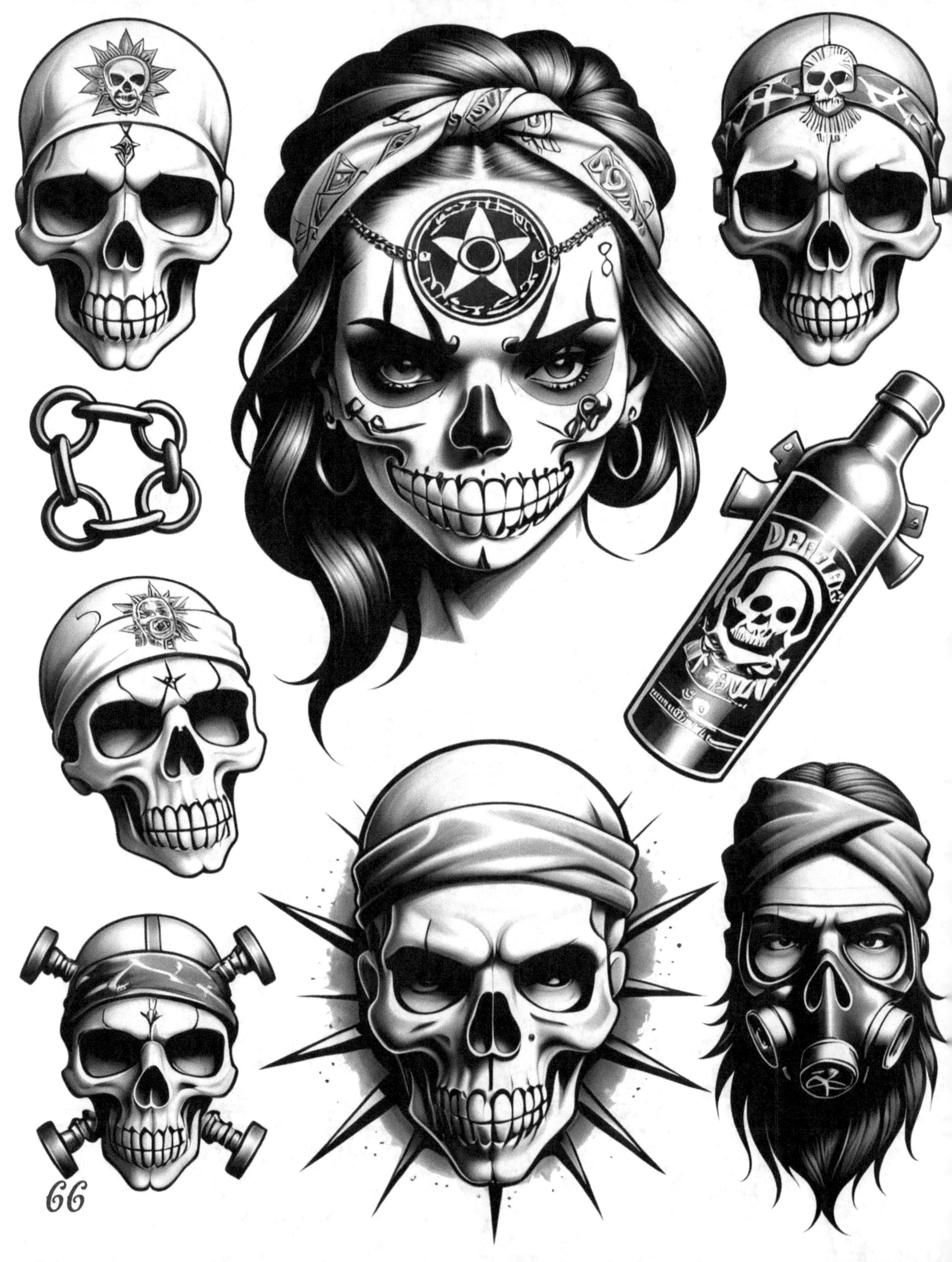

66

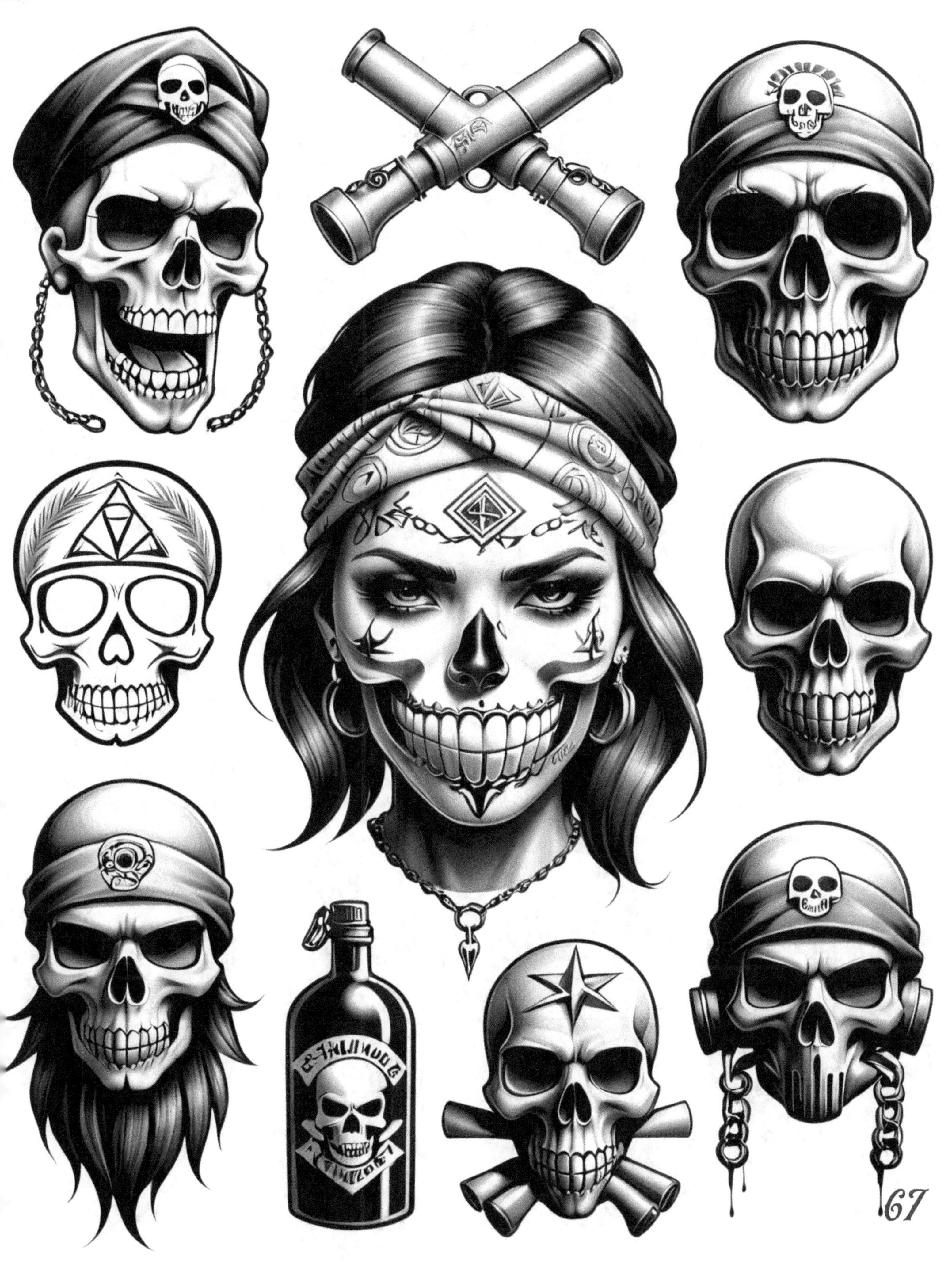

67

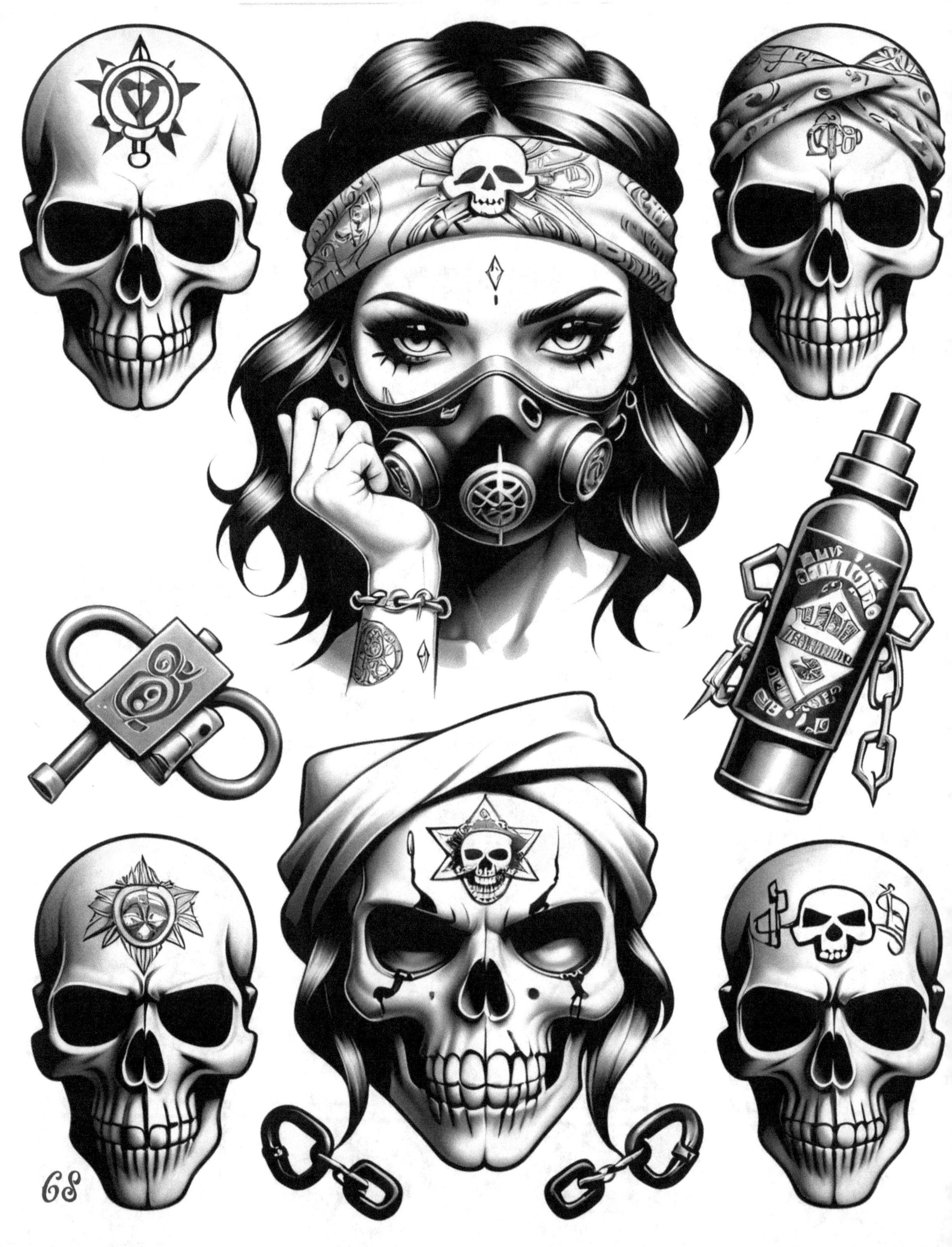

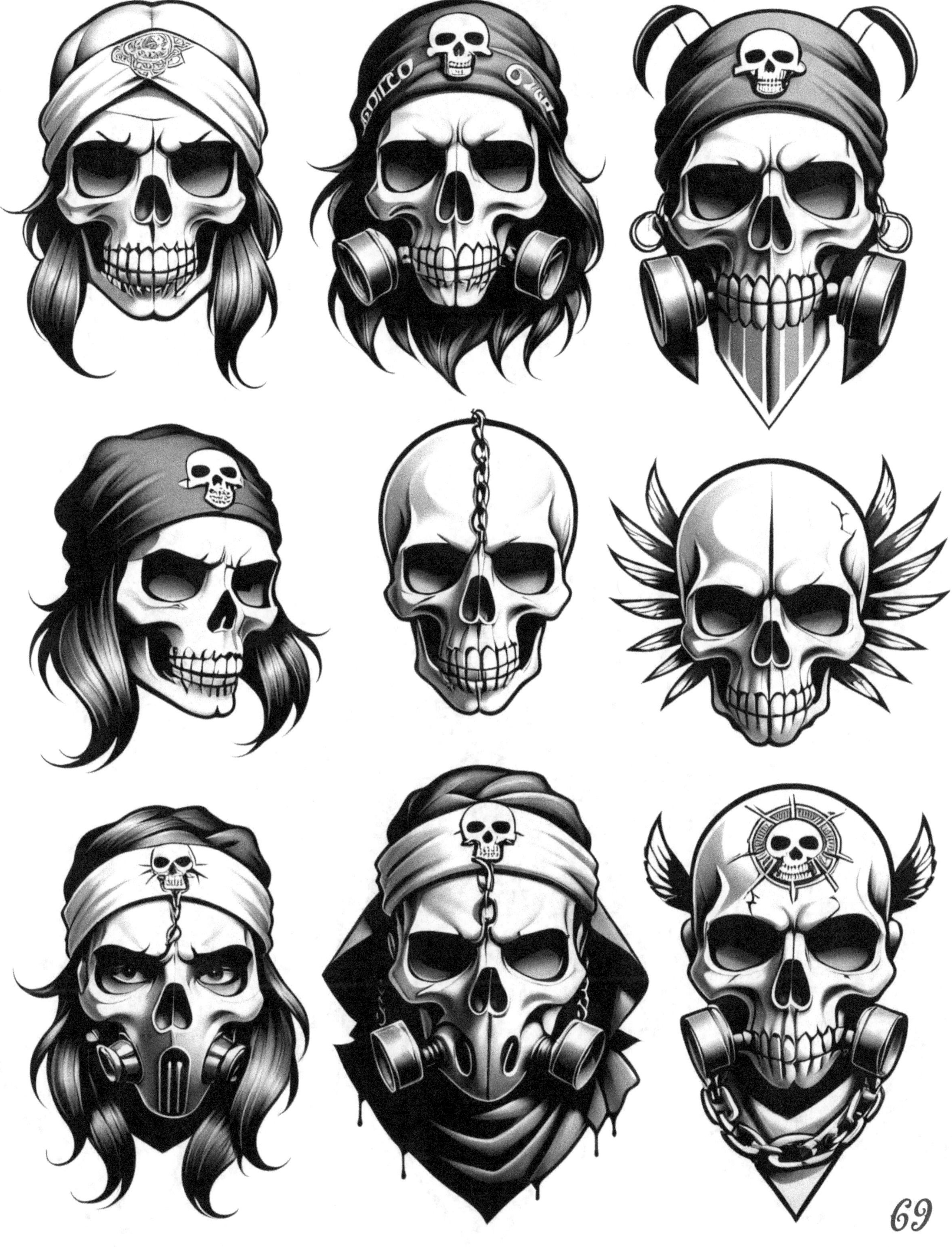

69

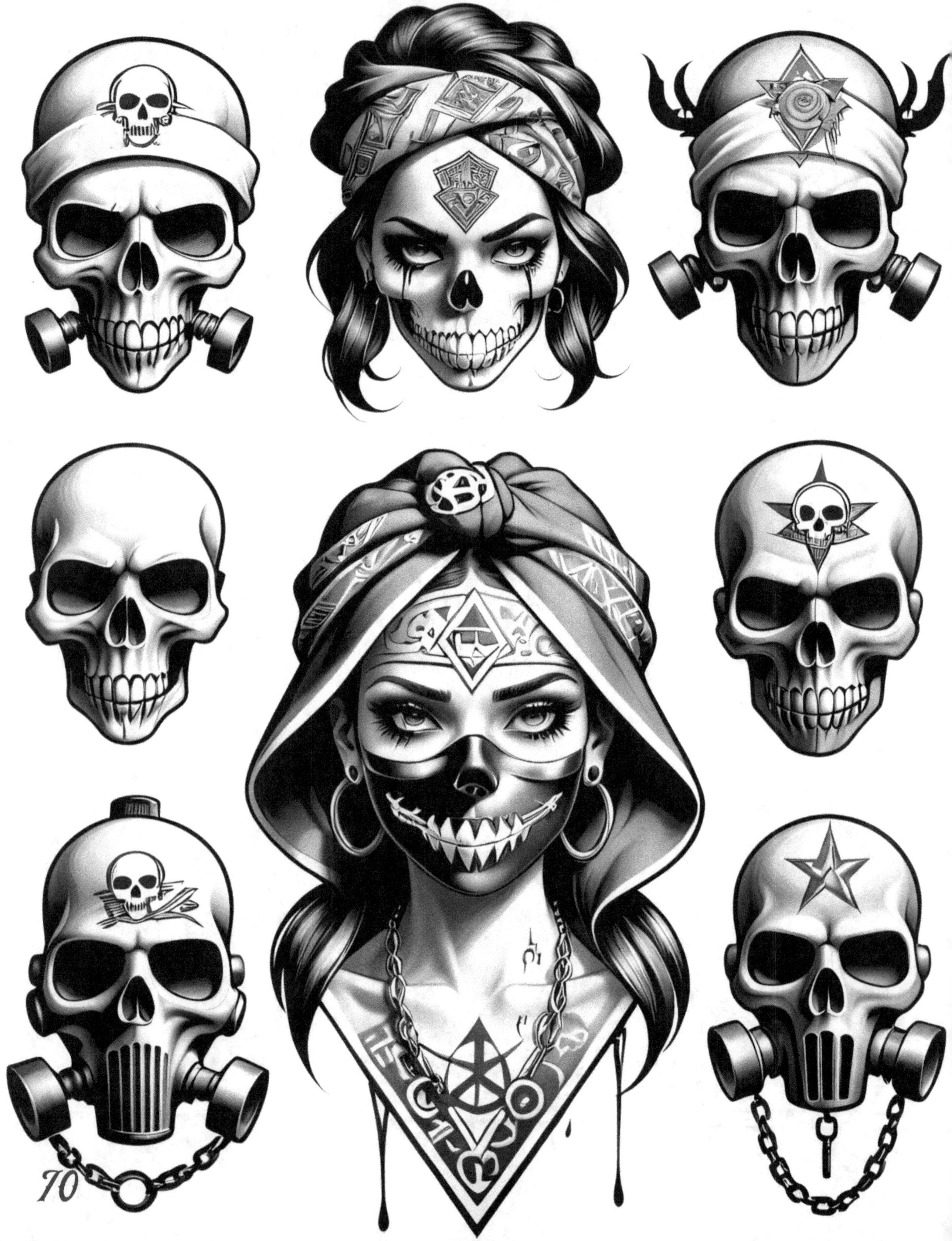

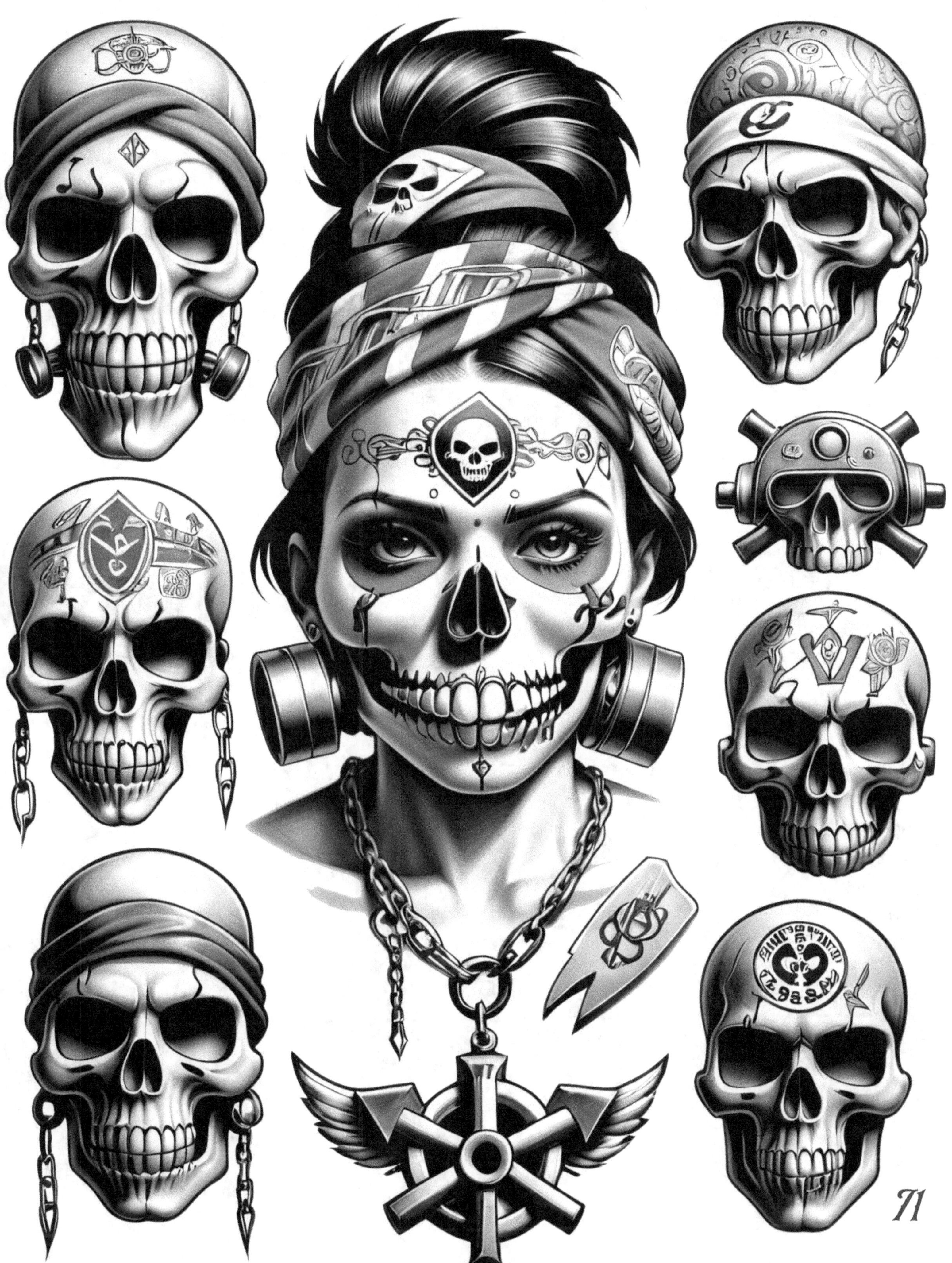

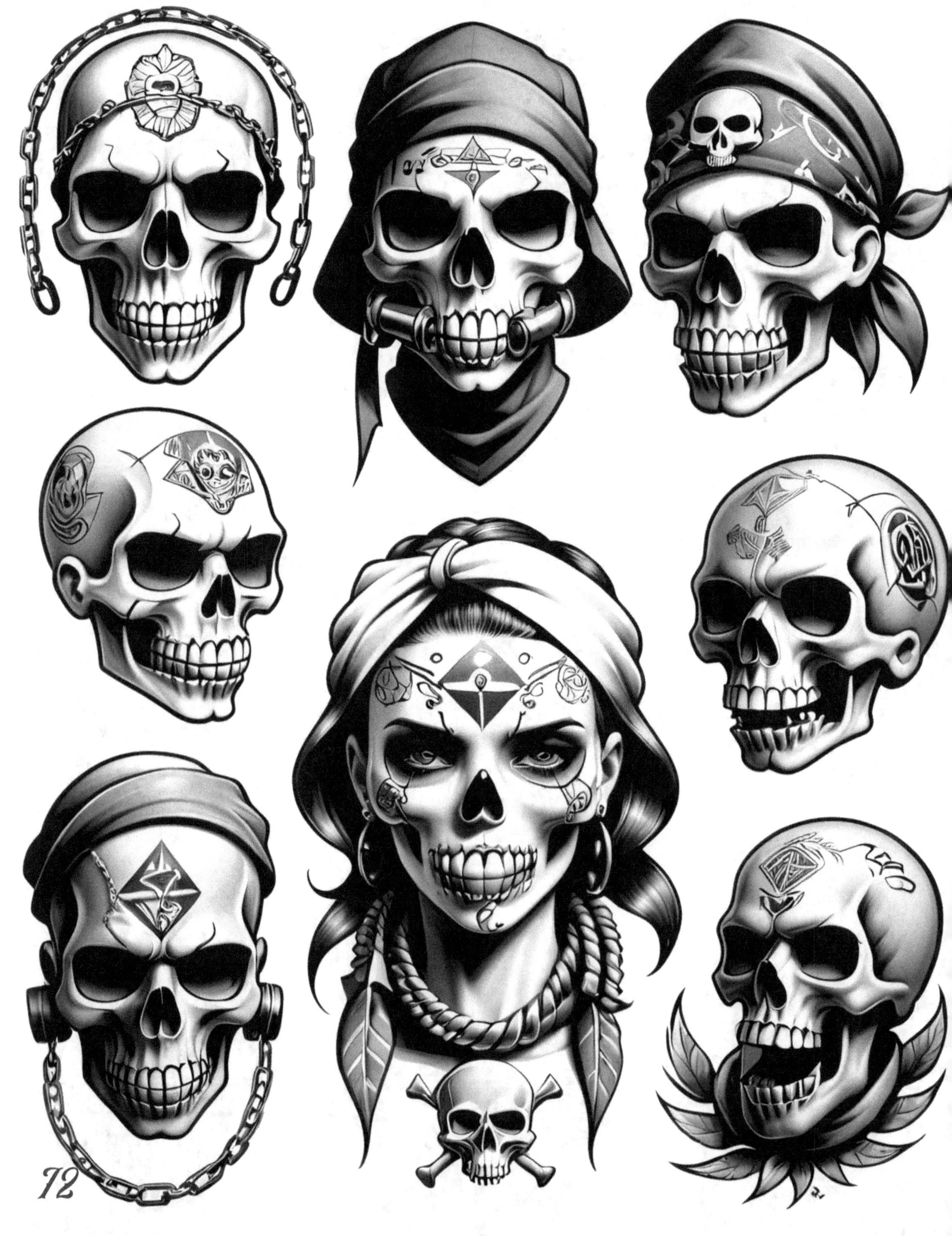

The Gothic

The Gothic theme in Chicano tattoos delves into the darker and more mystical elements of art and symbolism. Gothic designs often include skulls, grim reapers, and Gothic arches, infused with dramatic contrasts and intricate details. These motifs not only explore themes of death and the afterlife but also reflect on the existential musings and the darker side of human nature.

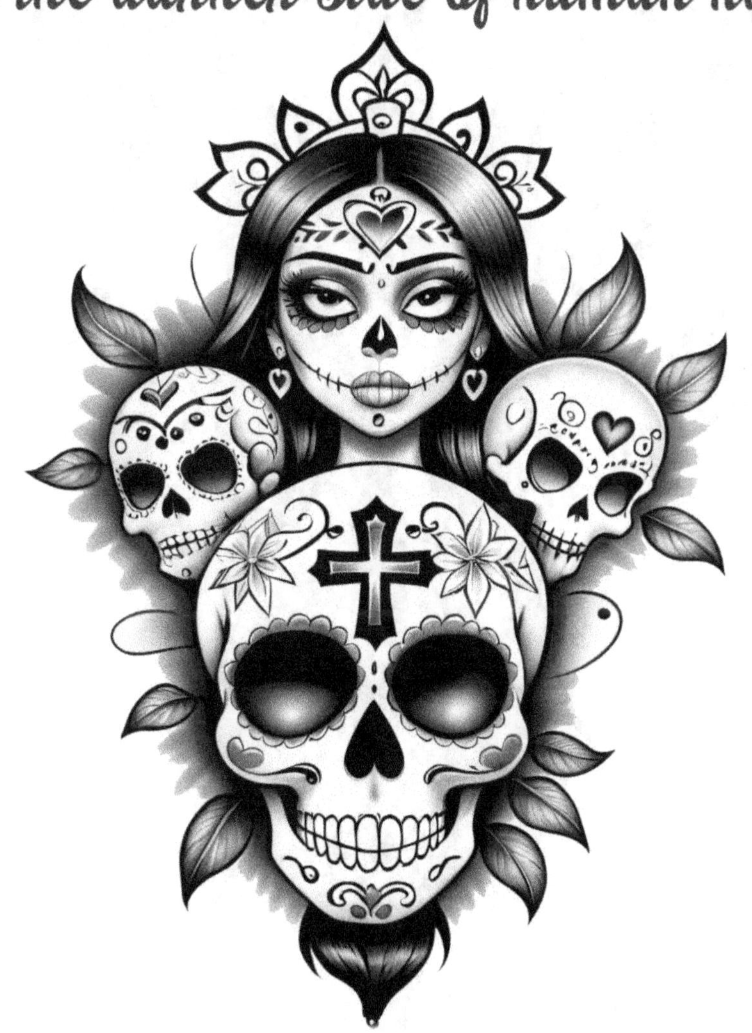

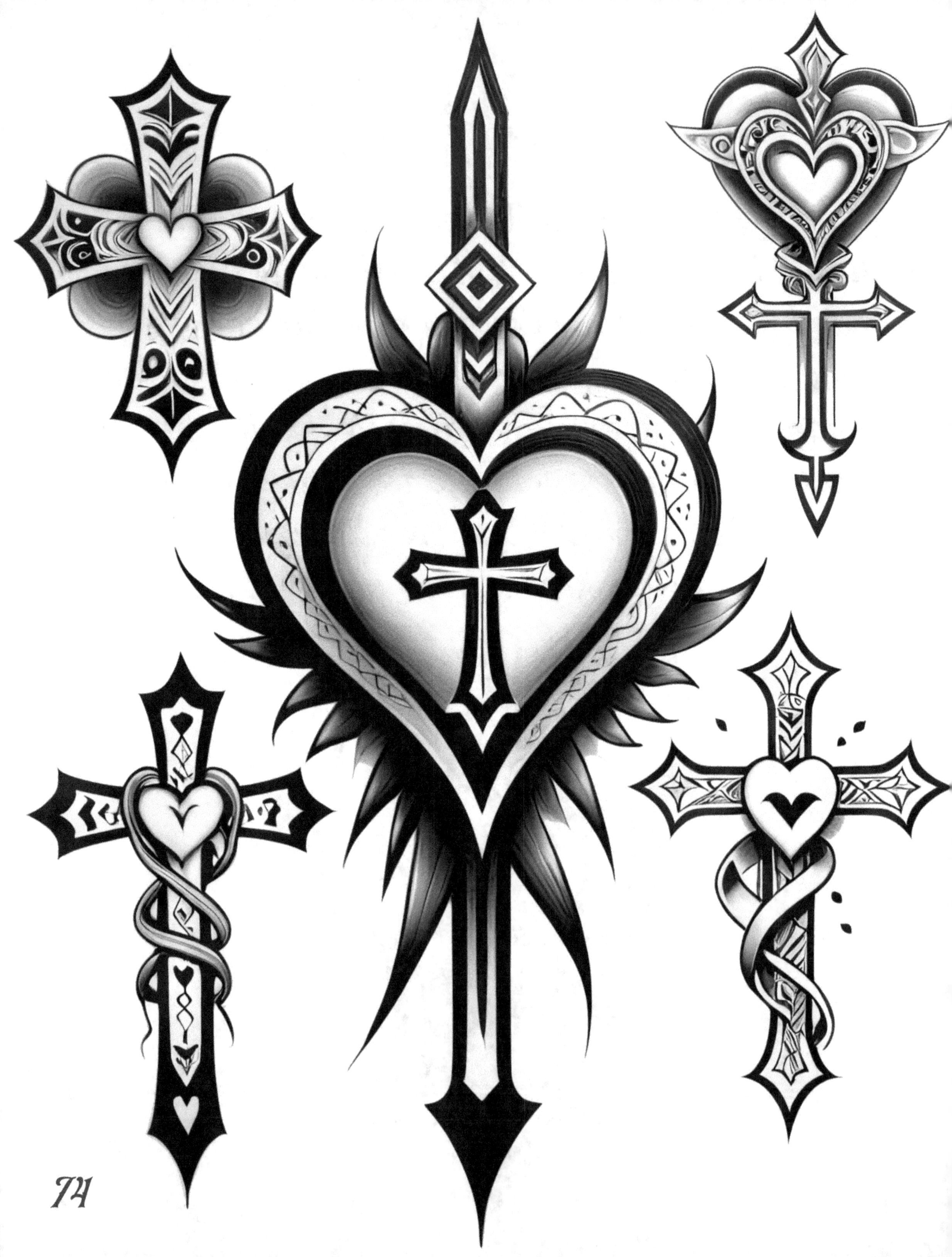

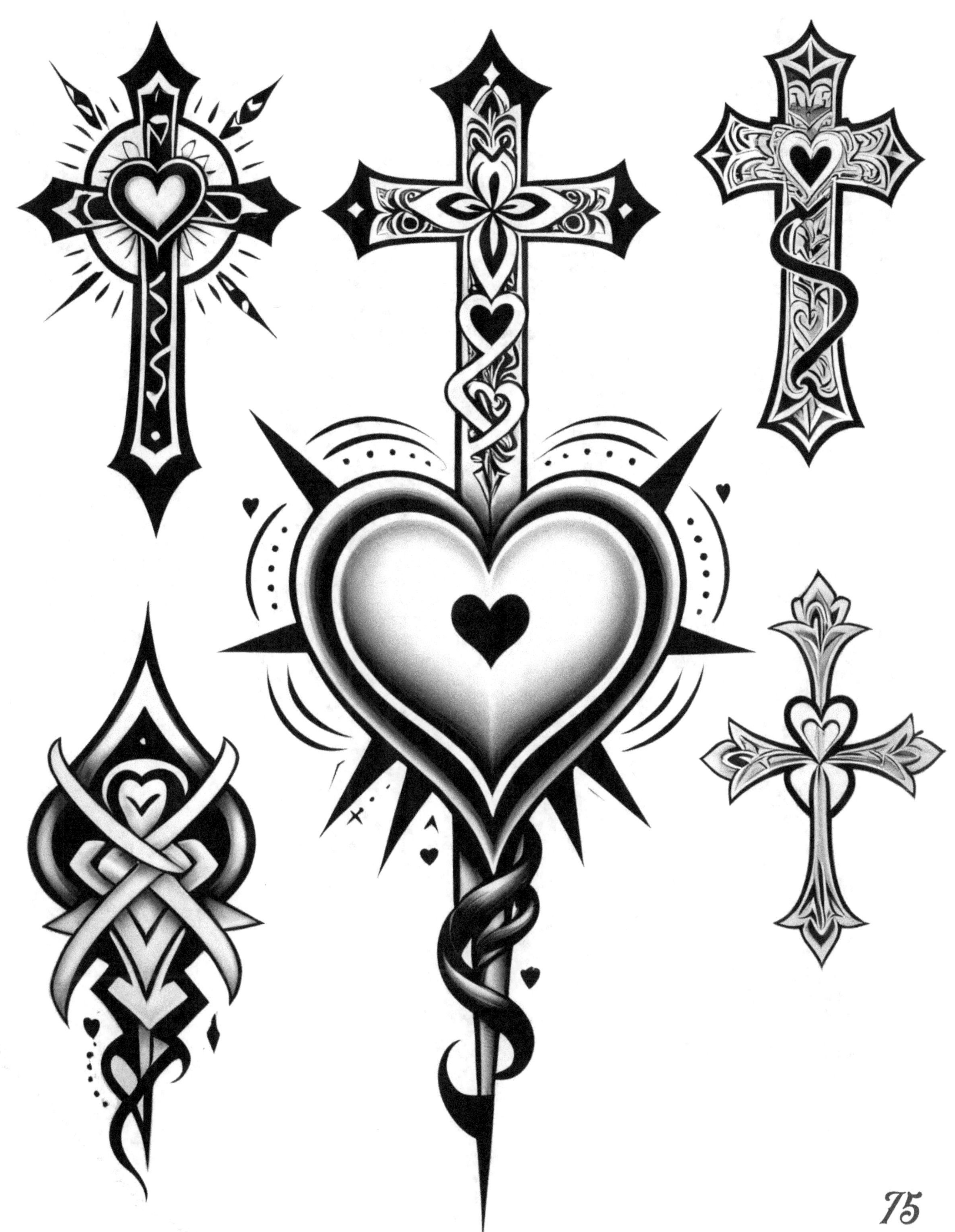

75

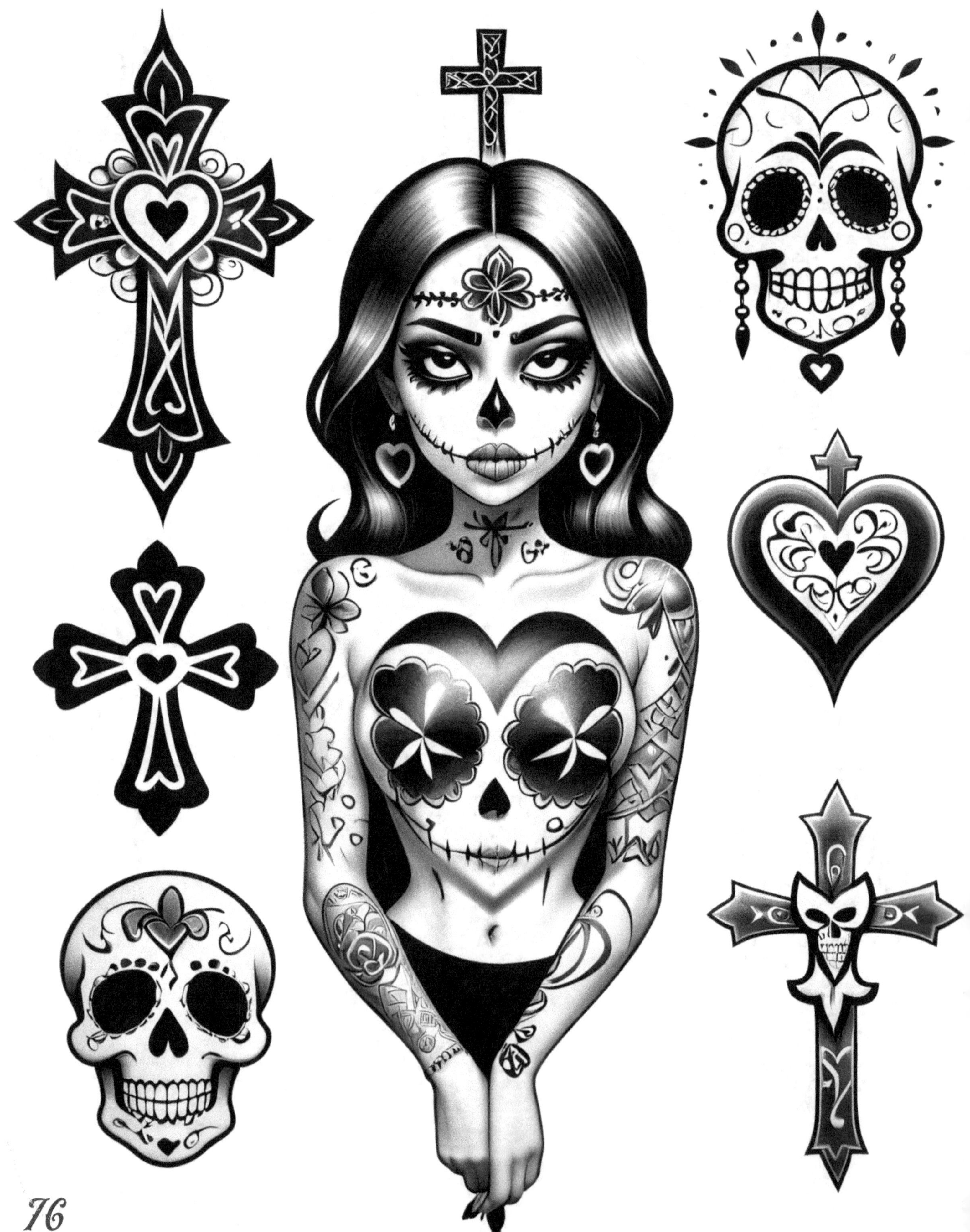

76

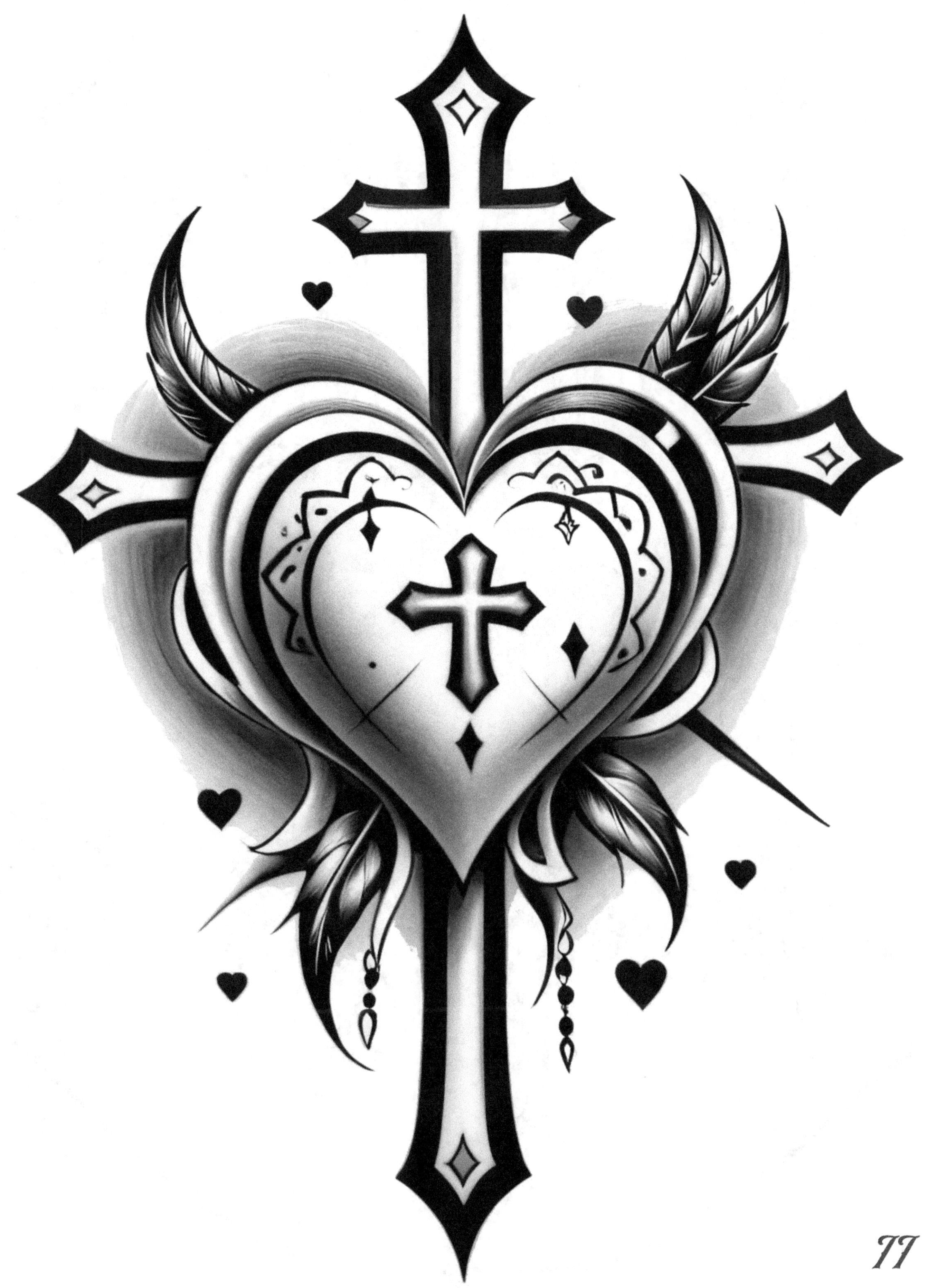

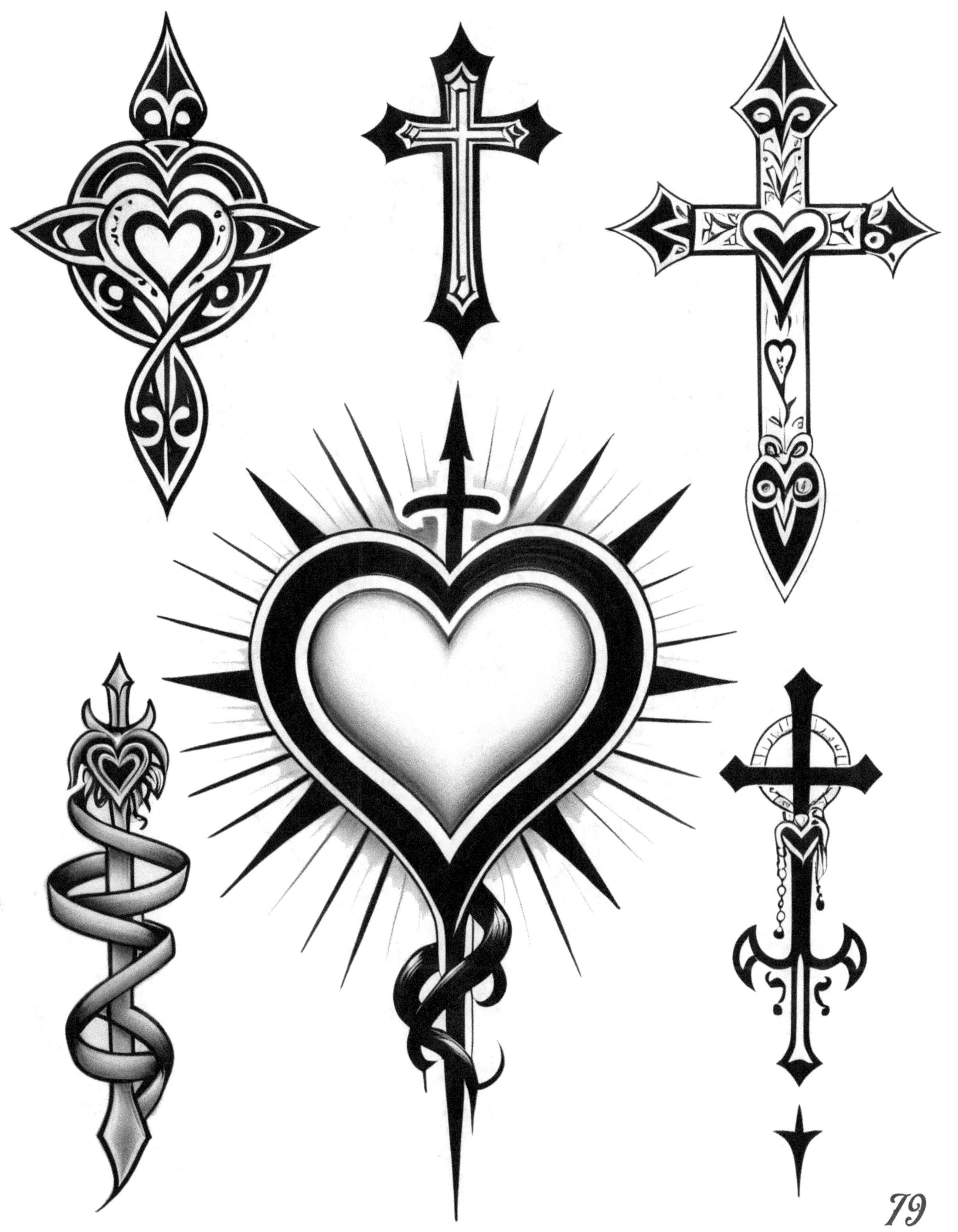

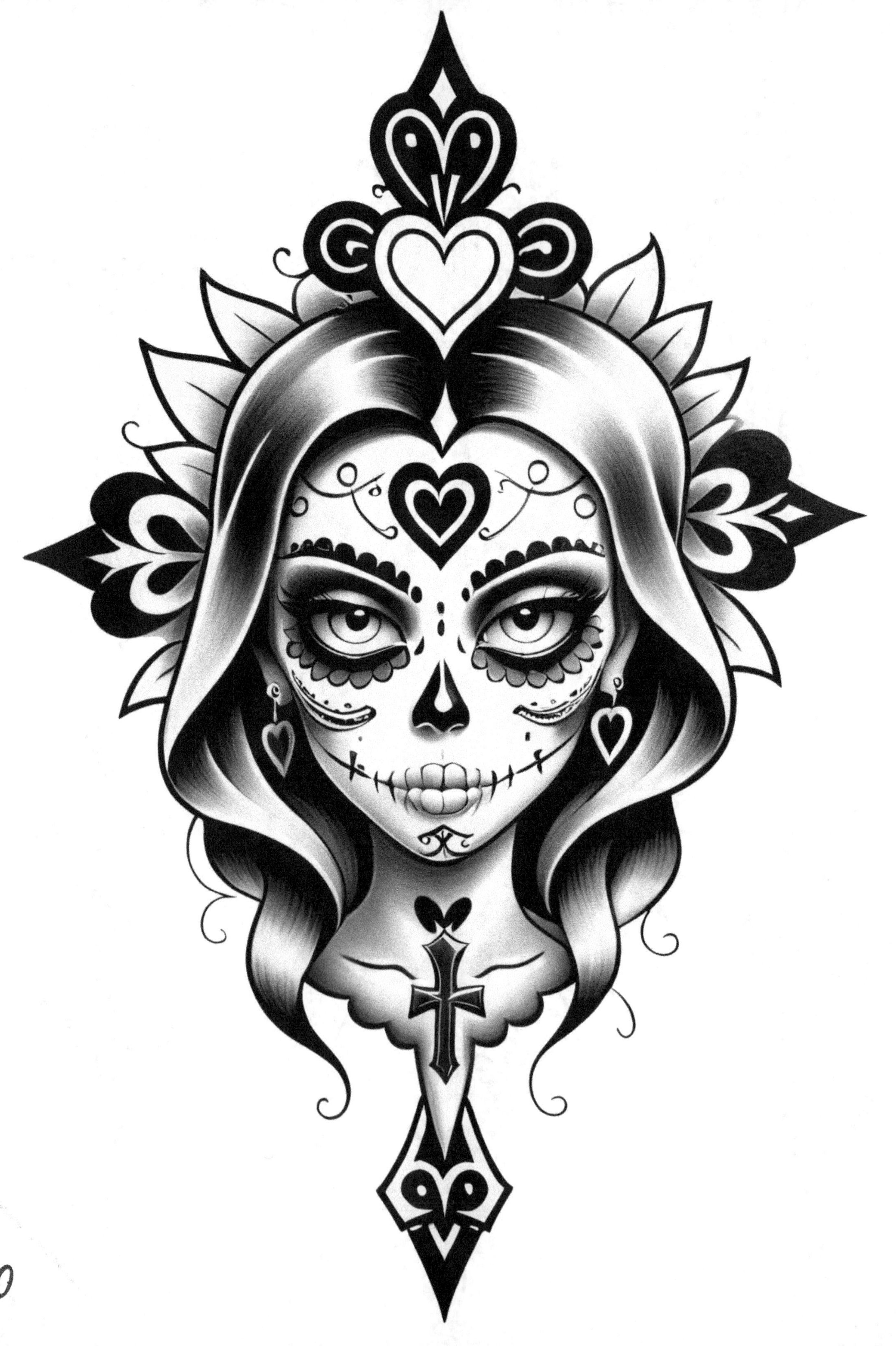

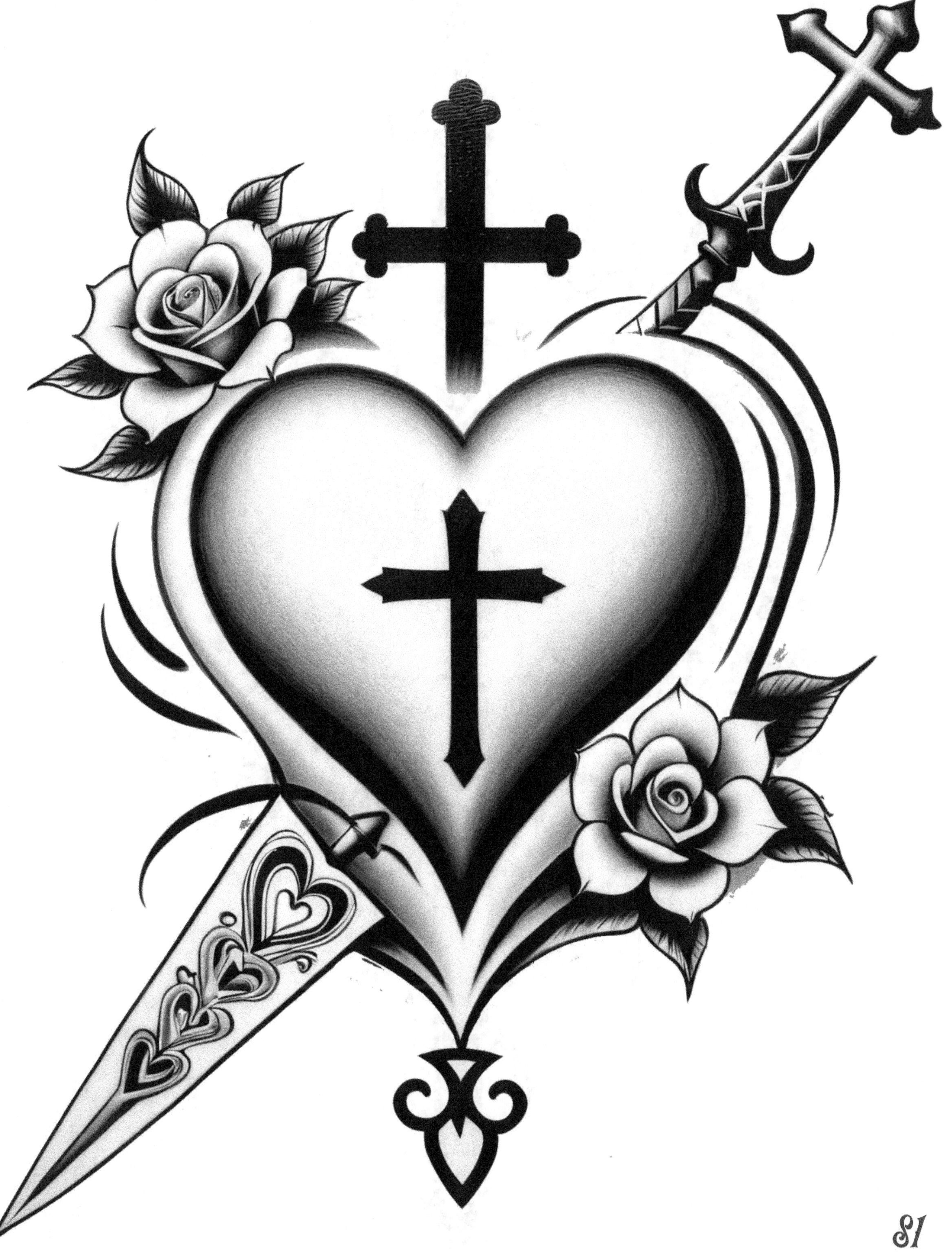

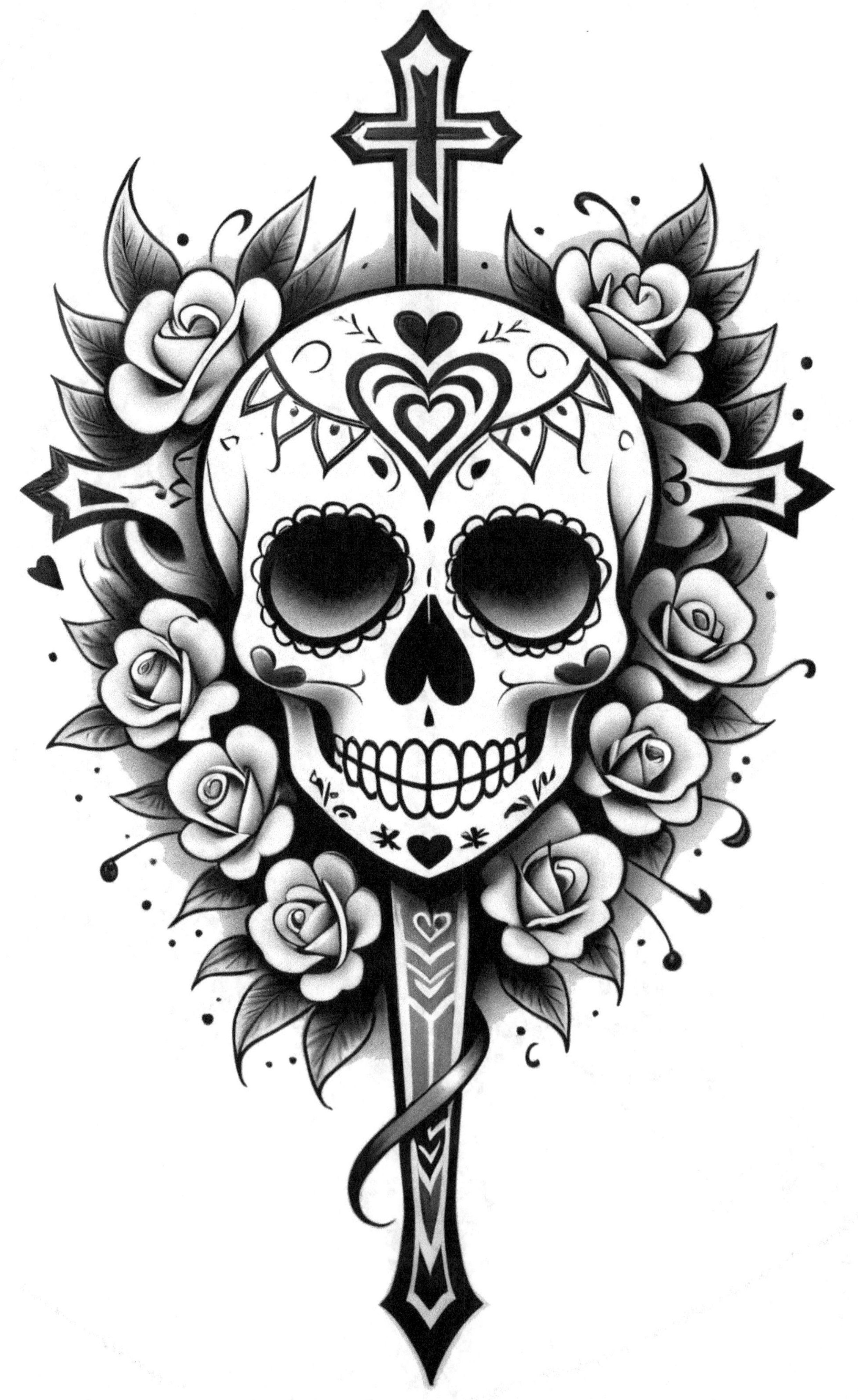

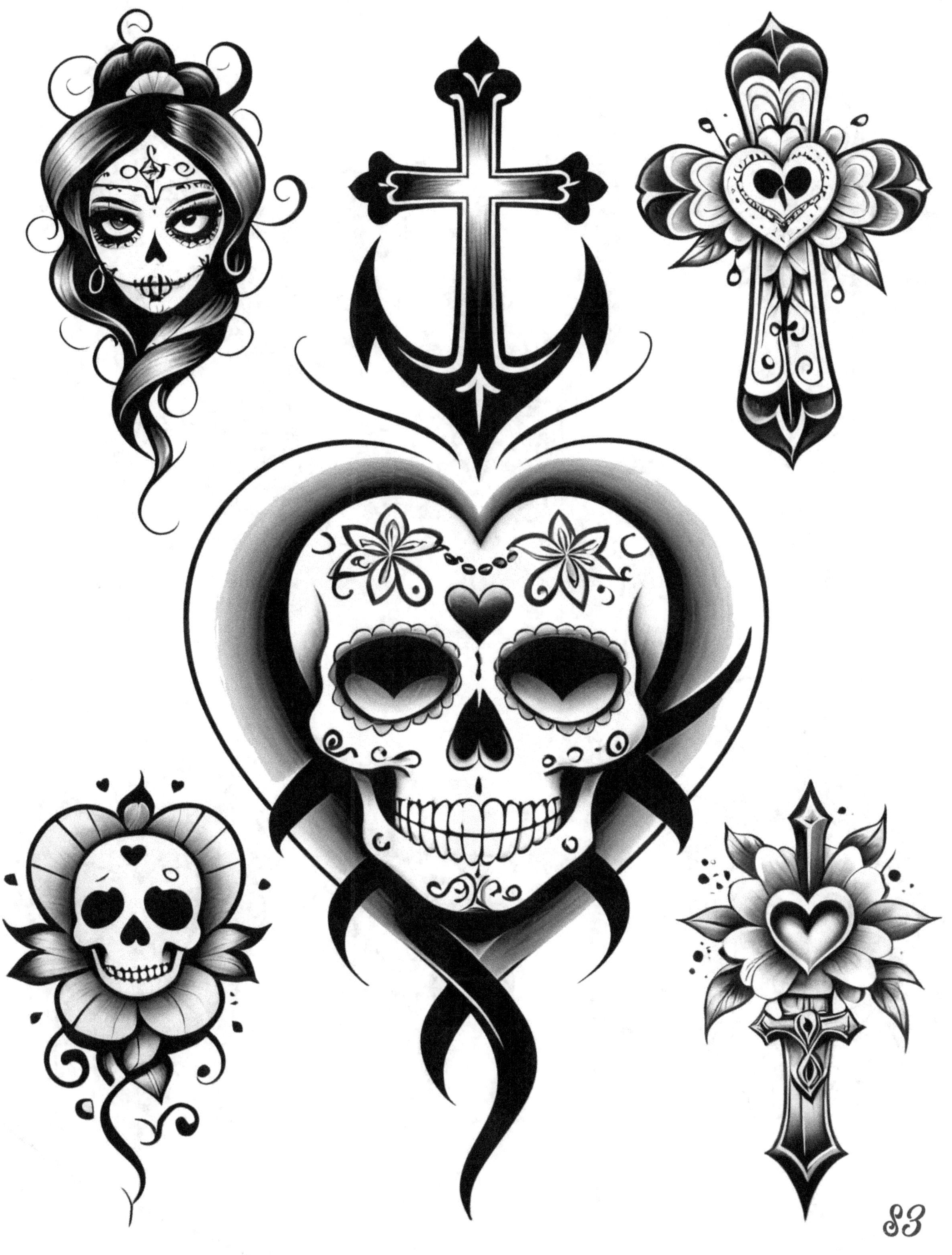

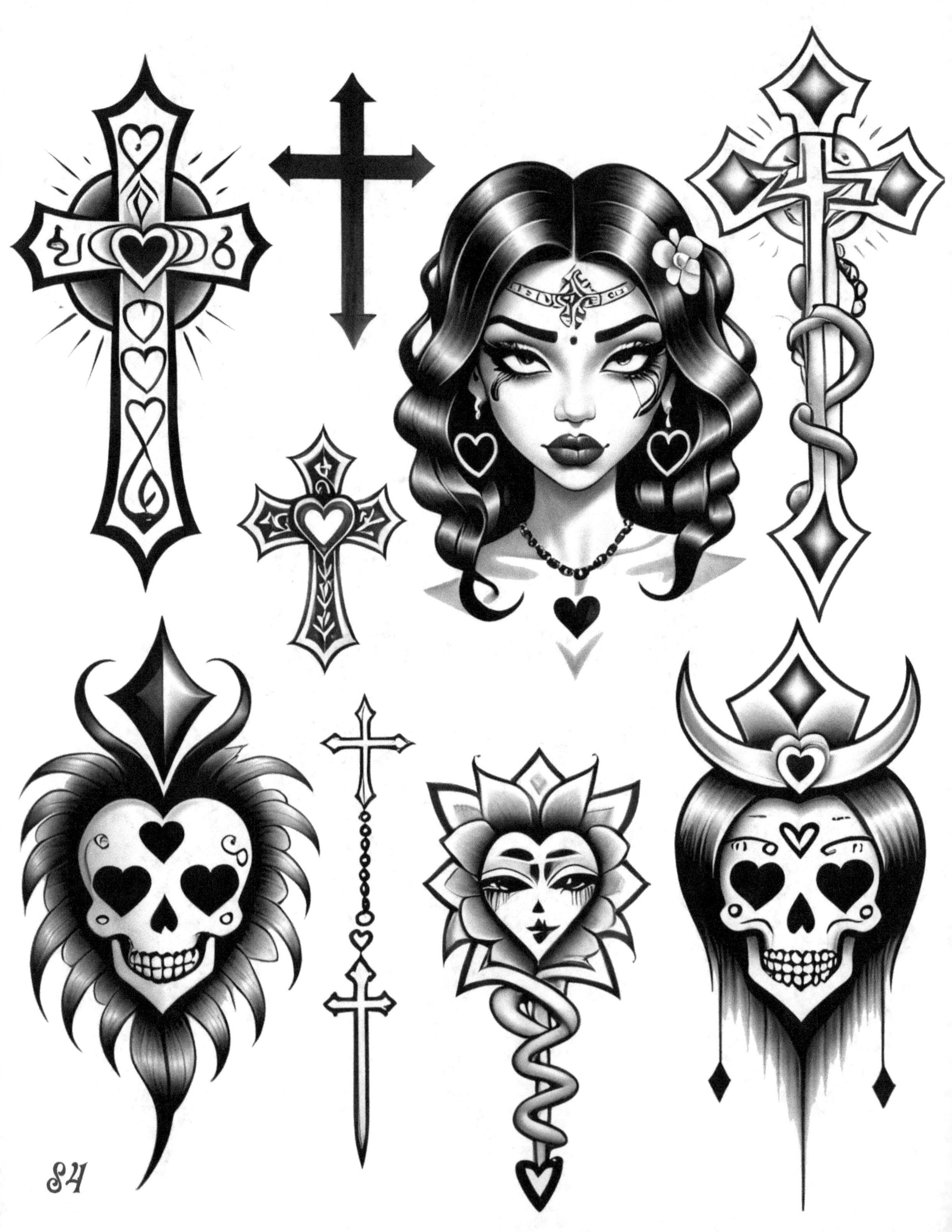

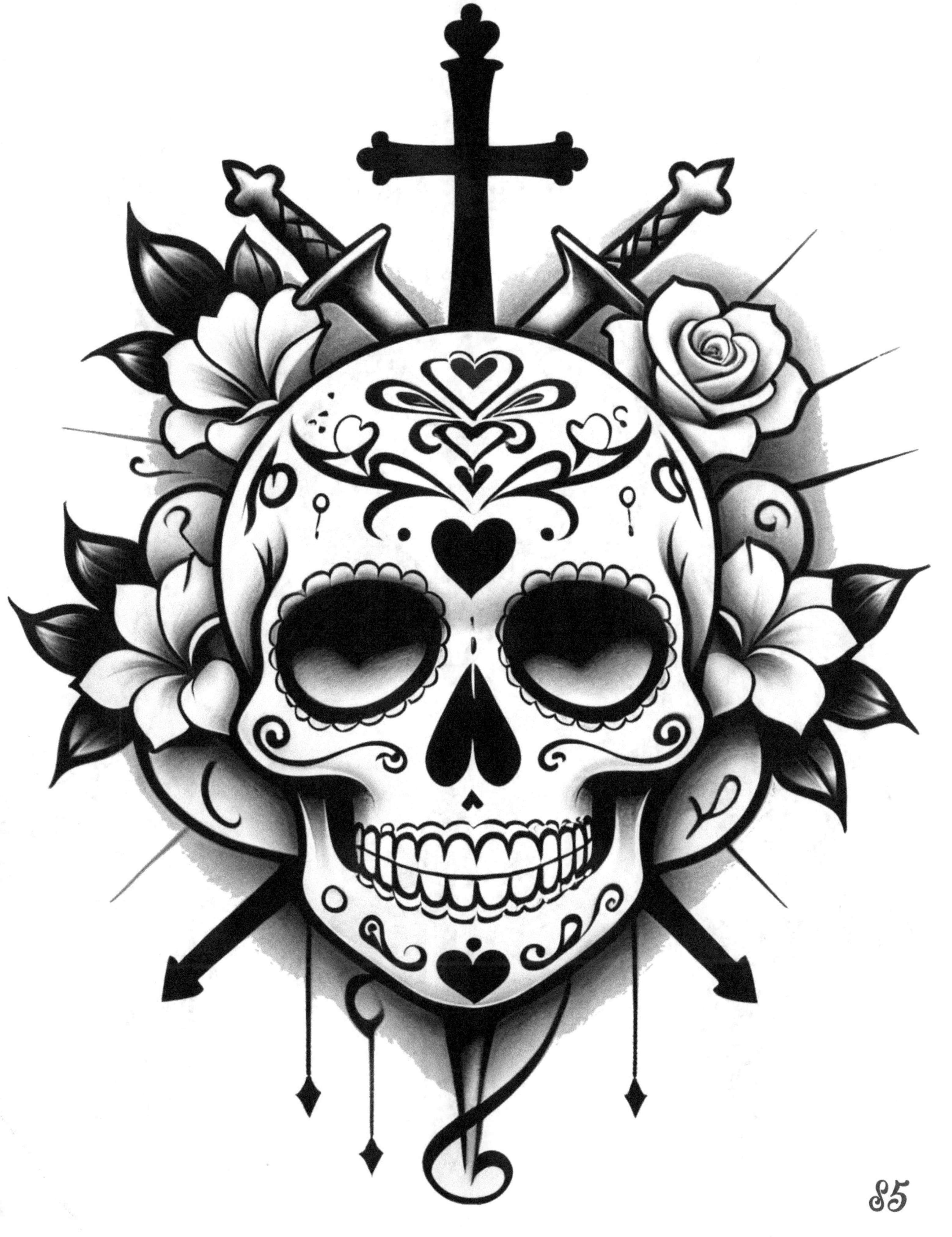

85

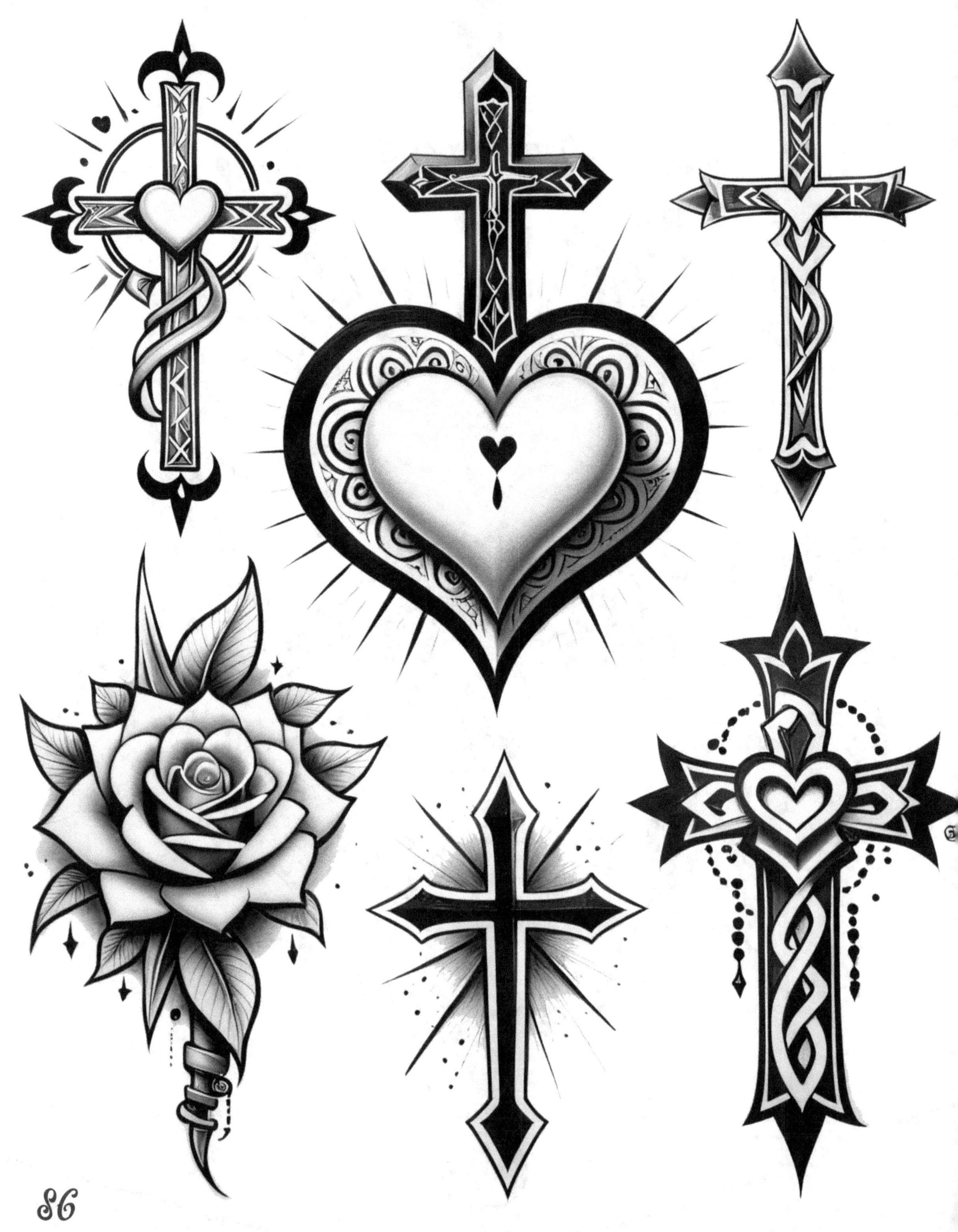

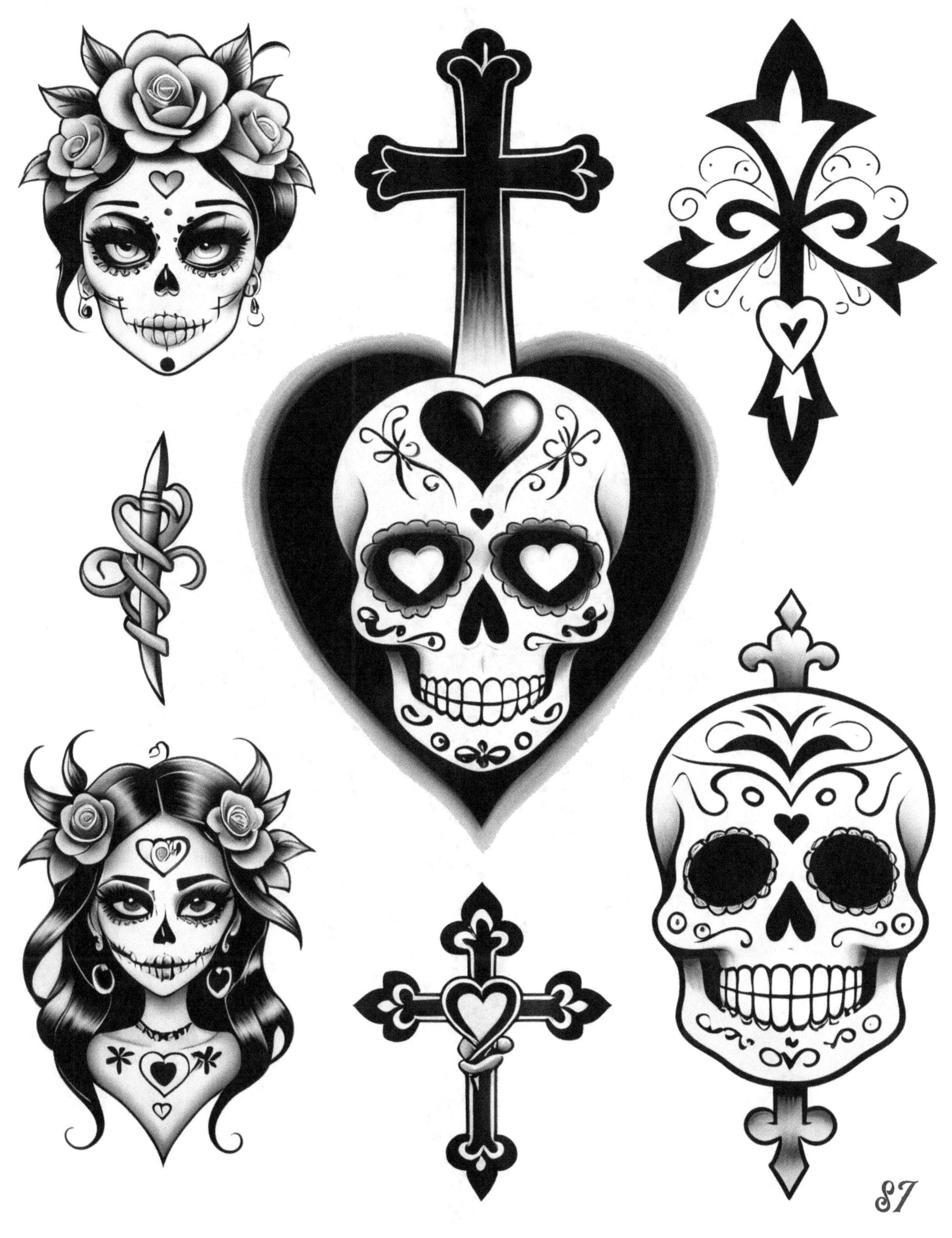

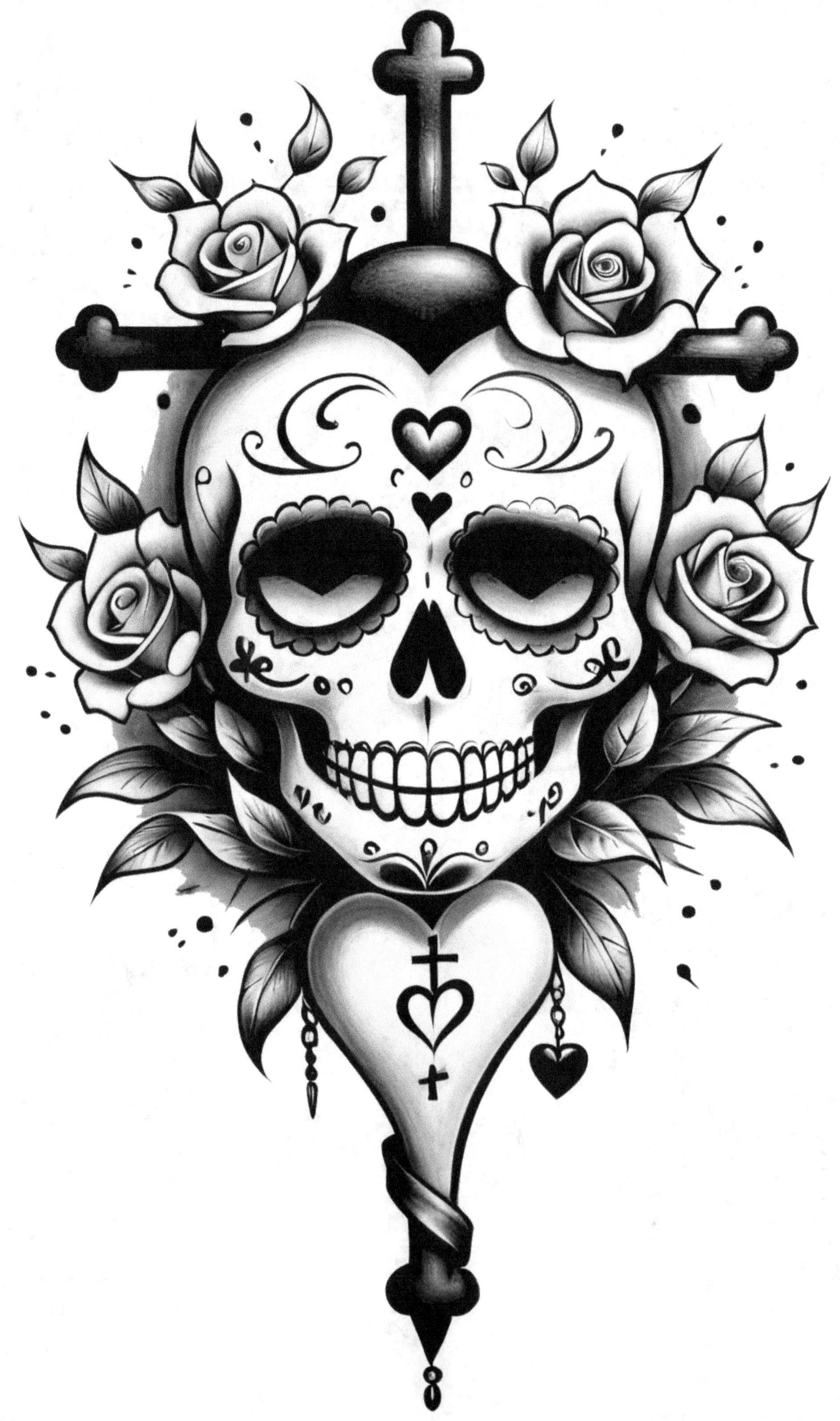

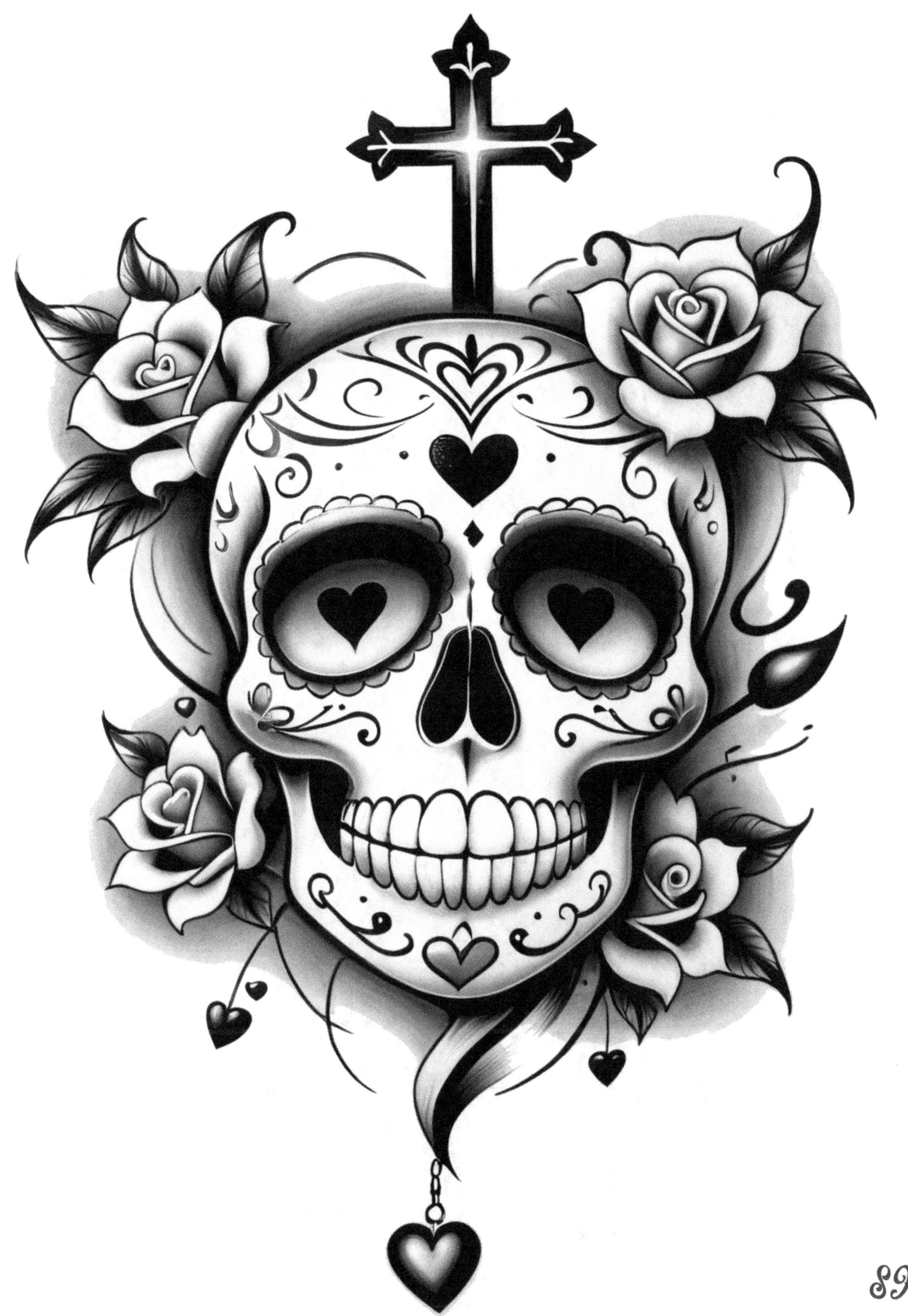

Sacred

Sacred themes in Chicano tattoos often focus on religious and spiritual symbols deeply embedded in the Chicano culture. This includes images such as crosses, praying hands, and religious figures like saints and the Virgin Mary. These tattoos serve as expressions of faith, devotion, and a personal sanctuary of belief, providing protection, guidance, and a sense of spiritual grounding.

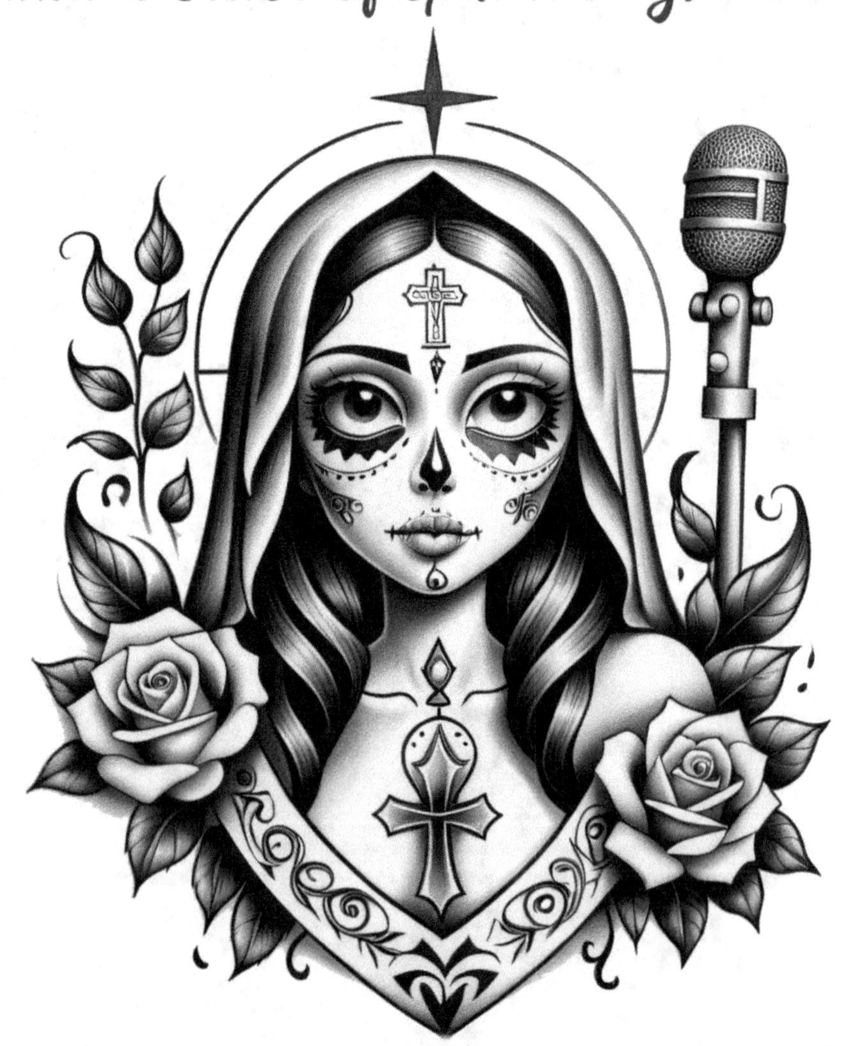

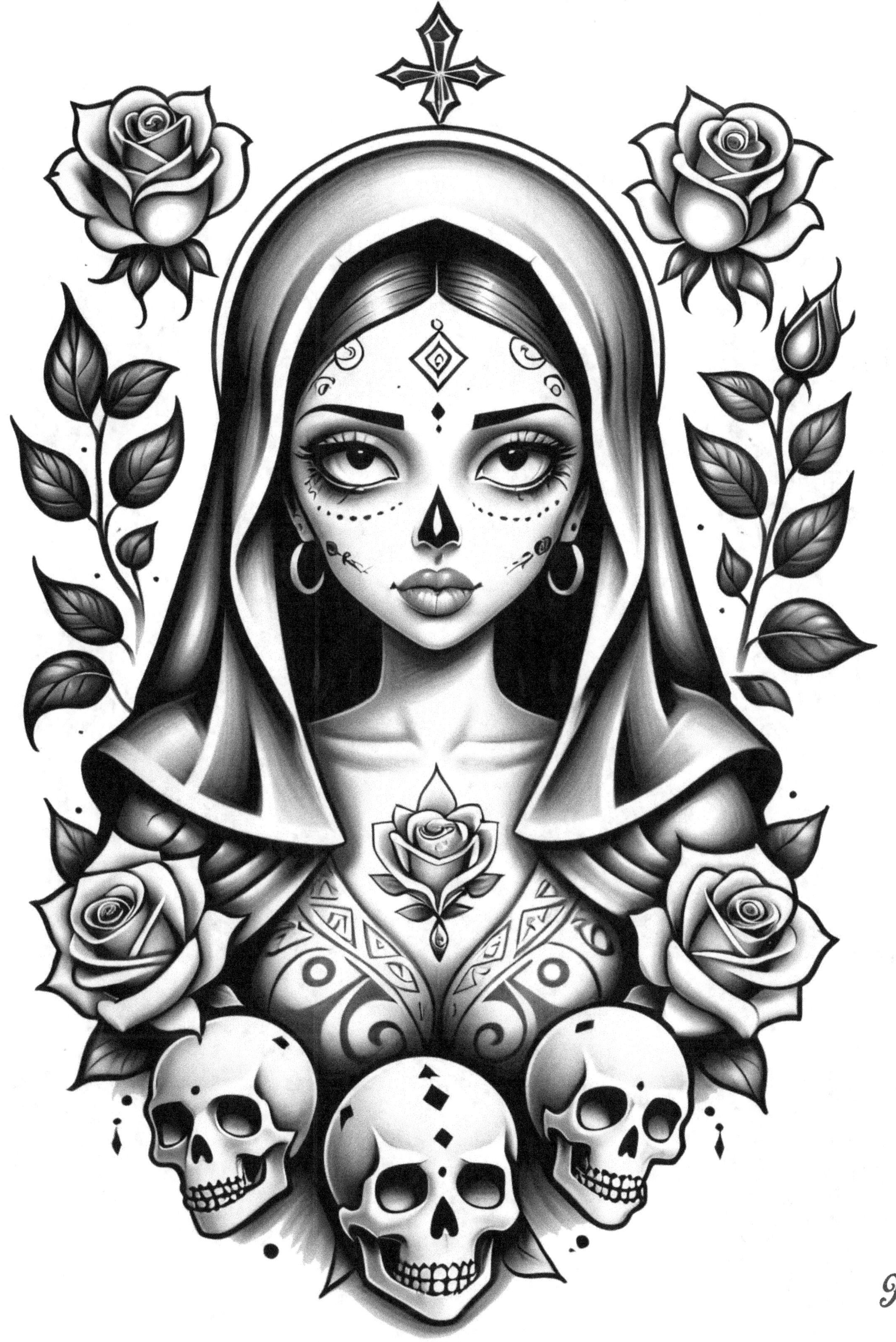

91

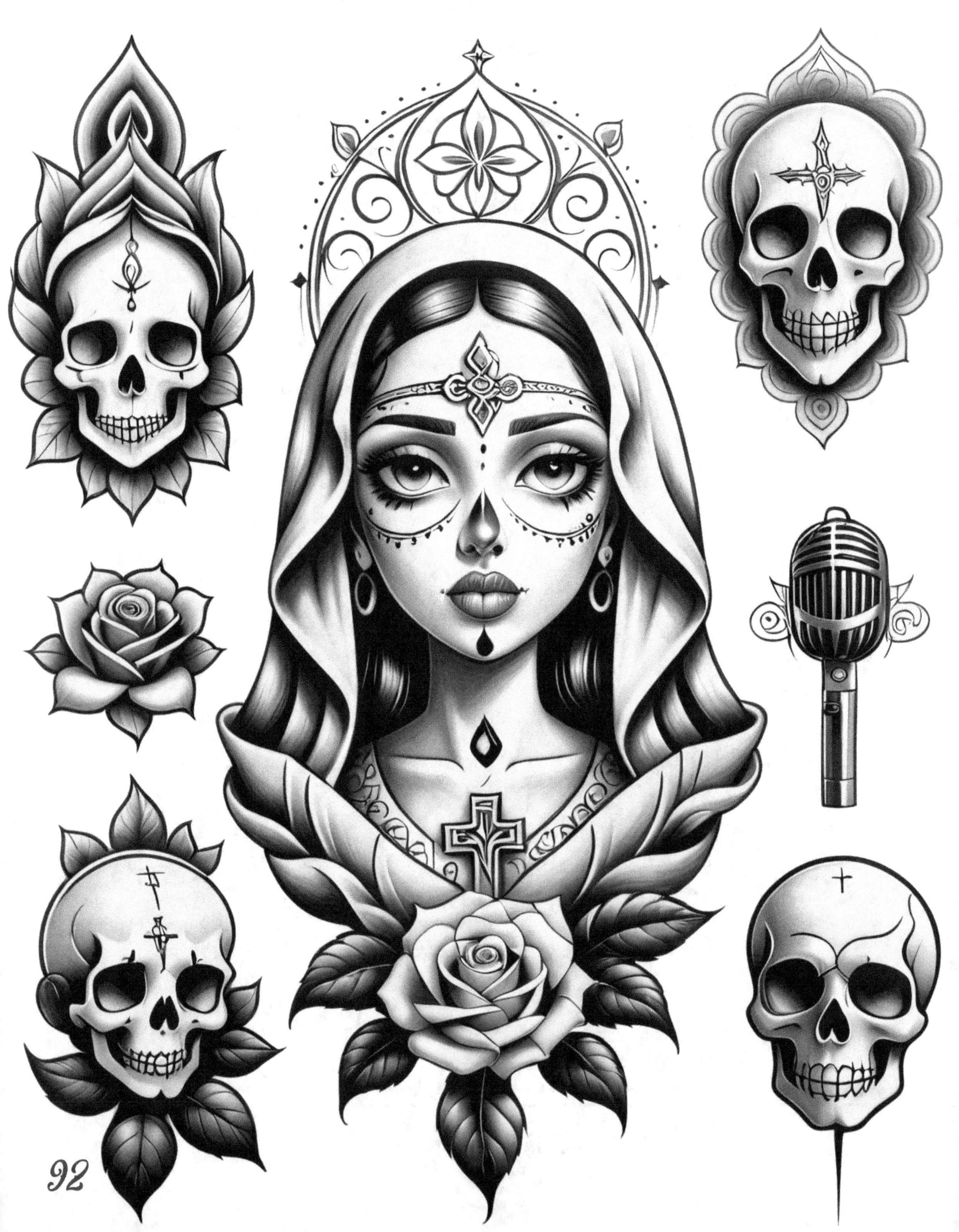
92

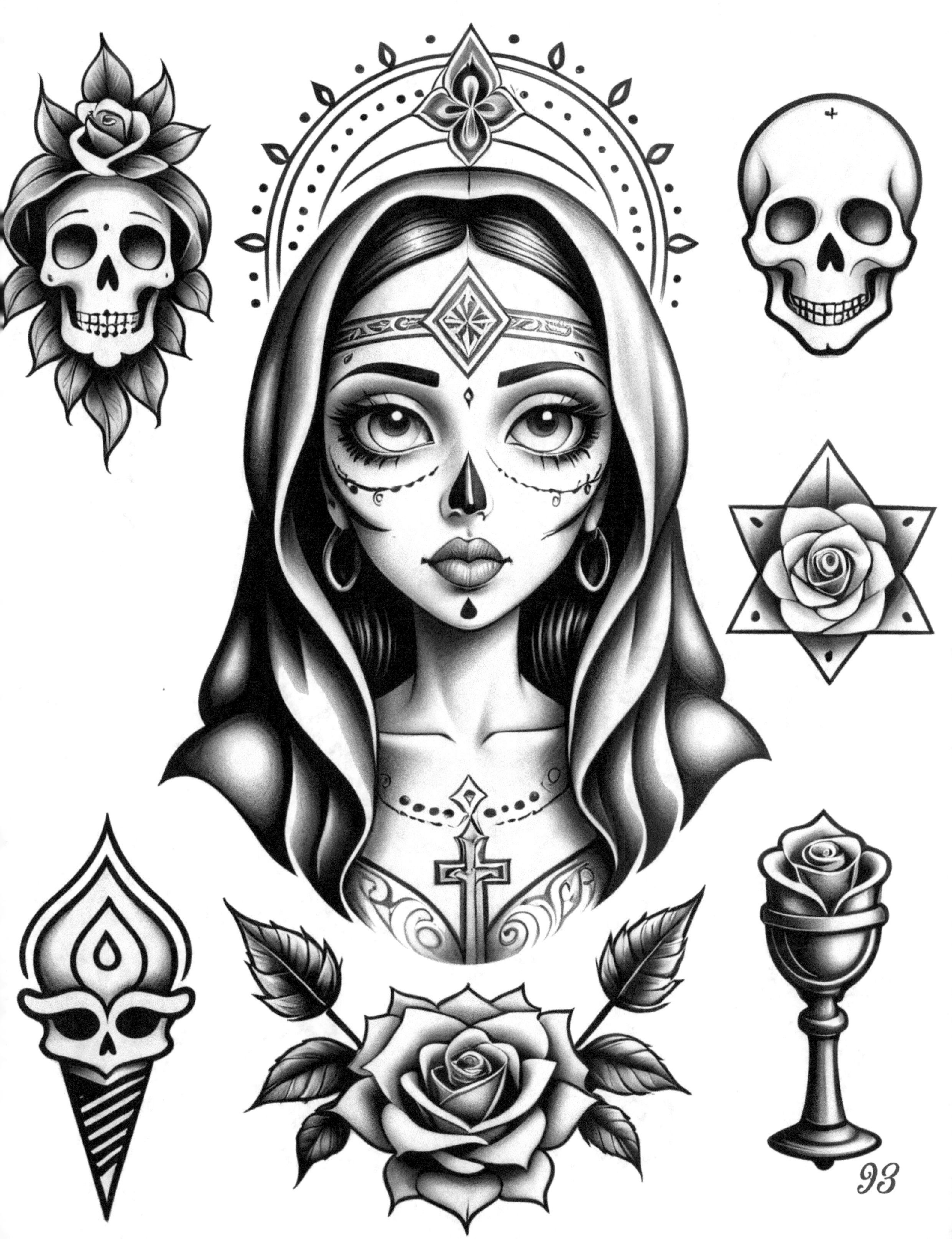
93

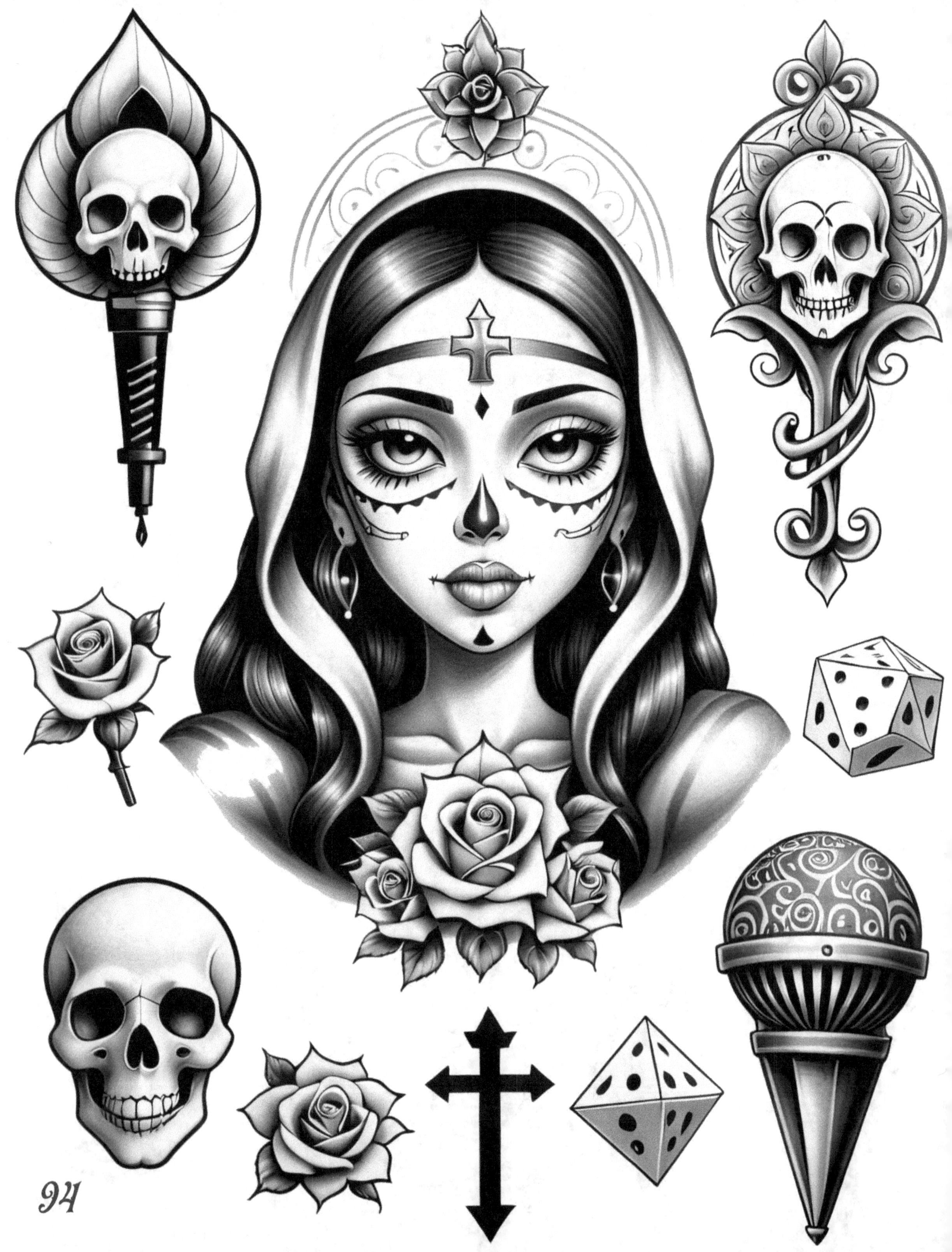
94

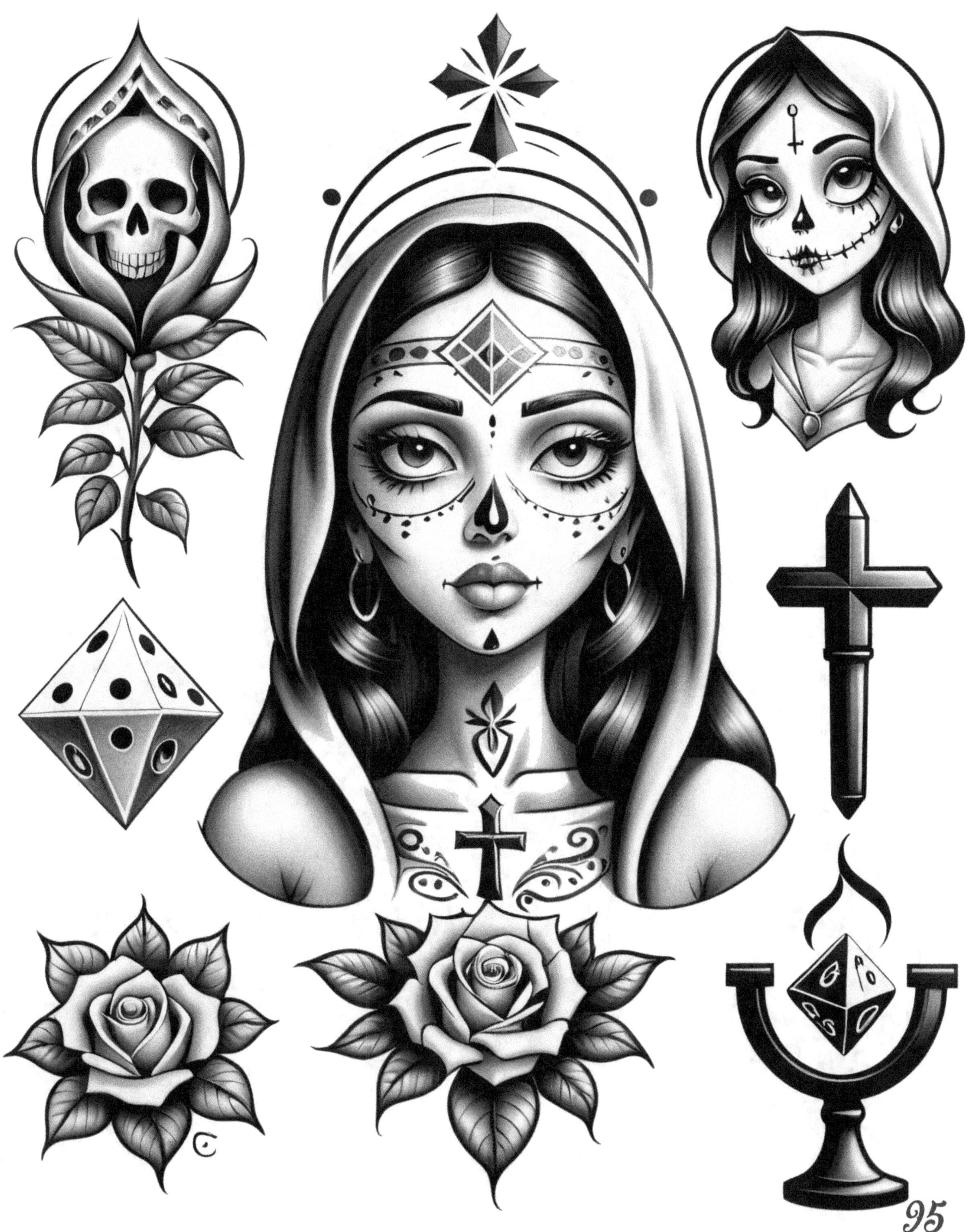

95

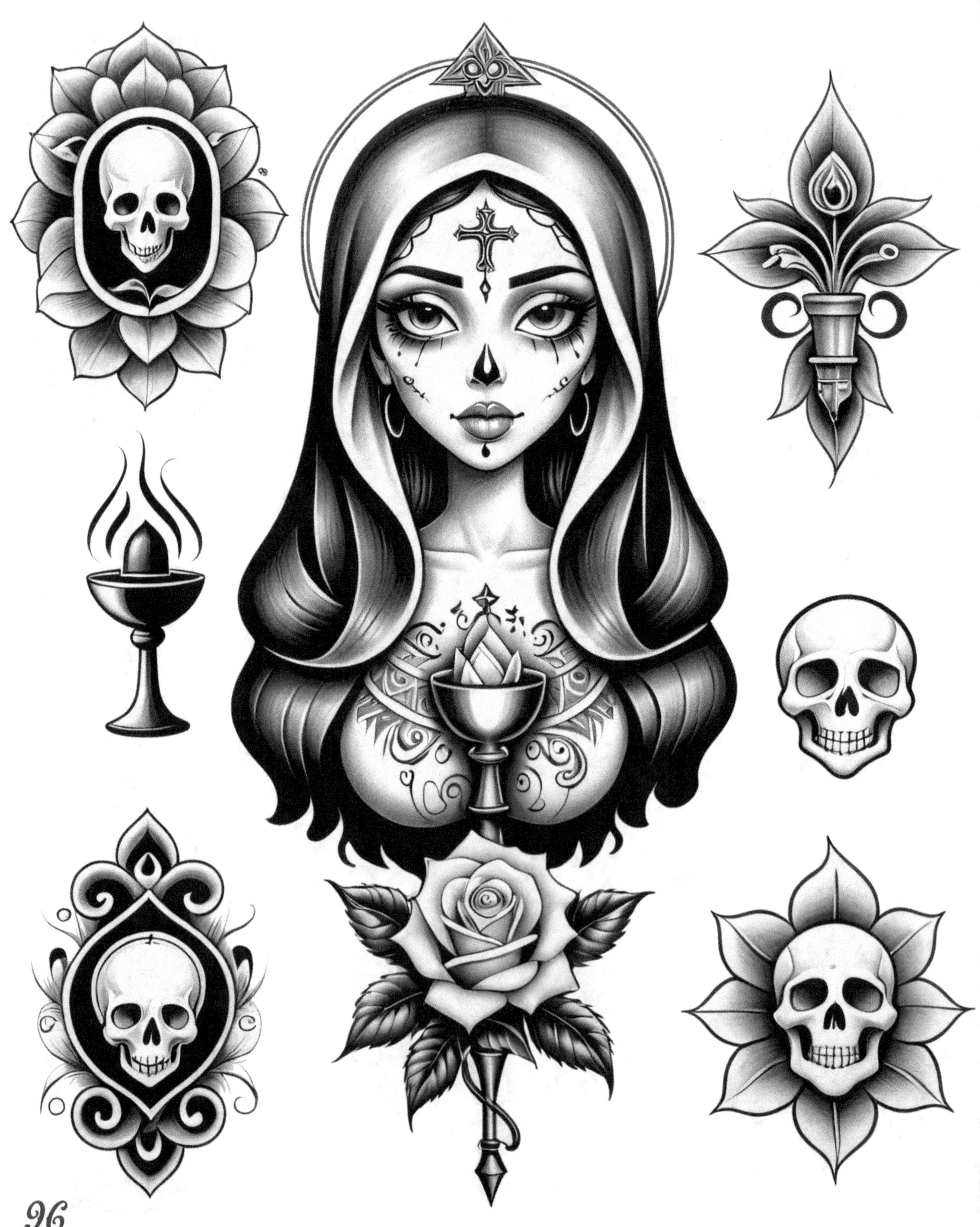

96

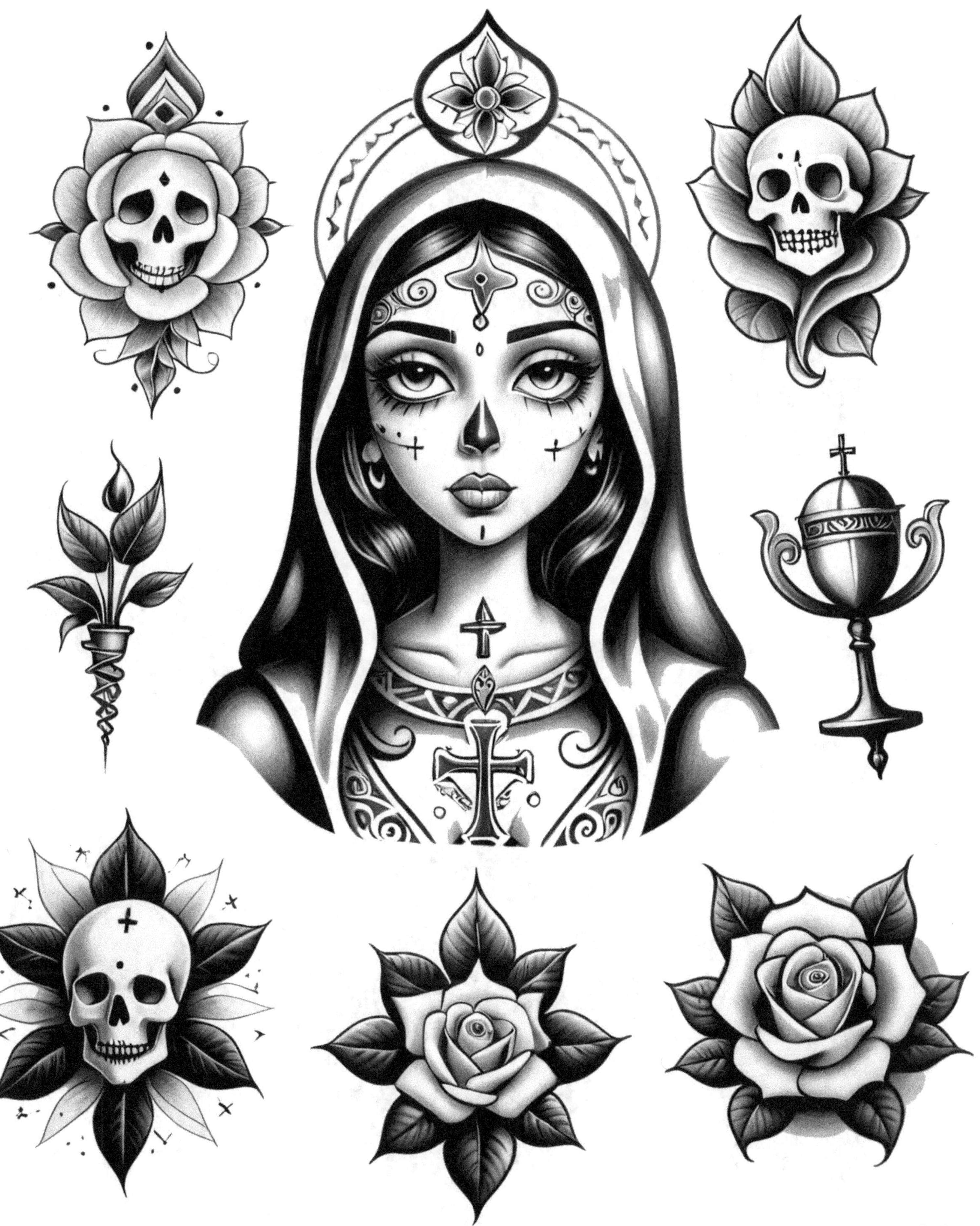

97

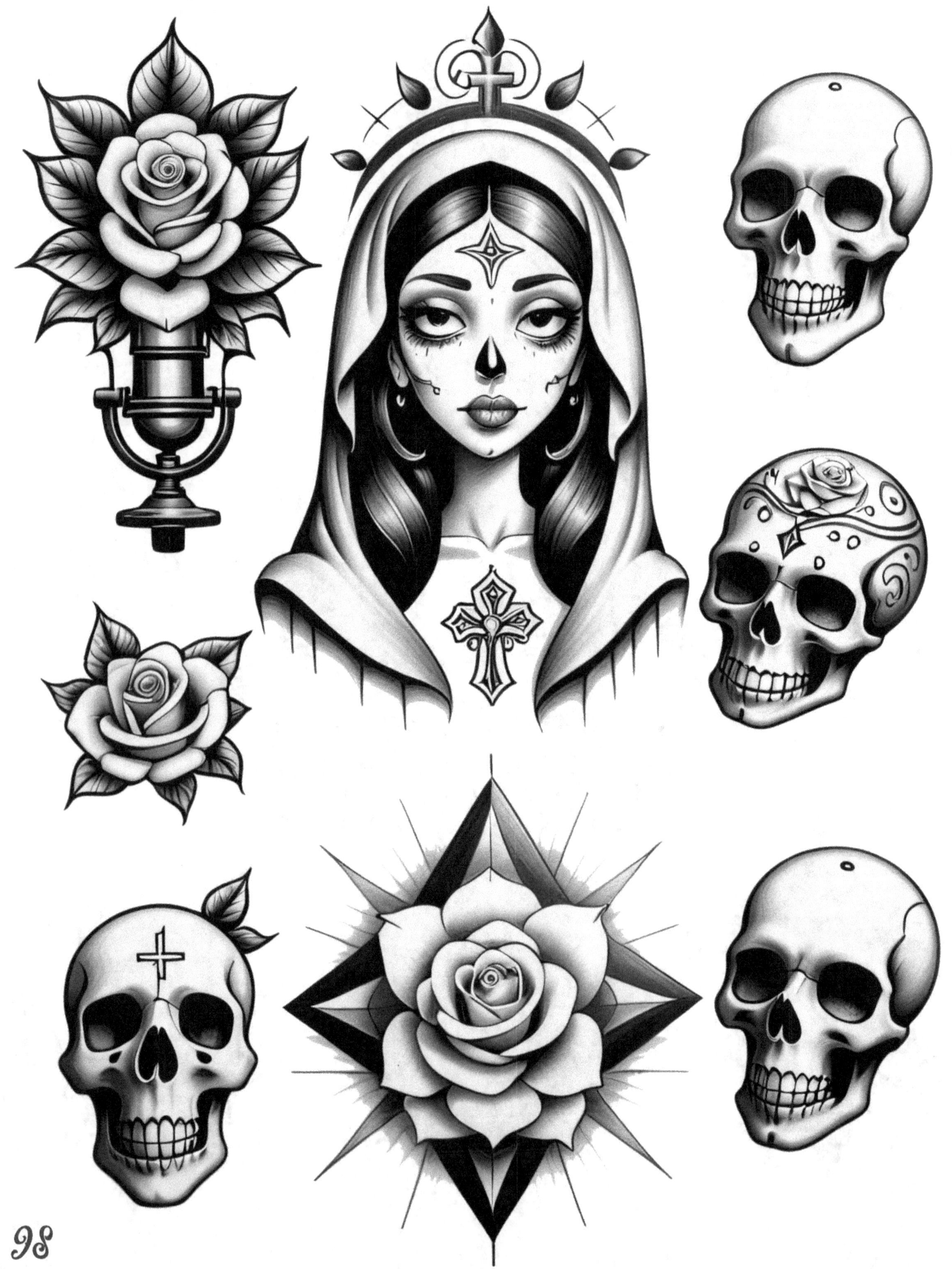

Floral

Floral motifs are popular across many cultures, and in the Chicano style, they often symbolize beauty, life, and transience. Flowers such as roses are frequently used to express love, emotions, or as a tribute to the deceased, embodying both celebration and mourning.

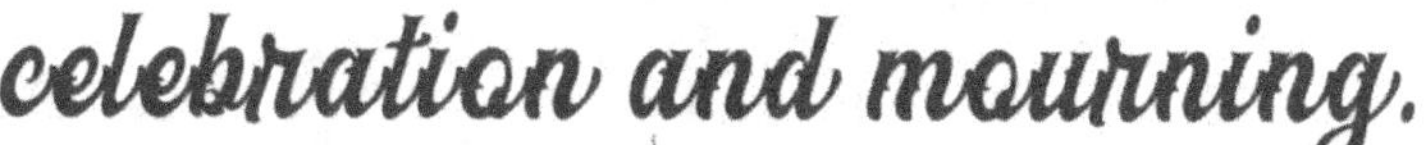

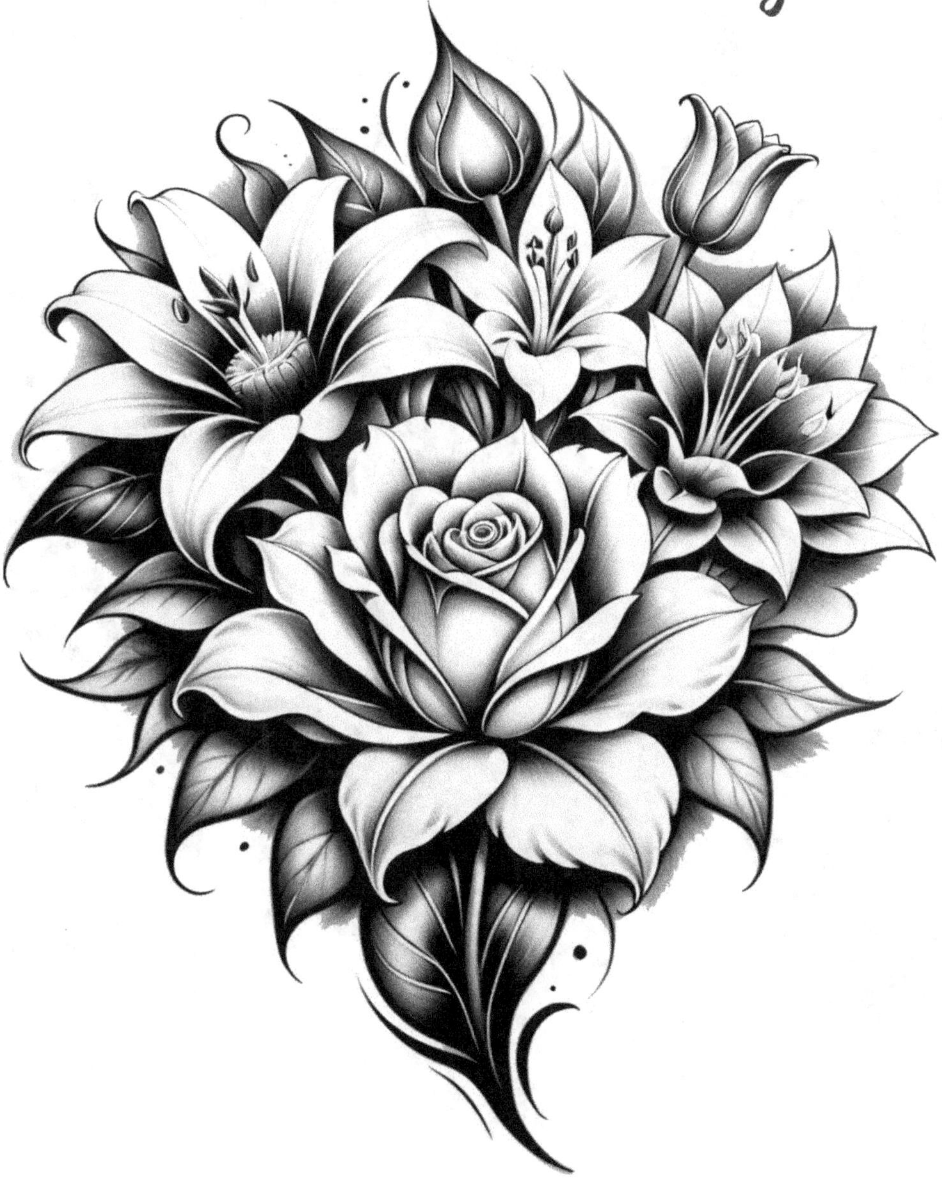

100

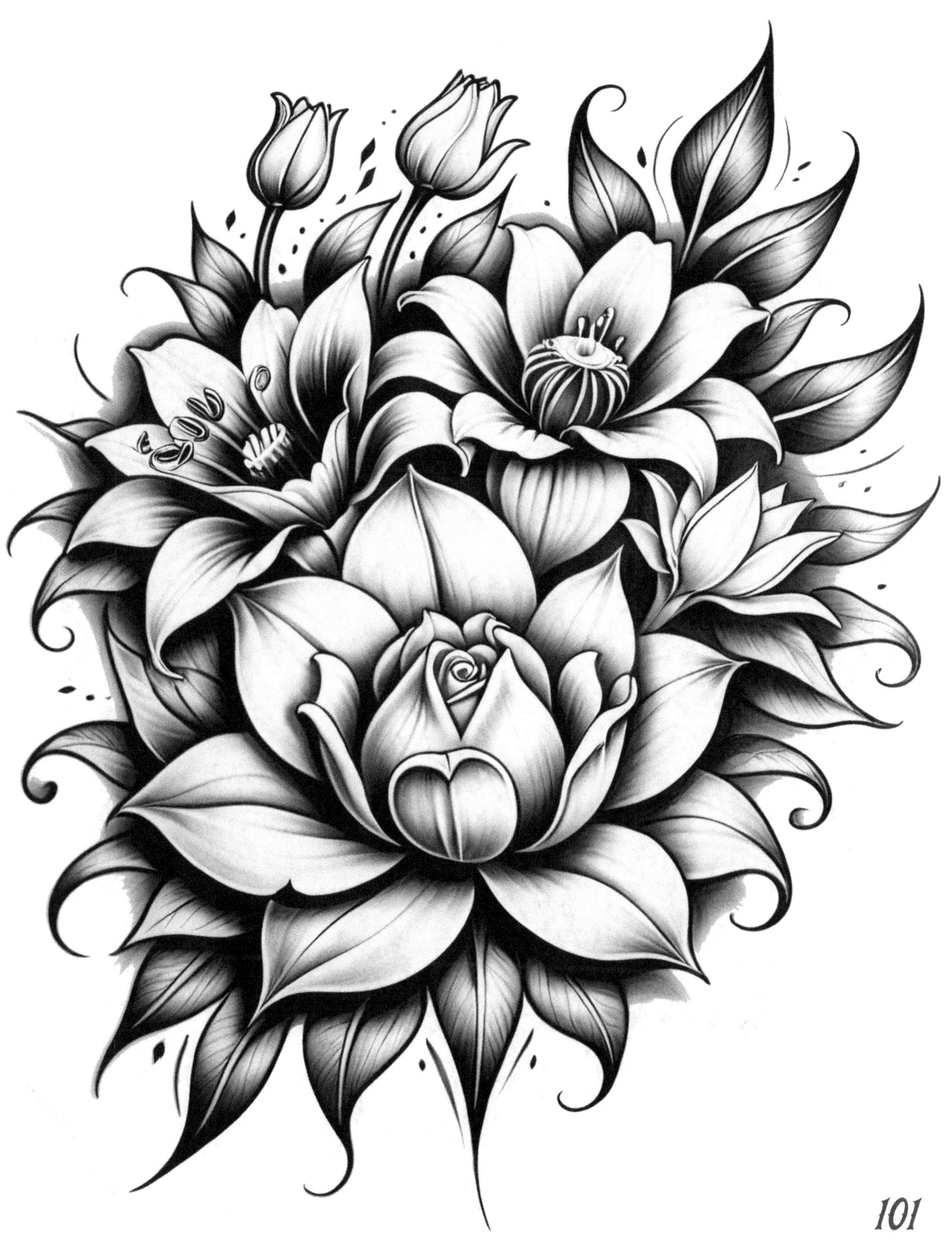

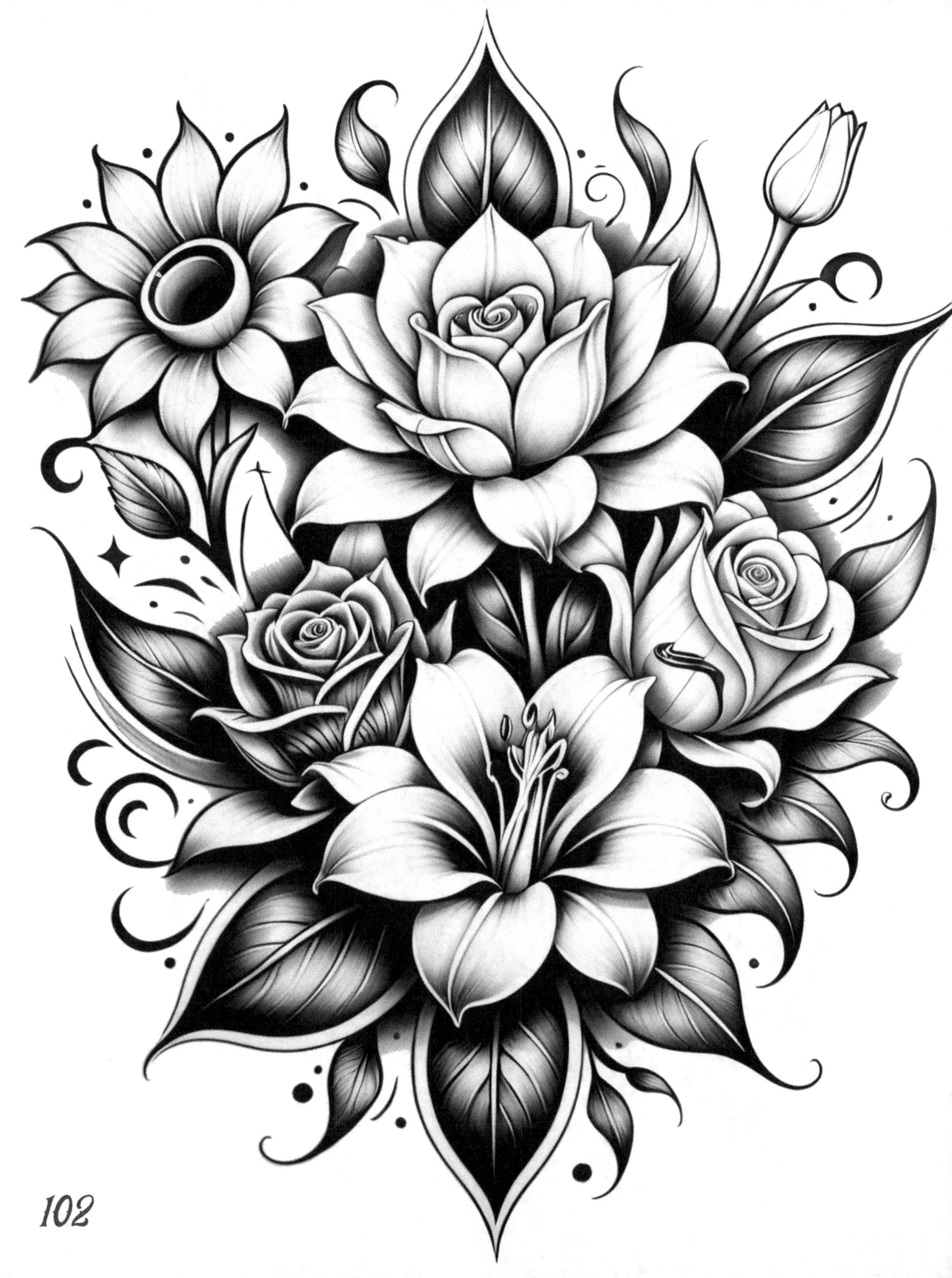

102

103

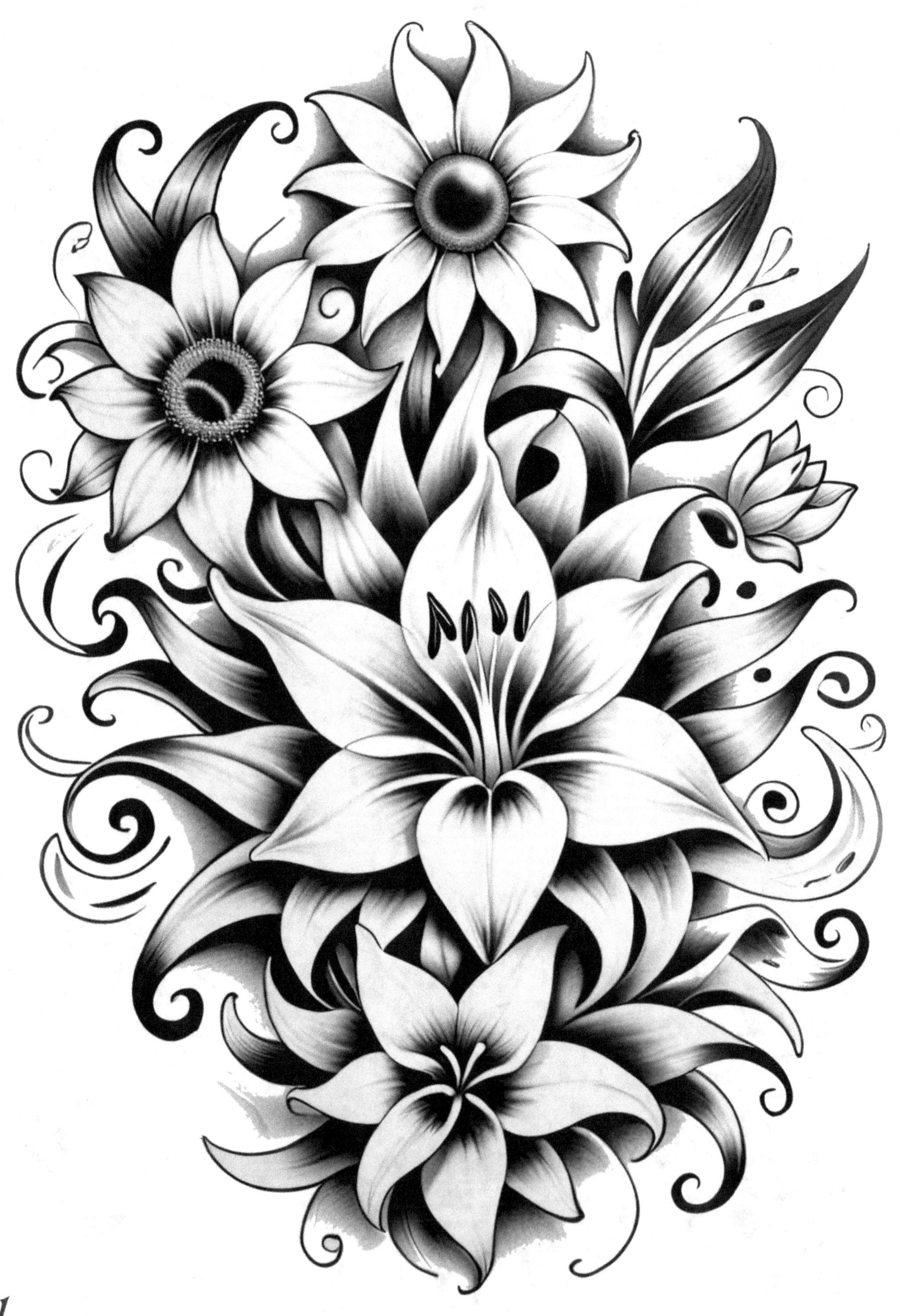

104

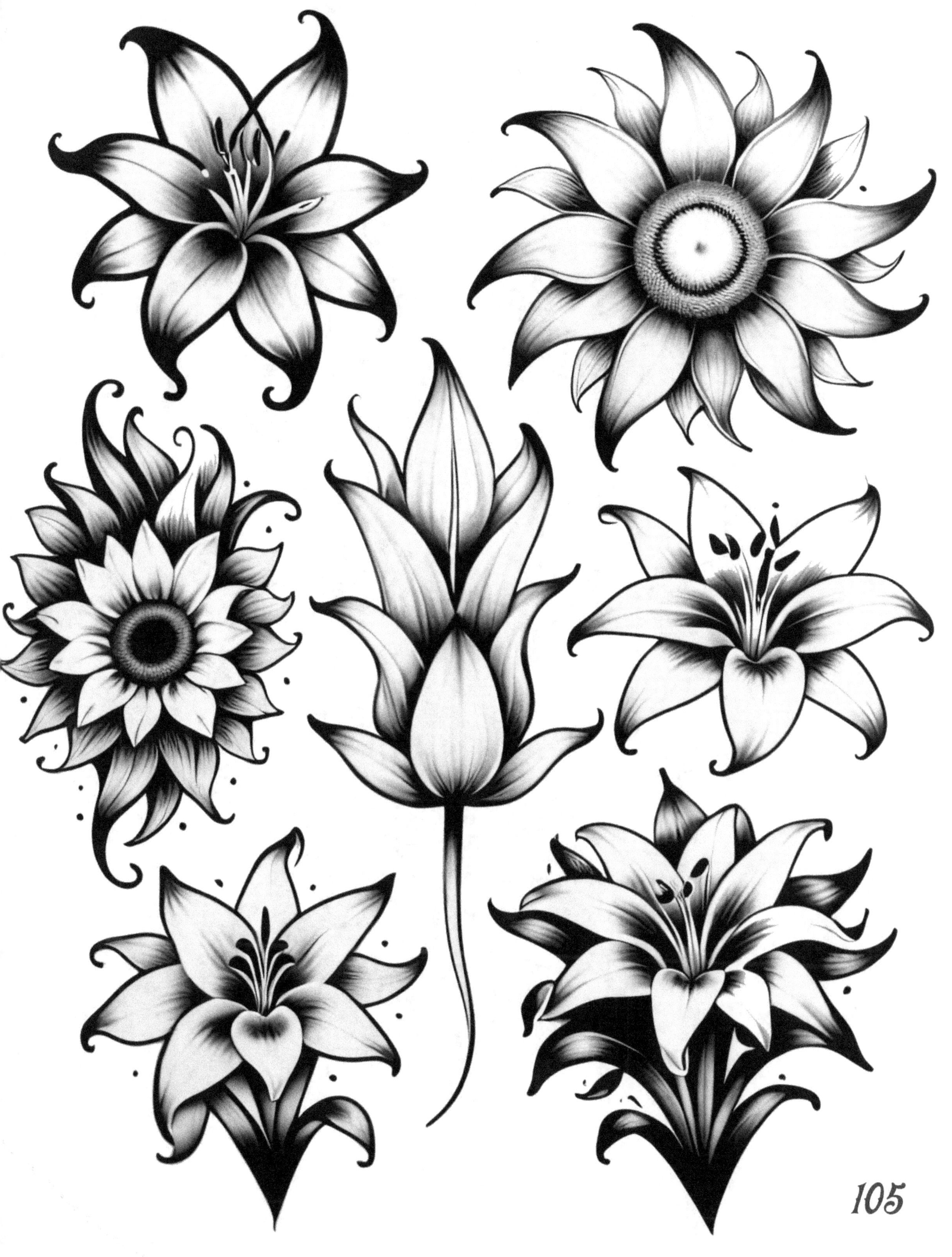

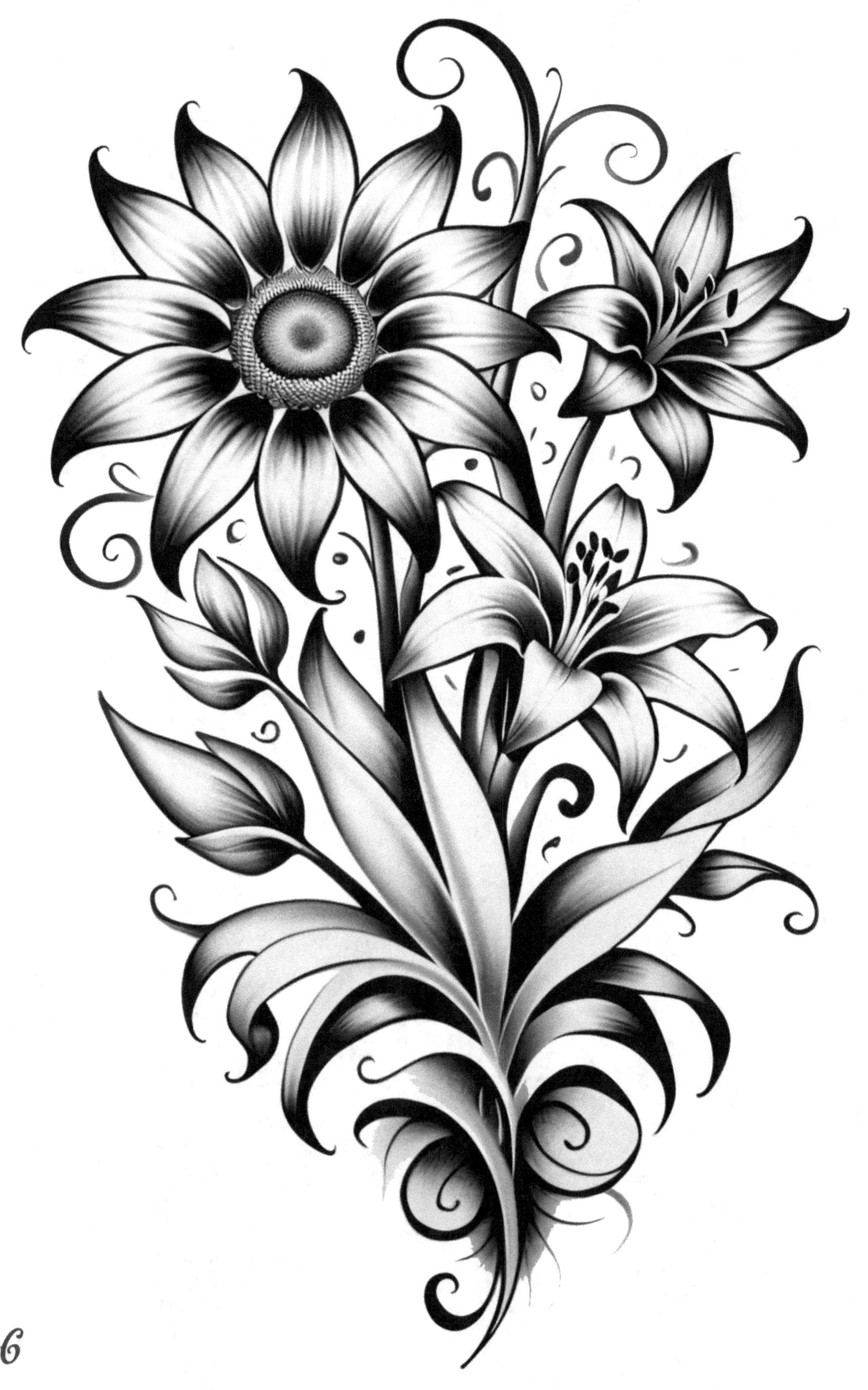

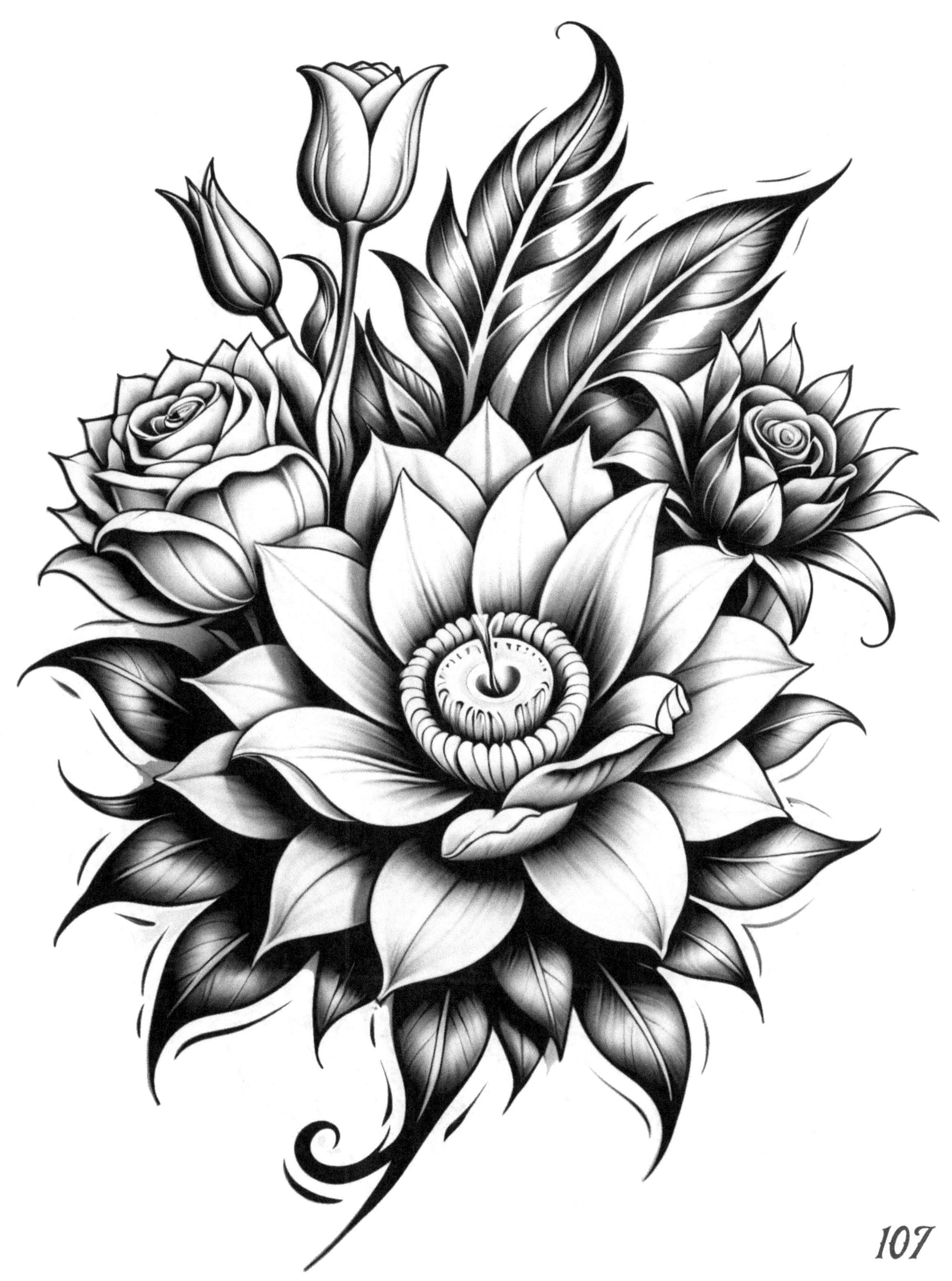

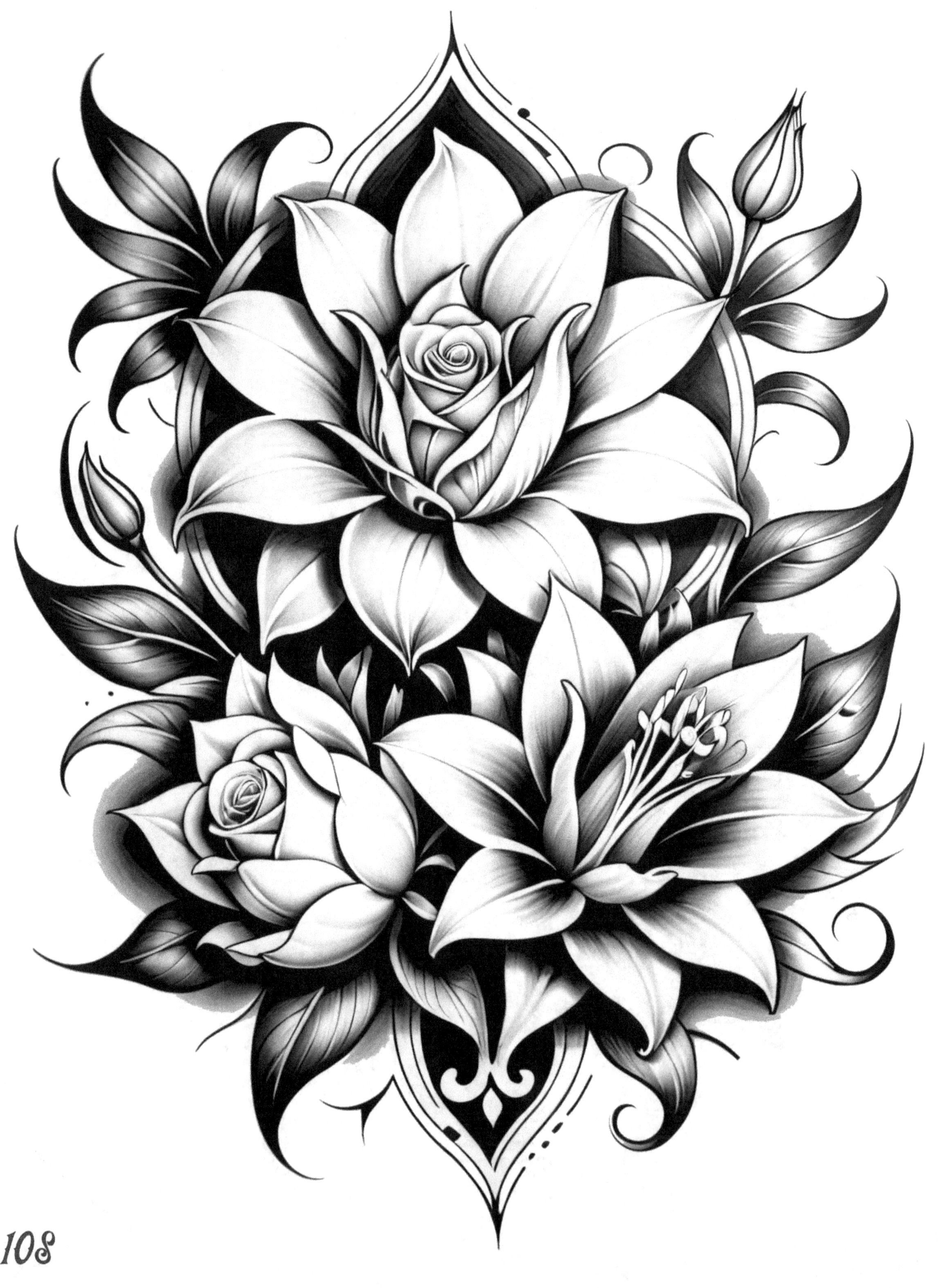

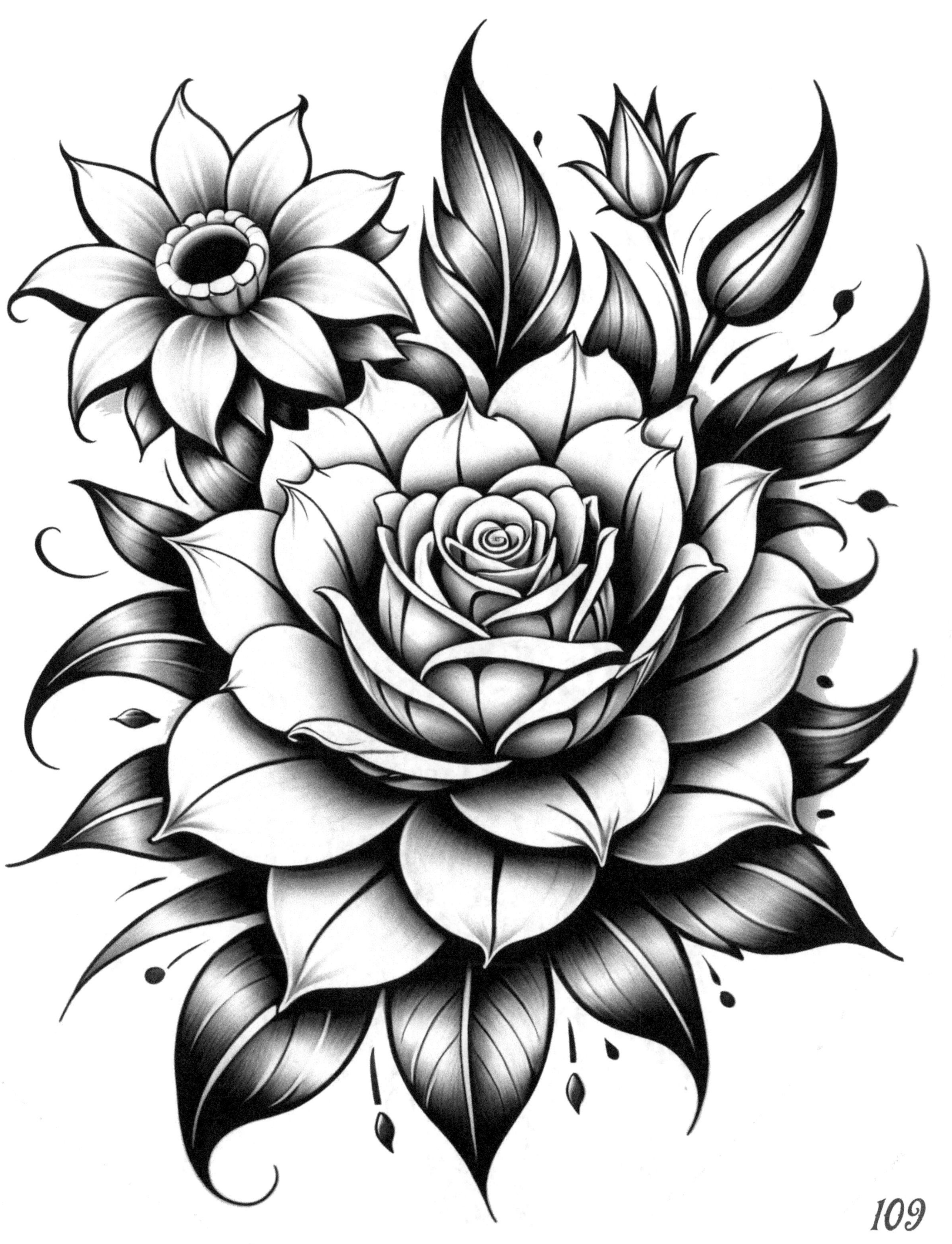

Nature

Nature motifs in Chicano tattoos often explore themes of freedom, spirituality, and the intrinsic link between identity and the natural world. Elements like dreamcatchers, bears, wolves, mountains, and rivers symbolize respect for nature, spiritual beliefs, and indigenous heritage, highlighting a deep reverence for the natural environment.

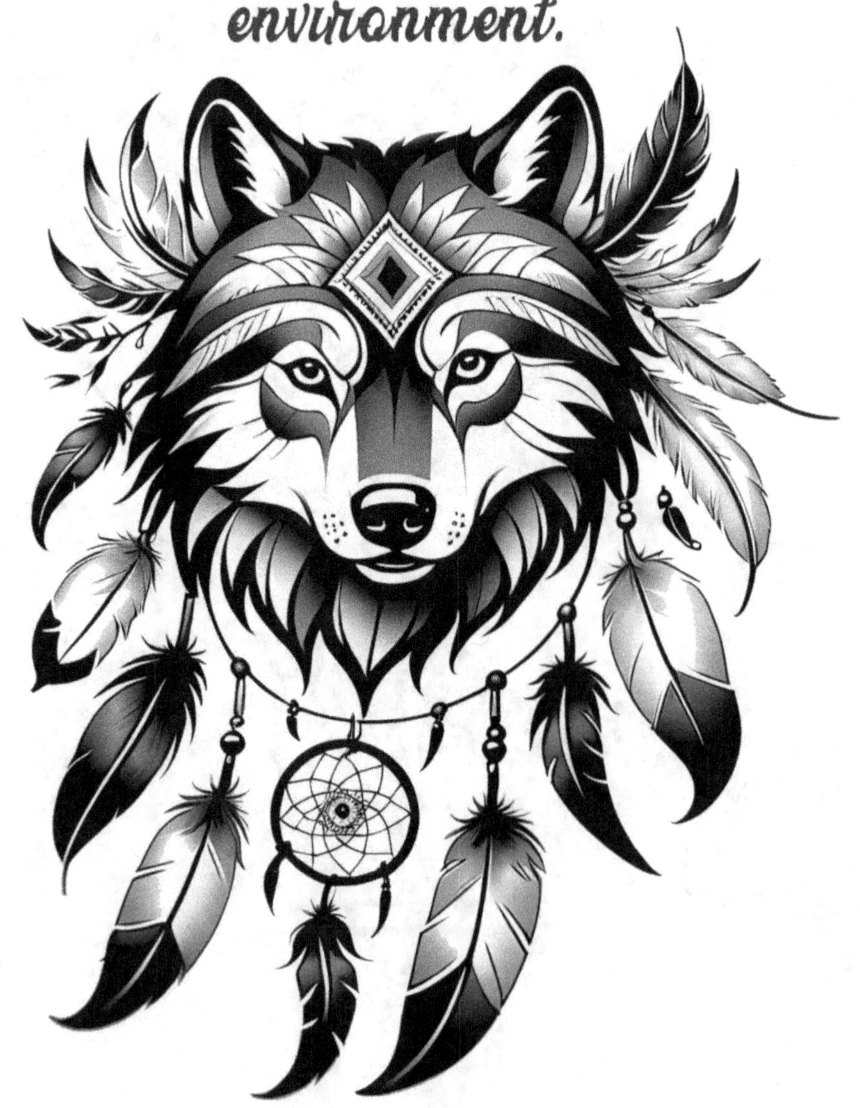

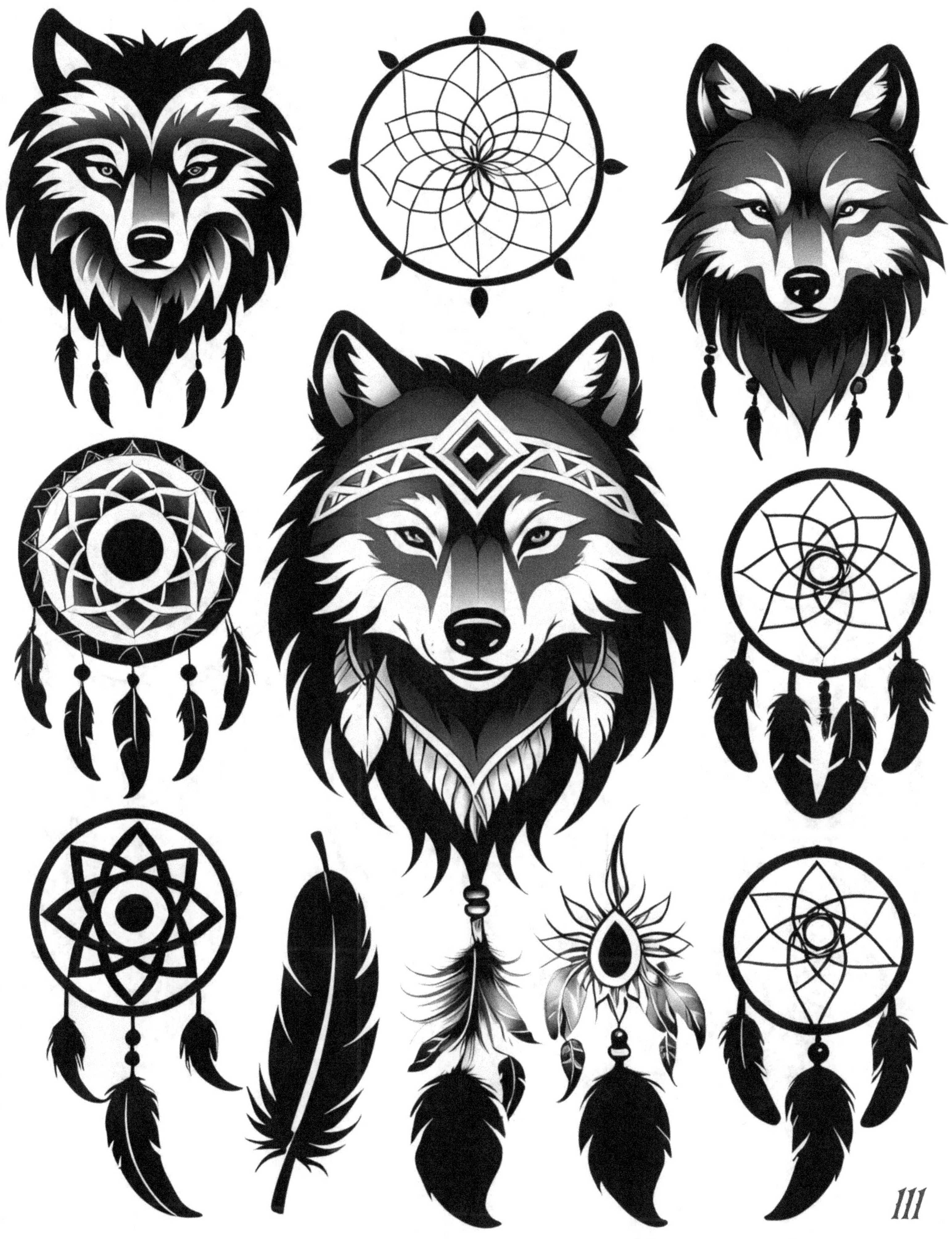

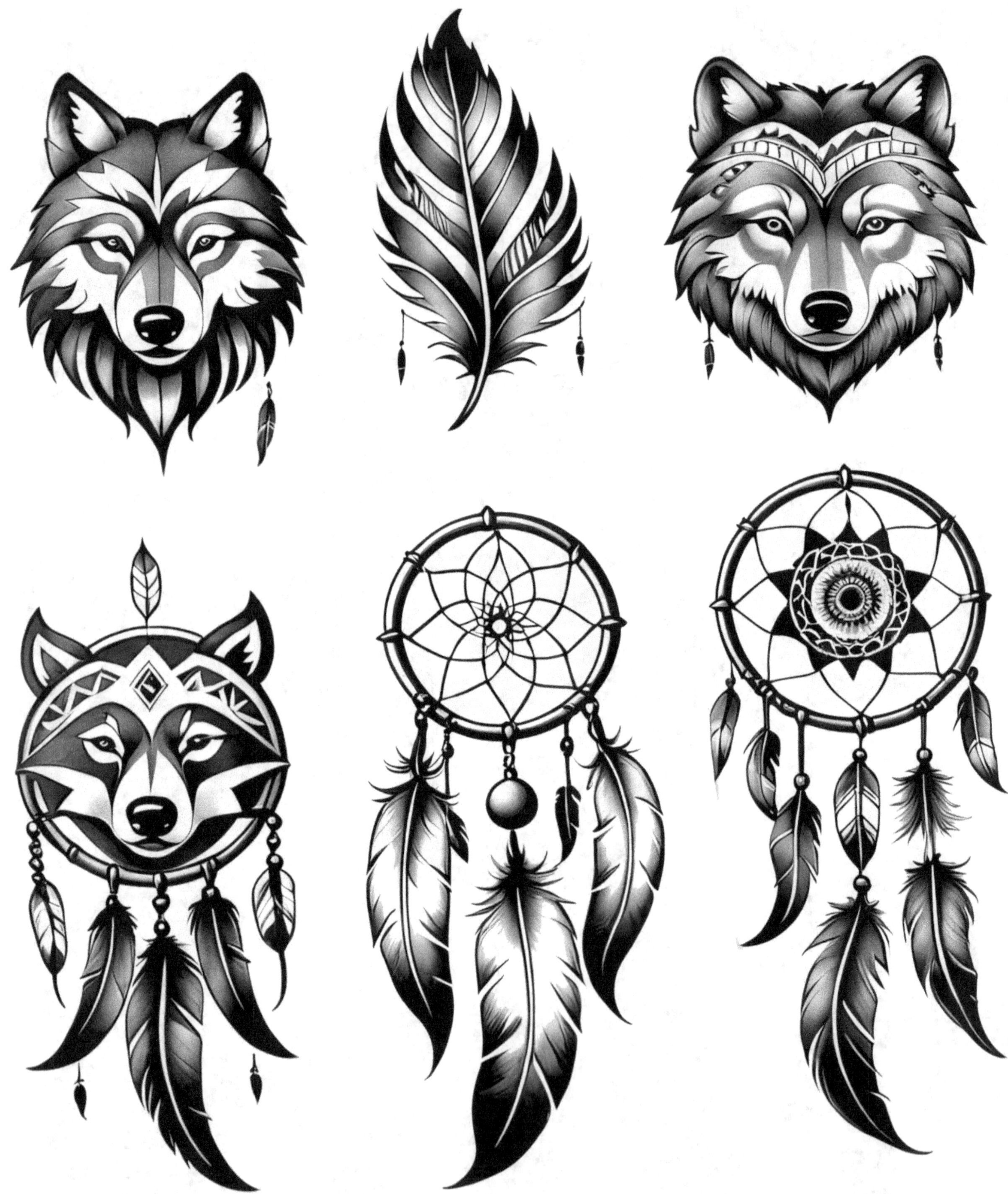

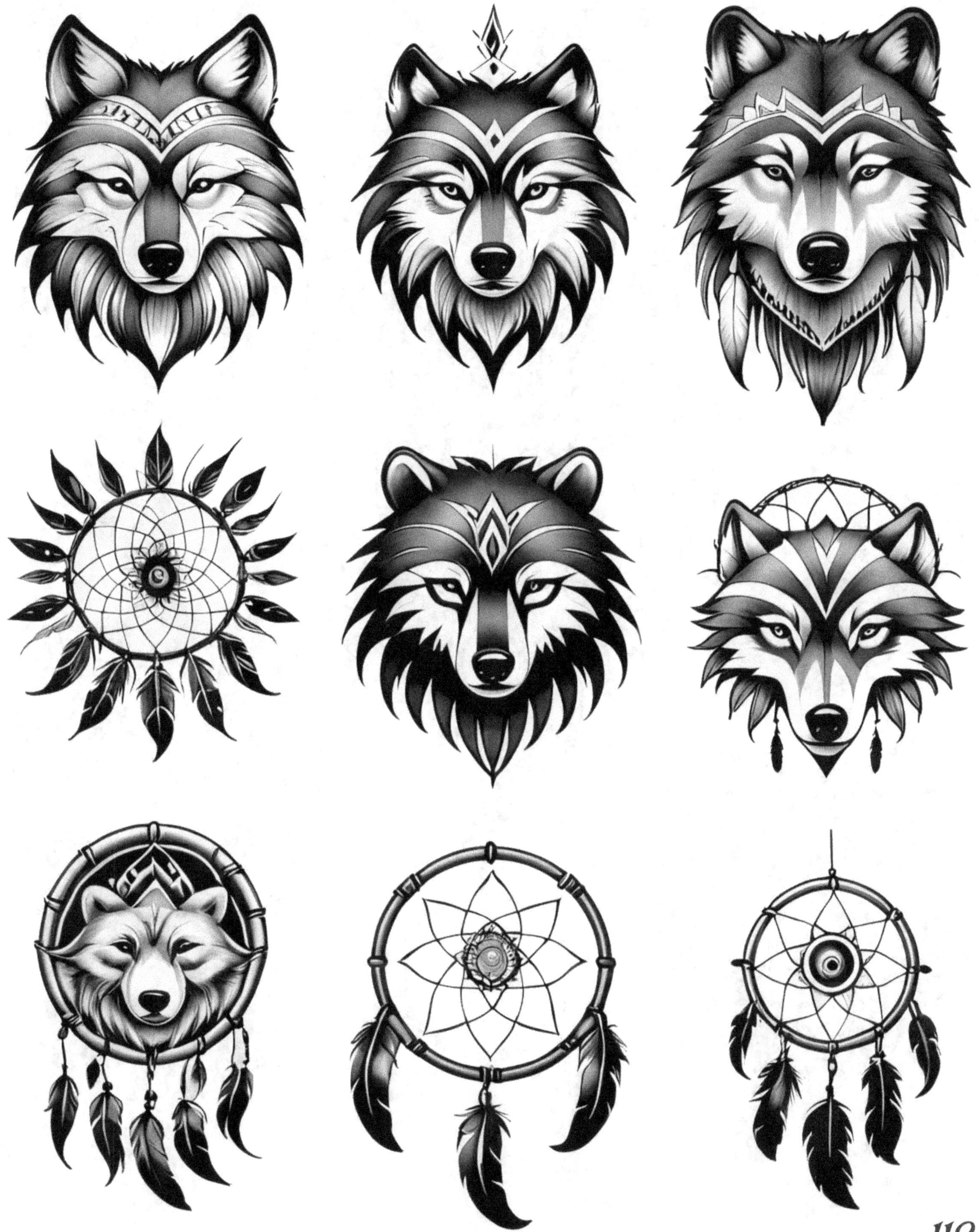

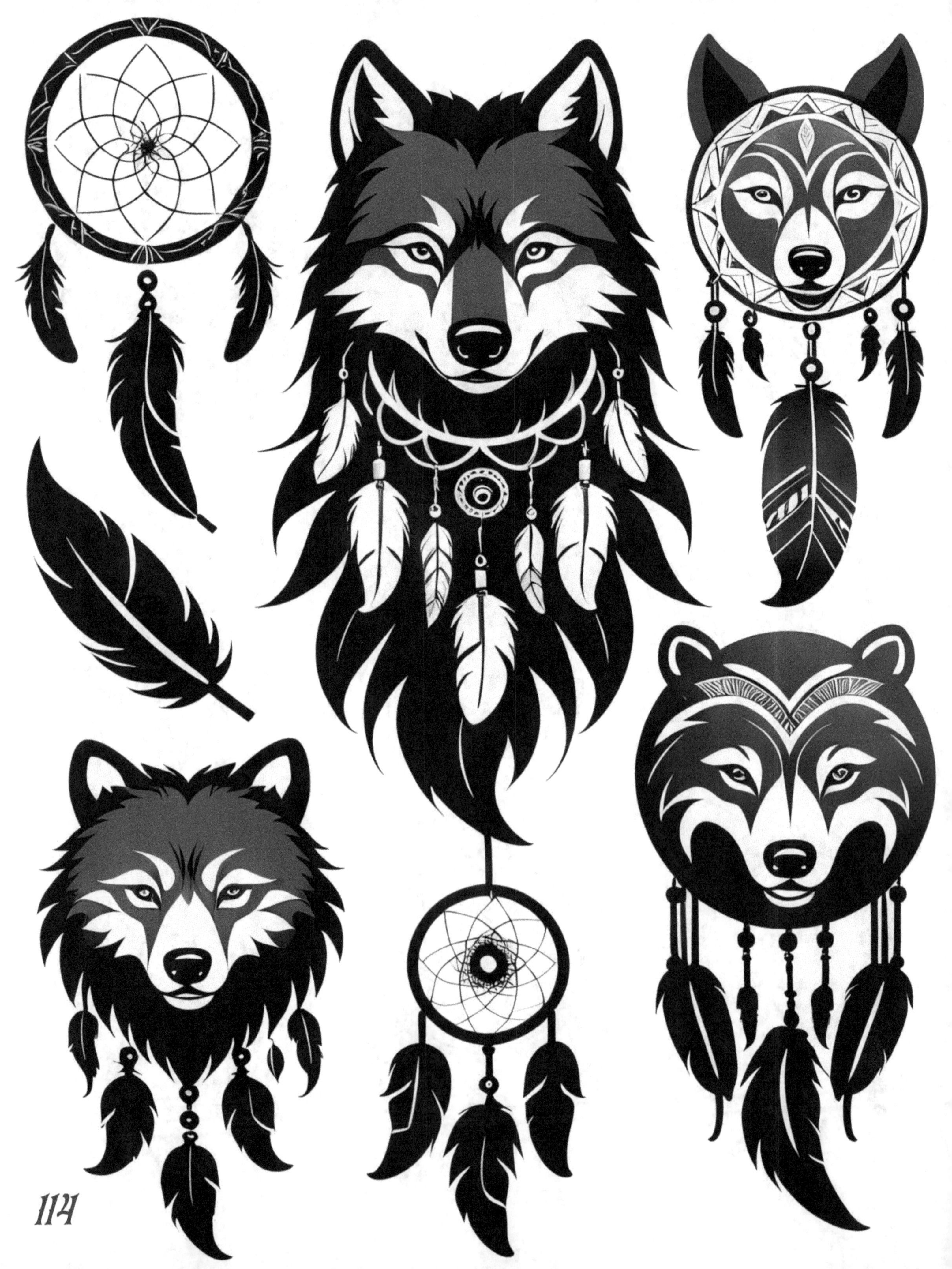

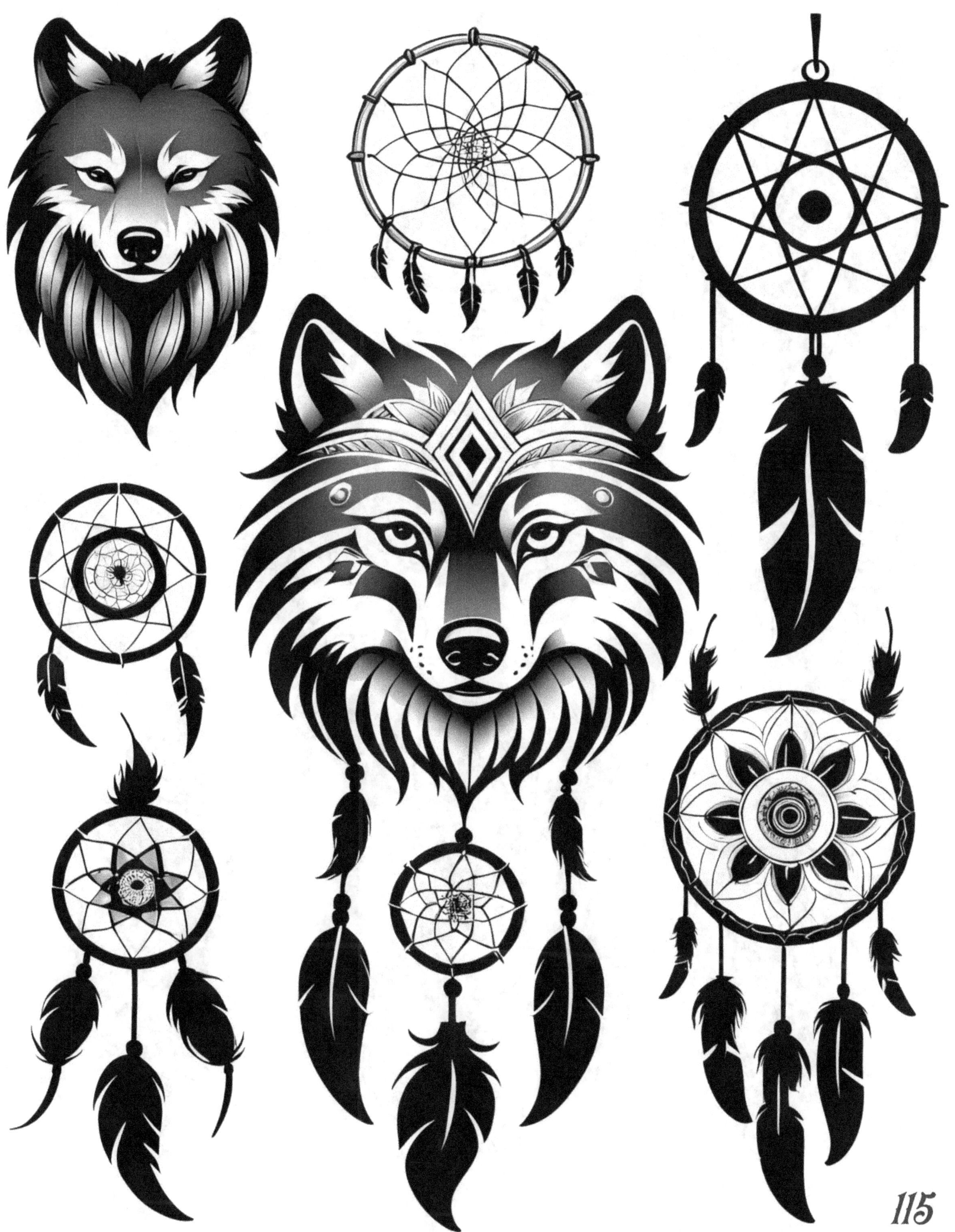

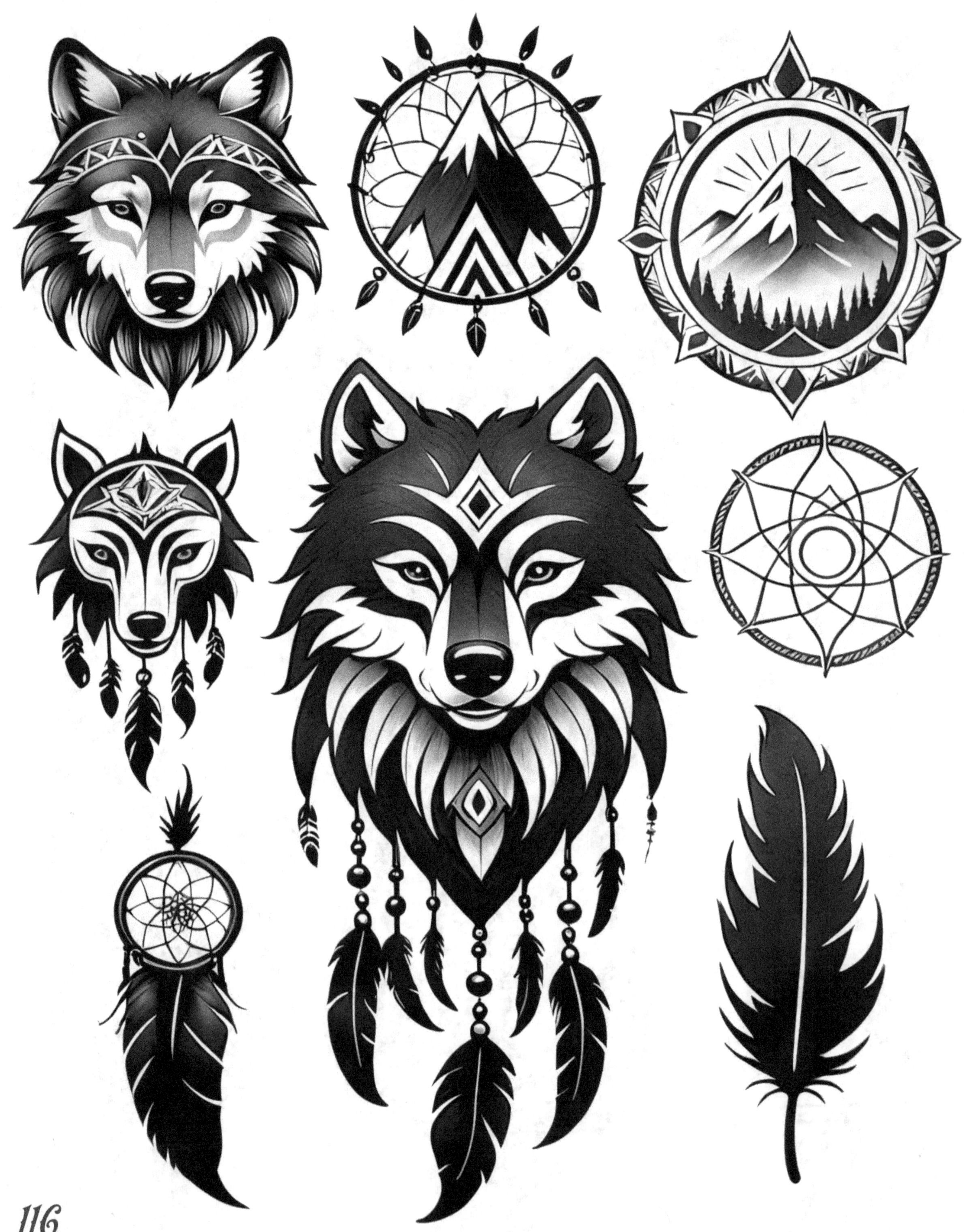

Classical

The Classical theme in Chicano tattoos draws on traditional and iconic Chicano imagery that has become foundational within the style. This includes roses, hearts, skulls, and religious icons like the Virgin Mary, which are often stylized with intricate black and grey shading, fine lines, and dramatic highlights. Classical motifs also include symbols of love, grief, and devotion, which are commonly interwoven with personal stories or cultural histories. These designs not only celebrate the rich artistic heritage of the Chicano community but also connect wearers to the timeless themes of human experience and the deeply rooted aesthetics of Chicano visual culture.

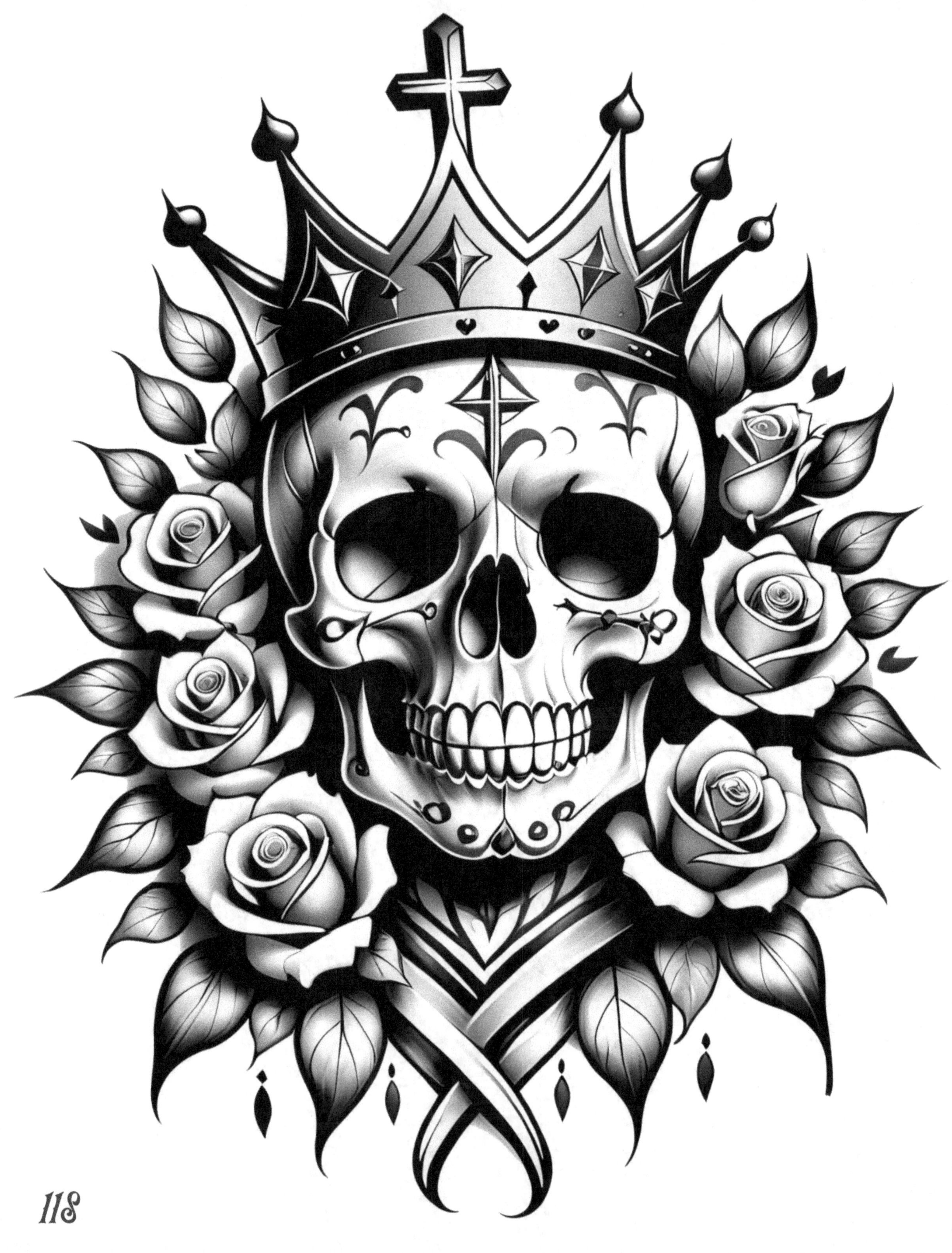

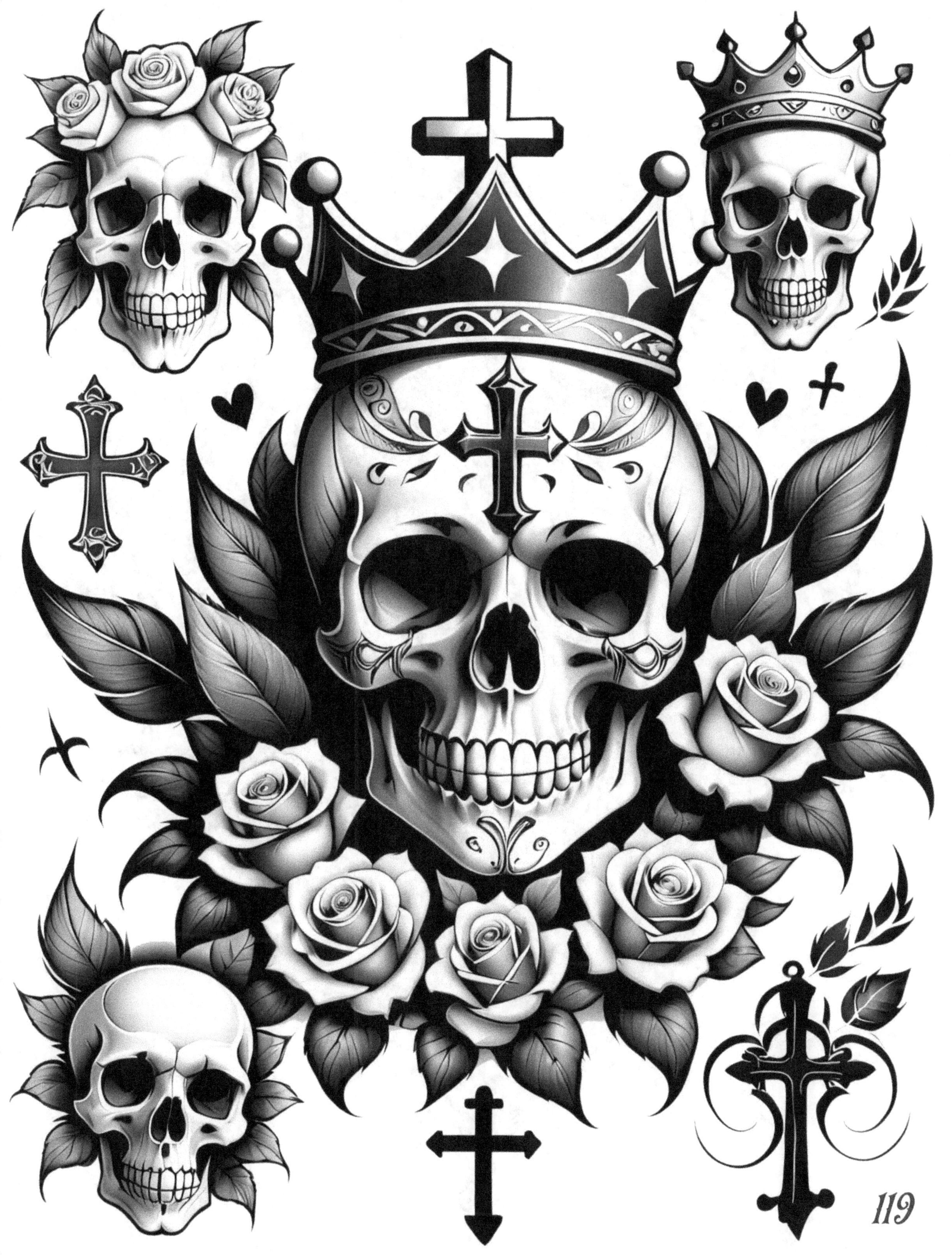

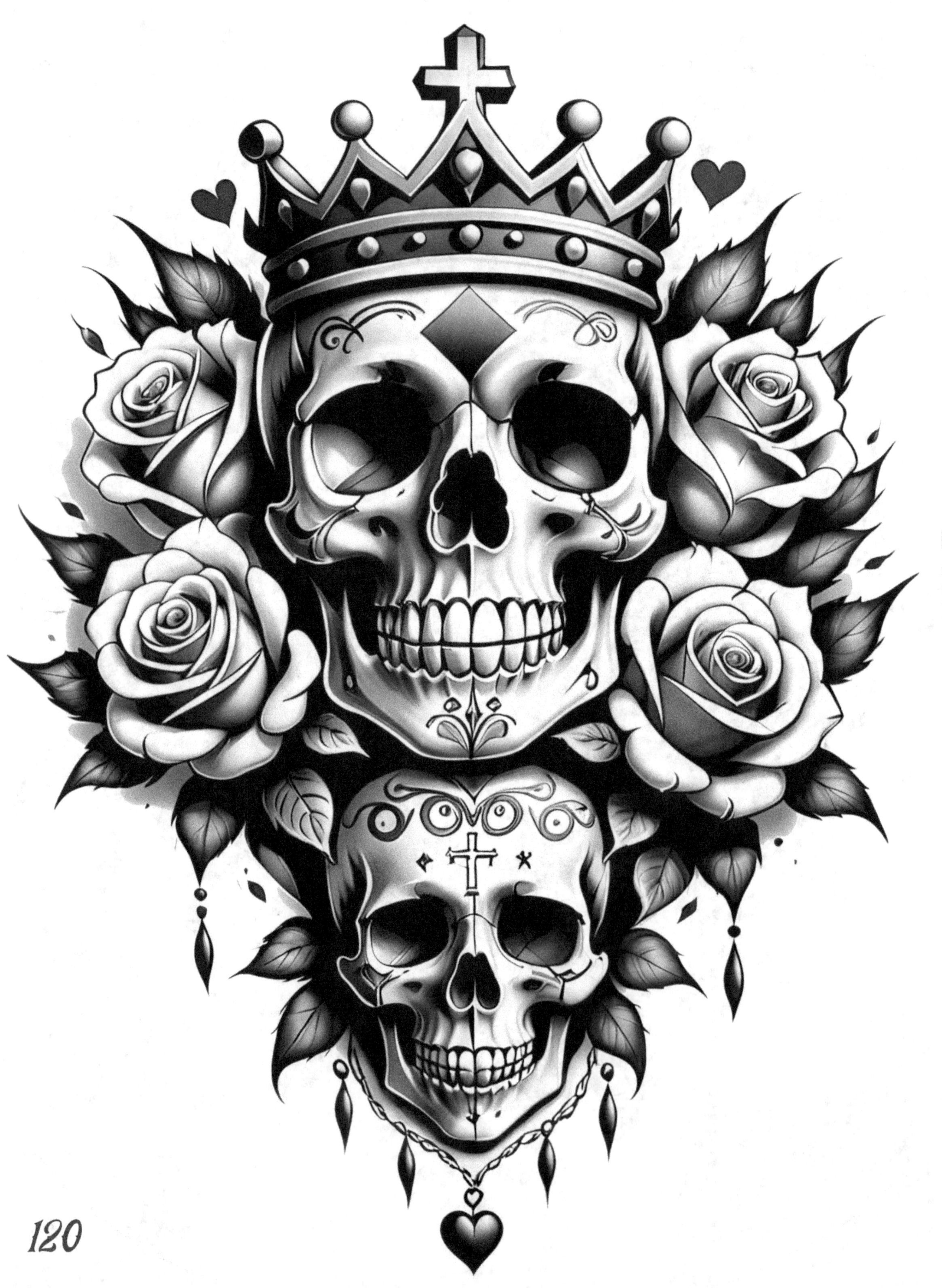

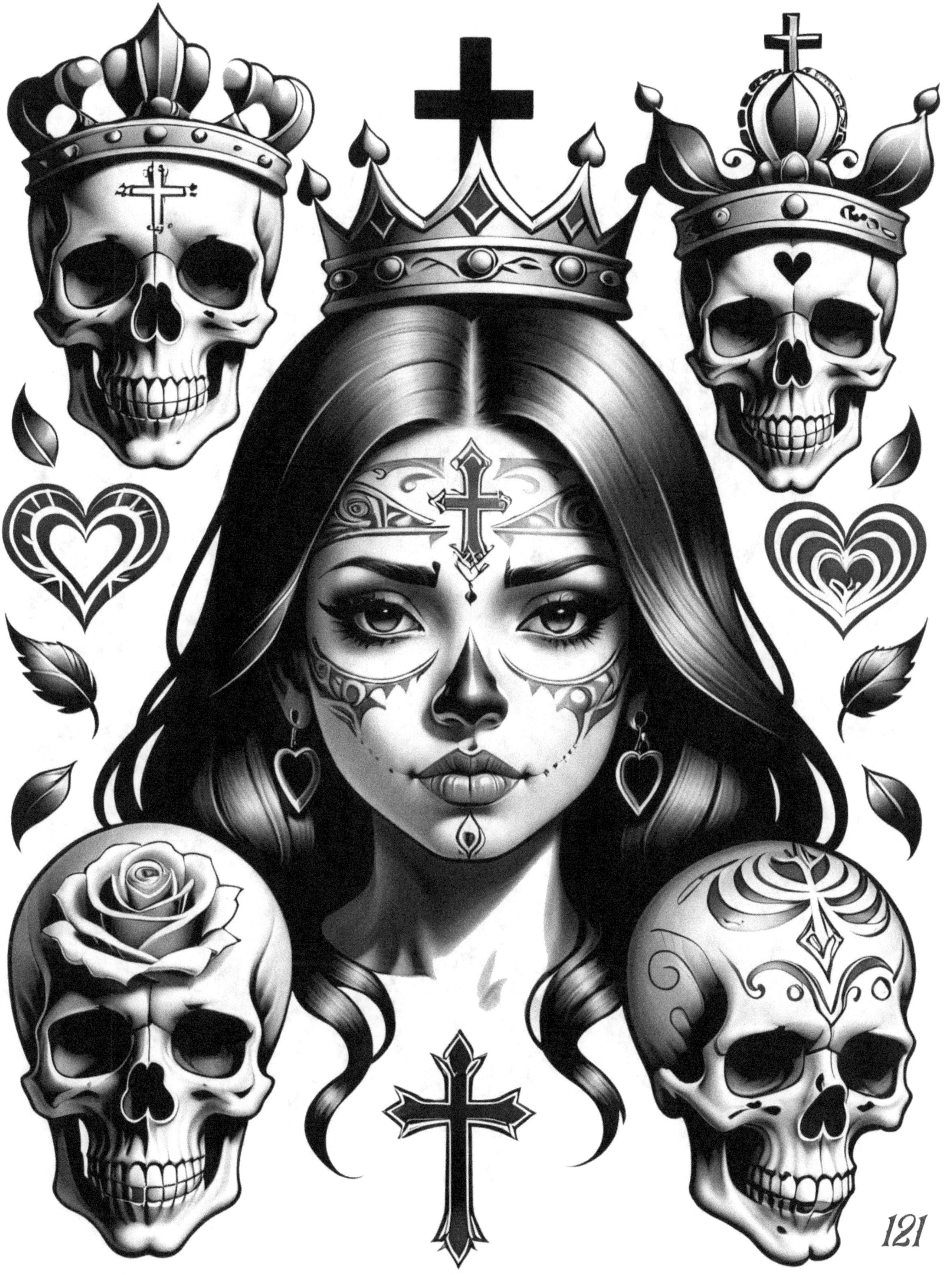

121

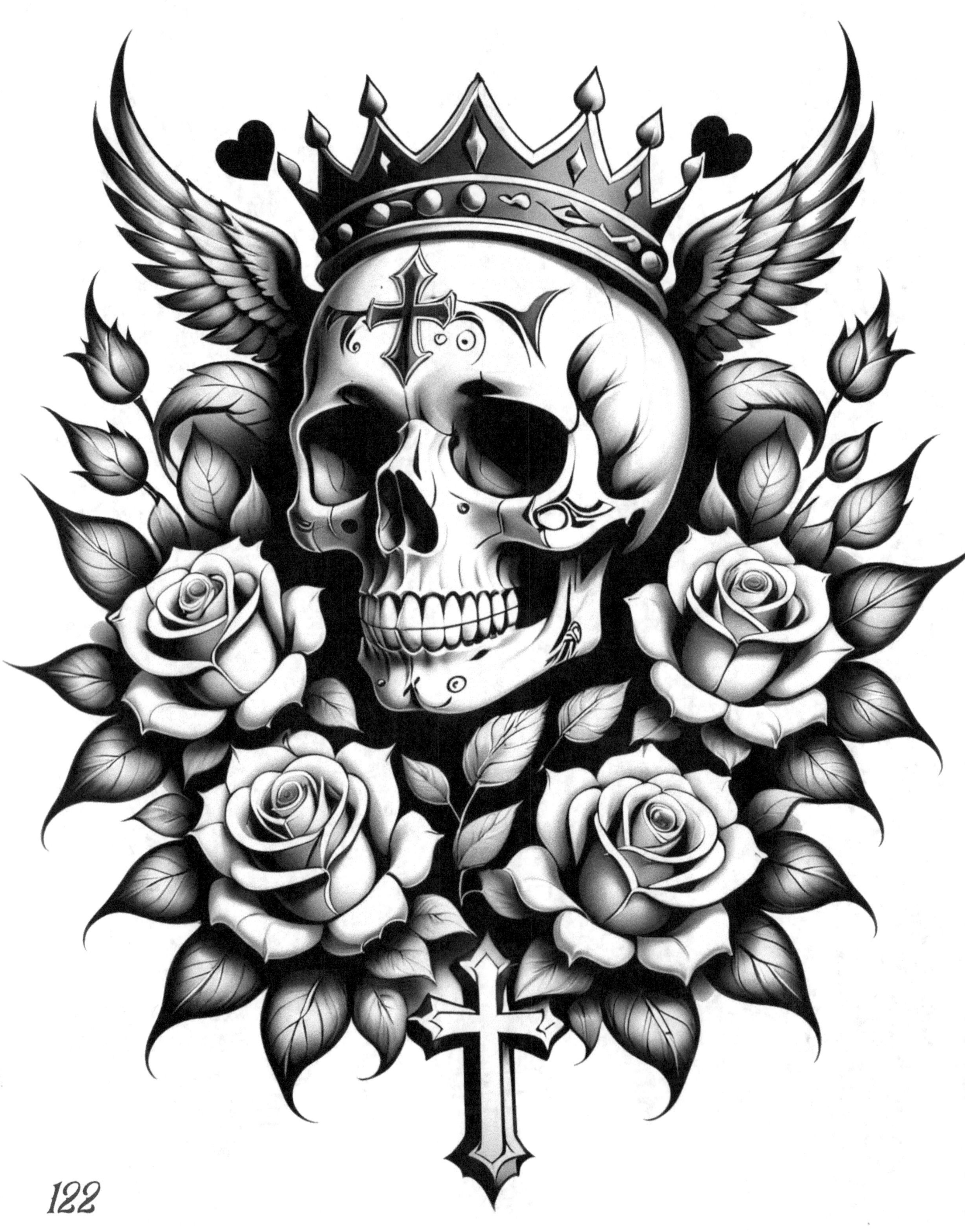

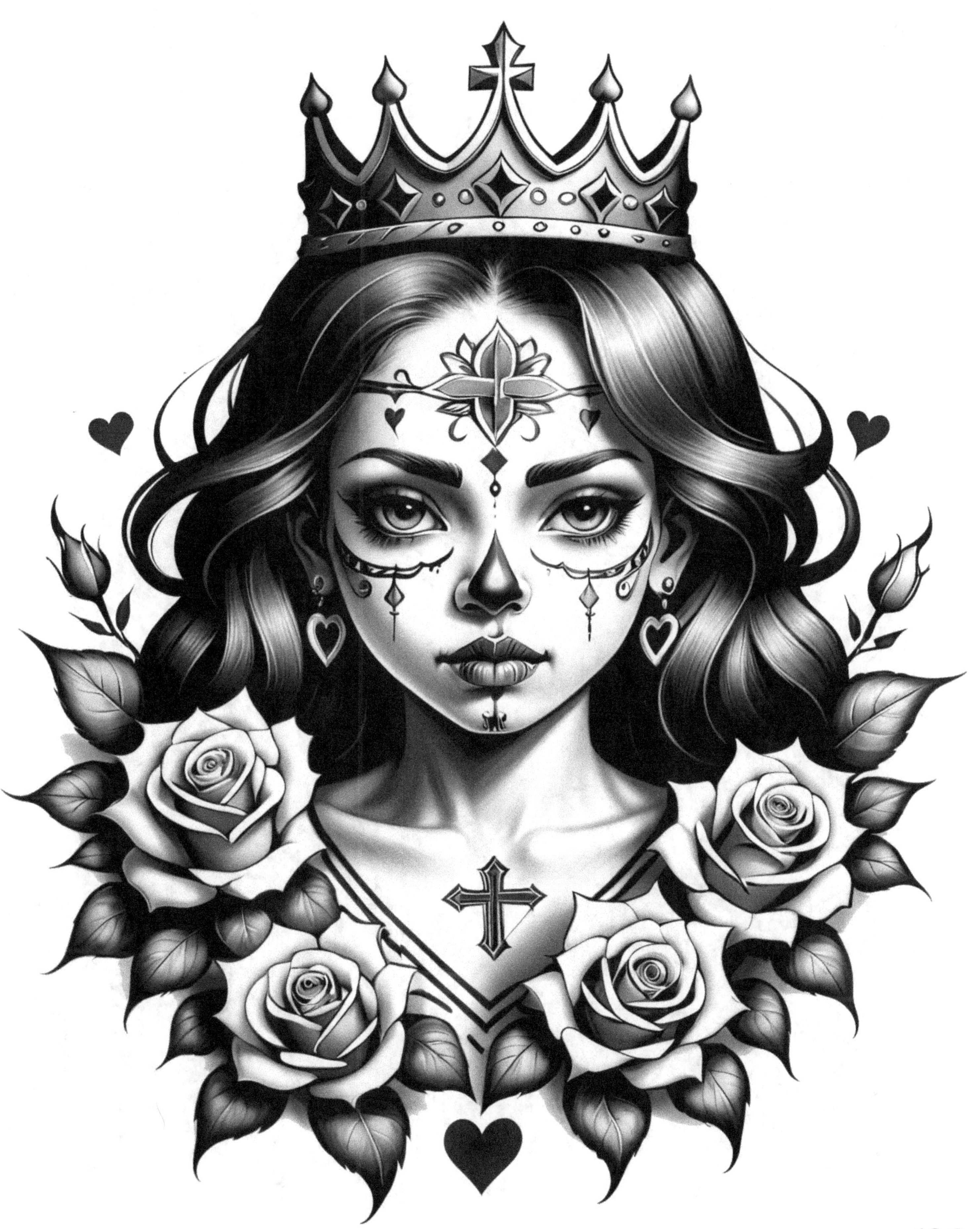

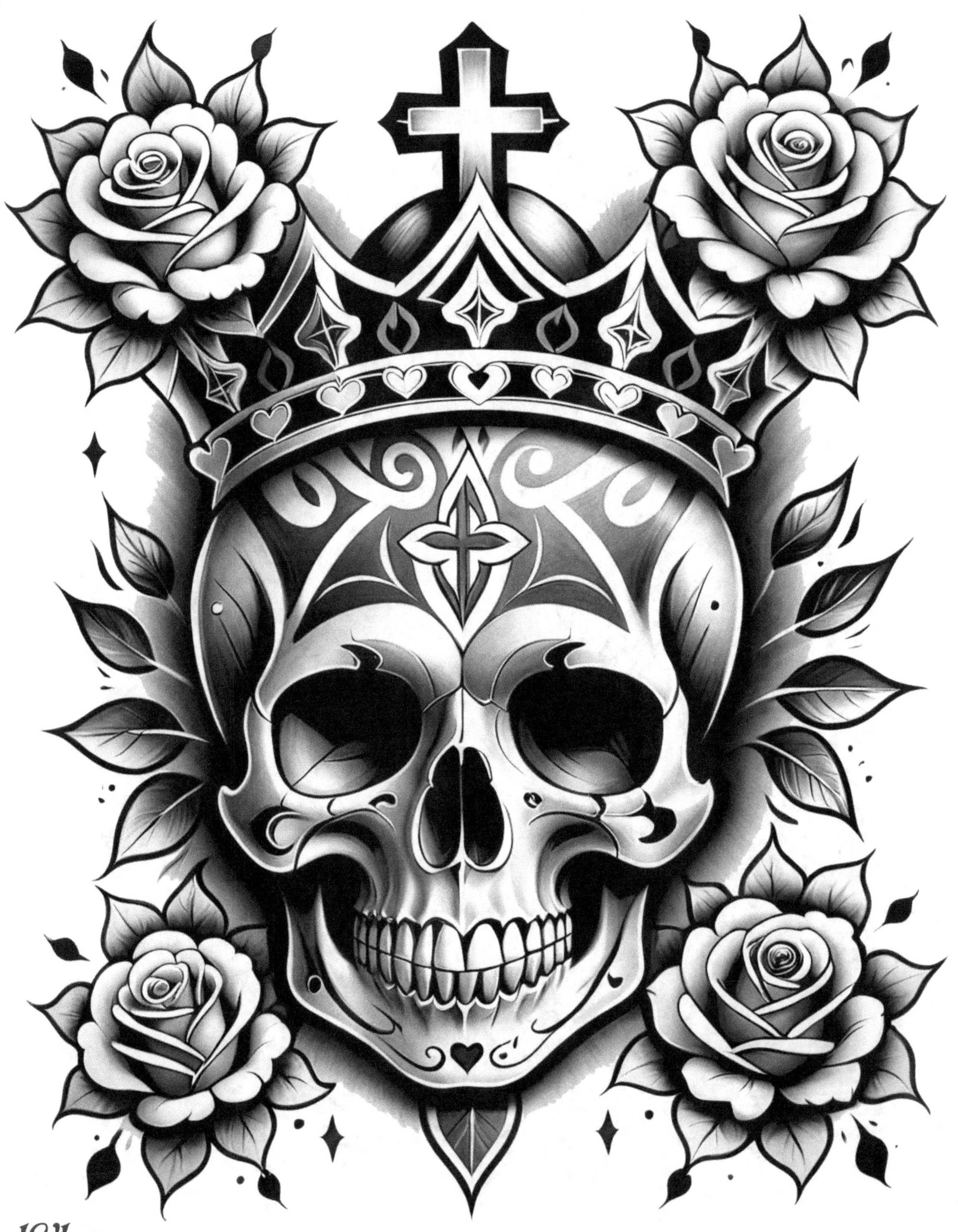

124

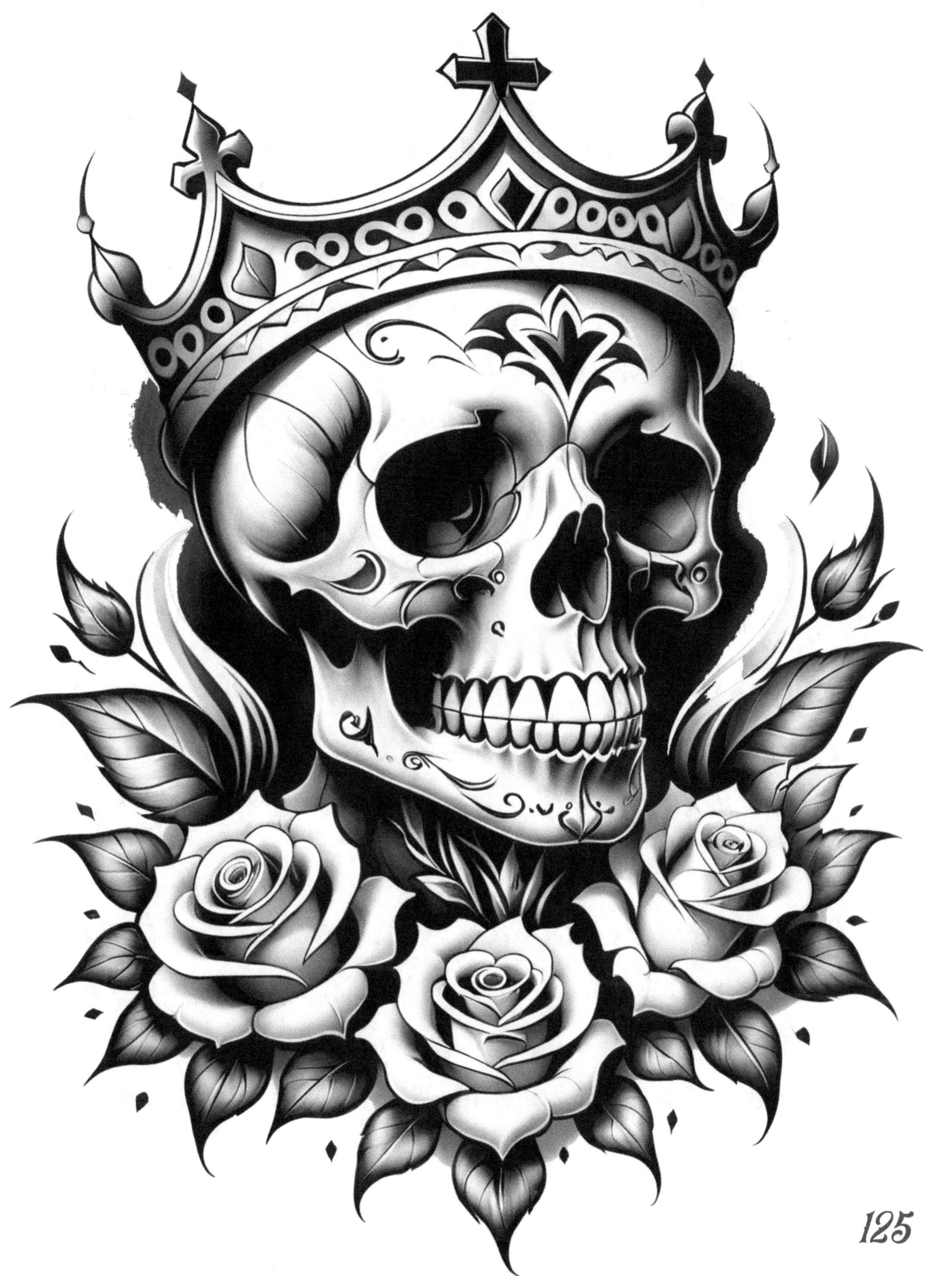

Conclusion

As we close this journey through the vivid and profound world of Chicano tattoo art, we reflect on the incredible depth and diversity these themes present. Each motif, from the sacred to the street, from the classical to the gothic, embodies more than just aesthetic appeal; they carry the weight of cultural histories, personal struggles, and deep spiritual beliefs. This book has aimed to not only showcase the artistry and craftsmanship of Chicano tattoos but also to honor the rich cultural tapestry they represent. We hope that the pages within have inspired you to appreciate the stories and significance behind each design, just as much as their undeniable beauty.

May this exploration of Chicano tattoo themes encourage you to look deeper into the symbols you carry or wish to carry on your own skin, finding connections to the universal themes of life, loss, and lasting legacy.

Thank You

Thank you for choosing to explore the intricate world of Chicano tattoo art with us. Your interest in this book supports not only the continuation of artistic exploration but also the appreciation of a cultural expression that speaks volumes about identity and resilience. We are grateful for your curiosity and hope that this book has enriched your understanding of a style that is as meaningful as it is visually captivating.

Remember, each tattoo has a story, and each symbol a history. May you carry forward the spirit of this art form, whether on your skin or in your heart.

With appreciation,
Life Style Daily